PLANNING AND DESIGNING

TRAINING PROGRAMMES

Leslie Rae

Gower

© Leslie Rae 1997

Published by
Gower Publishing Limited
Gower House
Croft Road
Aldershot
Hampshire GU11 3HR
England

Gower
Old Post Road
Brookfield
Vermont 05036
USA

British Library Cataloguing in Publication Data
Rae, Leslie
    Planning and designing training programmes
    1. Employees – Training of
    I. Title
    658.3'124'04

ISBN 0 566 07929 1

Library of Congress Cataloging-in-Publication Data
Rae, Leslie
    Planning and designing training programmes/Leslie Rae.
        p.   cm.
    Includes index.
    ISBN 0–566–07929–1 (cloth)
    1. Employees—Training of—Planning.   I. Title.
    HF5549.5.T7R248   1997   97–10302
    658.3'12404—dc21   CIP

Typeset in Palatino by Bournemouth Colour Press, Parkstone and printed in Great Britain by Hartnolls Limited, Bodmin.

Contents

Part One: Identifying and Analysing Needs

1   Introducing training needs identification and analysis   3

What is TNIA? – Training Needs Identification and
Analysis – Why perform TNIA? – The benefits and
disadvantages of TNIA – Responsibility for TNIA – The
Training Quintet – The TNIA clients – The stages of TNIA

2   Applying training needs identification and analysis   19

Case studies – The practical implementation of TNIA – A
pattern for identifying training needs – Who should perform
the TNIA? – Methods for analysis – Stage 1: Clarifying
requirements – Stage 2: Planning your TNIA – Stage 3:
Assessing the needs of the current situation – NVQ
competence standards

3   Identifying current training needs   39

Stages 4 and 5: Identifying errors and omissions in people
skills and identifying training needs – Project planning –
Outcome analysis – Moving on – Stage 6: Determining
training objectives and content

Part Two: Planning and Designing Training and Development Programmes

Part Three: Planning and Designing Training Sessions

Figures

Preface

The demands of industry and commerce are continually changing and are reflected in the activities of the training department and the training and development programmes. New approaches, skills, operations and procedures require either new training programmes or modifications of existing ones. This in turn affects the members of the training department – planners, designers, authors, trainers, administrators – who have to develop different programmes. Only too frequently the steps preceding the training event are rushed or inadequate and the training itself is entered into without an effective design.

The training process is complex and starts at a decision-making event. This might be a senior manager meeting at which a new operation or procedure is decided; a personnel report on suspicions of problems gleaned from performance reviews; line manager's concerns that they or their staff may be performing at less than total effectiveness; or staff themselves who realize that they need support, guidance and training to perform their roles or develop beyond their current levels. Whatever the source of the need requirement, if effective training and development is to result, the activities to achieve the needs must be planned in a capable manner.

The objectives of this book are to describe the steps necessary in this planning and design process to prepare a basic training and development programme. There is not room to describe all of the approaches fully: advanced detail is available elsewhere and an extensive further reading and reference list is given to help in this process. Although the planning emphasis is on direct training programmes – still the principal way in which large numbers of learners achieve many of their needs – the design and planning principles and techniques can be applied more widely to such approaches as open learning, interactive video programs and computer-based training programs.

The text follows a logical pattern:

- Part One – identifying and analysing needs
- Part Two – planning and designing programmes, including the setting of training objectives
- Part Three – planning and designing training sessions
- Part Four – evaluating training and development programmes.

There is some repetition in Chapters 7–10, but this was necessary to support the actions of the programme planners and the session planners. Training approaches introduced in Chapter 7 are summaries only, the detailed descriptions being given in the other chapters.

Throughout the text 'programme' refers to a series of training events over a complete training period – a training course or workshop, or linked series of courses or workshops; a complete open or IT learning package, etc. 'Session' refers to the more discrete event such as an input session or presentation; an activity, a discussion or other types of training approaches that, held together, form a coherent programme. The content of the book stops at the actual presentation of sessions as this is very personal to the training practitioner and is a subject demanding much more space. This is not to deny its importance and there are many self-instruction packages and training programmes that will serve the trainer's needs.

It is my hope that the book will encourage training managers, training programme designers and trainers themselves to look more closely at the requirements when new or modified training is required. In so many cases the demand is for the training to be provided 'yesterday', but at least a structured approach will reduce the time necessary and should improve the finished product.

I must thank Malcolm Stern of Gower, who gave me my start in the writing process, and members of his staff who have been most helpful in making the readers' understanding of my scripts easier with gentle suggestions for modifications and improvements – Solveig Gardner Servian has been particularly helpful in this respect, as always. My thanks also go to the army of managers and training practitioners with whom I have been associated for so many years and who were the sources of much of my practical training knowledge. Finally I must express my gratitude to my family who over the past fourteen years have suffered the throes of my writing and all that this implies (other authors will know what I mean!).

Leslie Rae

Part One
Identifying and analysing needs

Chapter 1

Introducing training needs
identification and analysis

This chapter:

    discusses the nature of a training needs identification and analysis (TNIA)
    describes the reasons for performing a TNIA
    describes the benefits of a TNIA
    suggests the range of responsibilities involved
    outlines the stages of a TNIA.

The design and planning of training and development programmes, of whatever nature, should not begin at the stage when the trainer or programme authors say to themselves: 'Right, we have to produce such-and-such a programme. What are we going to put in it? I like taking sessions on …'.

Apart from that last comment, which is completely the wrong way of approaching the design of a programme, the question should have been answered long before this stage. A number of factors are significant in the processes of training and development and one of the most important must be the initial identification of the training and learning needs that exist for individuals and the organization. Without an effective identification, how can we be sure that the learning opportunities we are providing are:

- needed by the organization?
- needed by the individuals?
- on a scale required?
- in the areas where some 'problem' exists, etc?

and the programme we are developing is appropriate and relevant?

Even if the learning opportunities provided are validated as effective, if their need has not been identified and the type of opportunity has not been investigated fully, the whole process may be worthless in terms of both effective learning and cost and value effectiveness.

What is TNIA?

As in many areas of training and development, jargon describing various processes in needs identification is rife. Umbrella descriptions include 'training need analysis' and 'training needs identification', or simply 'needs analysis' or 'needs identification'. The first two terms are excellent, provided we are sure that we are only identifying or analysing training; the other two common terms are too general to define the area of discussion.

We shall see later that when the needs of individuals and organizations are being investigated, the solutions are not necessarily those of training and development; in fact, many are (or should be) concerned with the motivation, commitment and practice of the people who should be carrying out the work *for which they have received training*. The failure in such cases is in the commission of training rather than its omission. Of course, the learning opportunity may not have been sufficiently effective to give the learners the skills to practise the area of learning back at work. Many barriers arise in the implementation of learning in addition to the failure of the training to provide the necessary knowledge, skills and attitudes:

- the negative attitude of the line manager to the introduction or implementation of new methods or techniques
- a similar negative attitude of peers and subordinates
- insufficient time to allow you to put your learning into practice
- organizational changes of attitude or practice might undermine the training that the organization itself had originally approved.

The identification, analysis and solution of people needs in an organization can obviously be an extensive project. When a need is identified the solution may lie within a wide range of politically sensitive areas of organizational development, e.g. the encouragement of (pressure on?) line managers to take their people responsibilities to a more significant level. This book concentrates on the need areas that have been identified and that can be solved by some form of training and development opportunity and the basic procedures that follow from this.

Training Needs Identification and Analysis

The initial process in the training and development cycle is twofold – identification and analysis.

- *Training needs identification* detects and specifies the training and development needs of individuals within organizations and of the organization as a whole.
- *Training needs analysis* follows on from needs identification and determines the most effective and appropriate ways in which the needs might be met. It can, of course, lead to decisions that there should be no training provision in view of the limited scale of the needs, the cost of provision, future development envisaged, and so on.

Within the identification and analysis of these 'needs' the actual nature of the need must be defined. A 'need' is not a 'want'. In so many cases in the past the 'identification' of an individual's needs has been a result of the question 'What sort of training do you want?'. Effective training and development in an organization depends on the need (i.e. requirement) for the improvement of human performance being identified and satisfied by the provision of appropriate development opportunities. 'Wants' can frequently be 'needs', but the analyst must be certain of the value of any aspect raised and eventually provided.

Why perform TNIA?

Any process in training and development, as in any other area of the working environment, is open to the question of value and reasons for doing it – needs identification and analysis is no exception.

The two statements most frequently made by practitioners when the subject of TNIA is raised are:

'We don't need to go to that extent: everybody knows what is required.'
'I would love to go fully into needs, but with the training itself and evaluation, there just isn't enough time'.

These are certain recipes for training failure. There is usually no evidence that the requirements are known automatically, and in fact this attitude usually results in necessary training not being provided. TNIA is as important in the training process as the training itself and subsequent evaluation. Time can certainly be a problem, but subsequent guidance will demonstrate ways in which the available time can be used more effectively.

Approaching the subject in a more positive manner, the value of TNIA can be summarized as follows (see Figure 1.1):

● It confirms or otherwise the stated problem. People often say that a 'problem' exists in the organization or with an individual, but there is little immediate evidence to support this statement. A TNIA will either show that a problem does exist or that it is an unsupported suspicion. It may also show that other, unsuspected, problems are in fact present. Without a TNIA the unsubstantiated suspicions must remain as such, or, if action to provide training on this basis is taken, considerable costs might be introduced unnecessarily.

IT CONFIRMS OR OTHERWISE THE STATED PROBLEM

IT IDENTIFIES A PROBLEM OF TRAINING OR COMMISSION

IT ASSURES EFFECTIVE DIRECTION TO TRAINING

IT SAVES MONEY BY ENSURING APPROPRIATE AND EFFECTIVE ACTION

Figure 1.1   Why have a needs analysis?

- It identifies a problem of training or commission. We have seen earlier that performance problems may be due either to an absence of or failure in training and development opportunities, or to other non-training causes. It is too easy, when a problem arises, to decide that the people involved should be 'sent on a training course', as if this is a cure-all solution. In fact, investigation may show that they have received the training previously, but have not implemented their learning for a variety of reasons. If this situation arises with you and the people for whom you are responsible, an effective approach is usually to investigate non-training solutions first. Of course, where the introduction of completely new tasks and operations is concerned, training is usually the obvious path – but even then, beware. Some of the people that you might assume need this new training, may have received it previously elsewhere.

- It assures effective direction to training. An effective TNIA not only identifies a problem and that it may be one of training, but also specifies the areas in which training and development should be followed. This enables the line manager to identify the most effective learning opportunity – coaching, mentoring, self-instruction, open learning packages, training courses both external or internal, or any of the other learning approaches. These final decisions are the last stages of a TNIA and overlap with the design and planning of learning opportunities.

- It saves money by ensuring appropriate action. This benefit follows on from the selection of effective work-based solutions vis-à-vis training solutions, since the most effective will cost the least amount. Organizations need to control their finances effectively, including a critical examination of training and development needs, but without using cost as an excuse for refusing necessary training.

The benefits and disadvantages of TNIA

Most methods, techniques and approaches have advantages and disadvantages and TNIA is no exception.

Benefits

The benefits of a TNIA when a problem has been identified or raised as a suspicion, include the following (see Figure 1.2):

- It pinpoints the problem(s). In many cases of line operation, there is a suspicion that something is wrong in a particular area of work, but the specific problem is not known or understood. A TNIA investigation will clarify this suspicion and, if carried out effectively, will detail not only the exact nature of the problem, but

IT PINPOINTS THE PROBLEM(S)

IT IDENTIFIES THE SIZE OF THE PROBLEM

IT IDENTIFIES THE SCALE OF THE NEED

IT INDICATES THE TYPE OF SOLUTION

IT PROVIDES TRAINING OBJECTIVES

Figure 1.2   The benefits of a needs analysis

also suggest the best ways to solve it. In this respect it is a problem-solving technique and consequently can be applied to general work situations which are not operating effectively, and where the reasons are not evident.

- It identifies the size of the problem. A number of 'problems' when investigated are so insignificant or have such little effect on work that they are seen to be hardly problems at all, or their solution requires minimum action.

- It identifies the scale of the need. In many companies, problems are frequently not isolated to one part of the organization. A TNIA that is applied to a range of departments, sections, sites, etc. will identify whether the problem is an isolated one, or is a more universal need requiring a much larger solution effort, whether this is training or non-training.

- It indicates the type of solution. Once the extent, size and nature of the problem have been identified and analysed, guidelines are suggested to the most appropriate solution. As we have seen, the basic choice is between training or non-training solutions. Further divisions are possible so that the most appropriate, exact non-training approach can be brought into operation or the type of learning opportunity can be identified. For example, the problem might involve the dysfunctional behaviour of one person: the straightforward solution in such a case might be a counselling interview between the line manager and the individual. Or a computer program problem might be occurring among a number of people resulting from an updating of the program for which they have received no training. A localized, small group problem of this nature might be solved by an arrangement with the organization's IT trainer to hold an in-house, on-site short updating program, perhaps by using the network rather than by bringing the group physically together.

- It provides training objectives – a specific statement and outline of the content of the training programme. A TNIA will describe in detail the needs of the task or job, the gap between these requirements and the level of skills, knowledge and attitudes among the group of people in question, and consequently the training gap or needs in detail. It then becomes a simpler task for the trainer to design a programme around these identified needs, rather than provide a universal programme with some aspects which might not be necessary.

Disadvantages

The list of disadvantages is considerably smaller than the benefits or advantages. The only one of any significance is the need for a skilled person to be employed and consequently the use of that person's time. This has been quoted earlier as one of the common criticisms of TNIAs. If the trainer alone is responsible for conducting the analysis in addition to all the other areas of work for which they are responsible, this may be a justifiable criticism. But before new training is embarked upon, or existing training continues, the need for this training must be identified. Failure to conduct any form of TNIA, in the same way as failure to validate and evaluate the training programme, leaves the organization open to criticisms of over-use and waste of money spent on unnecessary training, so every attempt must be made to identify and analyse the needs accurately. This leads to the question 'Who is responsible for TNIA?'.

Responsibility for TNIA

A number of activities in training and development are not performed because the responsibility for them is not fully accepted by any group. This can certainly apply to TNIA. Line management considers the function as the responsibility of the training department 'since it is concerned with training' (even though the end result may be a non-training solution); trainers (often quite truthfully) say that they would like to do it but the time allocated to training is not enough; senior management when they decide (often arbitrarily) that a training programme should be introduced do so without requiring a TNIA to be performed.

In fact, there is a common and joint responsibility shared by a number of groups. I refer to this grouping as the Training Quintet (see Figure 1.3).

The Training Quintet

The Training Quintet consists of senior managers, line managers, training manager, trainer and learner, all of whom must play their full parts in training including training needs identification and analysis.

Senior management

Although not directly involved in the performance of TNIA itself, senior management must play a significant and active part principally by:

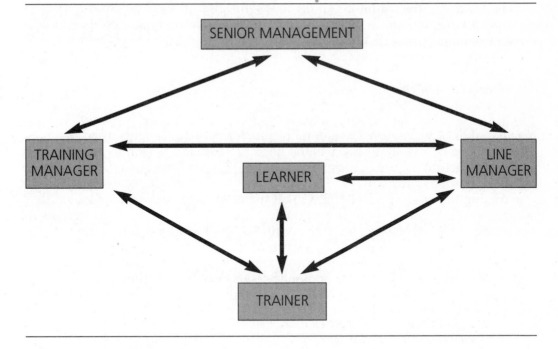

Figure 1.3   The Training Quintet

- requiring a TNIA to be performed whenever new training programmes are proposed or there is any doubt about the relevancy of existing programmes (they should recognize or be made aware of these at an early stage, preferably as part of the initial discussions)
- authorizing resource to enable it to be performed rather than simply saying that it has to be done (implying within already stretched existing resources)
- taking a real and analytical interest in the results, requiring the presentation of reports and recommendations about the identified needs.

This is summarized in Figure 1.4.

SENIOR MANAGEMENT

■ REQUIRE TNIAs TO BE PERFORMED AS NECESSARY

■ AUTHORIZE NECESSARY RESOURCES

■ TAKE A REAL AND ANALYTICAL INTEREST IN THE RESULTS

Figure 1.4   The role of senior management

There is little little value in clients and sponsors of training offering only a superficial interest by stating that they support a realistic approach to training without demonstrating their support in a practical manner.

The training manager

The training manager must act as a moving force in the progress of the development of training for which he or she has a responsibility. This manager

---

THE TRAINING MANAGER

■ INVOLVEMENT AND LINKING WITH SENIOR MANAGEMENT AND ENSURING ACTIVE INTEREST

■ AGREEING TRAINING NEEDS IDENTIFICATION AND ANALYSIS PROJECTS

■ ENSURING PROVISION OF SKILLED RESOURCES FOR TRAINERS INVOLVED IN TNIAs

■ REPORTING TNIA RESULTS TO SENIOR MANAGEMENT

Figure 1.5   The role of the training manager

acts as the link between the senior manager clients and the trainers, by reminding the former of the key nature of TNIAs and by ensuring that the latter are fully equipped with skills and resources to perform them. Training managers must analyse and collate the TNIA results prior to authorization of training or the presentation of reports to senior managers. This role is summarized in Figure 1.5.

The line manager

The line manager is often underused in the training and development area, and certainly so in the TNIA process. Many line managers will assert that they are already overloaded with work without adding further activities that they claim are the province of the trainer. The simple response in every case to these claims are that they cannot afford *not* to be involved. Whether or not they are making direct financial contributions to the training and development of their staff, training is costing them money – loss of productive resource during the training period – and hence a devaluation of their department's production. To what extent is the line manager aware of the need for the proposed training?

There are four TNIA activities for line managers:

1. Initial identification of problems that appear to have a training need.
2. Participation in TNIAs that involve their staff.
3. Participation in TNIAs with a wider application than those involving their own staff.
4. Action to resolve problems that have non-training solutions.

Trainers may complain about the apparent lack of interest by line managers in the training programmes. Involvement of whatever extent in TNIAs should resolve this problem, particularly when the managers realize that it is for the benefit of their staff and the end results will be increased efficiency and reduced costs of their units.

Organizations that have good interrelationships between the training department and the line management commonly involve line managers in the training plans at the earliest opportunity – certainly at the planning stage and also at the content design stage. This co-operation will ensure that the manager feels some ownership of, and hence commitment to, the training.

Similarly, when the TNIA approach is being considered, the line manager should be invited to contribute and in so doing, with the accompanying commitment, can be encouraged to take a more active part. Training department plans should include a programme of activities to obtain the active support of line management, for example:

● invitations to the line managers to help in the planning of the training programme
● invitations to the line managers for involvement in the initial consideration of the TNIA process
● visits to line managers to discuss training matters with them to agree these involvements – an expensive approach with a large number of managers, but the results will be well worth the expenditure
● invitations to attend training courses as observers so that they can learn at first hand what happens to their staff
● attendance by the trainers at meetings of line managers to make a contribution to the meeting describing what is happening in training; training plans and objectives; the desirable roles and responsibilities of different role-holders; how the line manager can help training and how the trainers can help the line management; and so on
● offers by trainers to give active support to the managers at different TNIA stages
● workshops for line managers where discussions can take place and agreements made about roles and responsibilities.

These roles are summarized in Figure 1.6.

The trainer

The trainer plays a crucial, if not always central, role in a TNIA. There must be significant involvement because the end result of the TNIA may be the provision of training programmes or the revision of existing ones in which the trainer is

THE LINE MANAGER

- INITIAL IDENTIFICATION OF POSSIBLE TRAINING NEEDS

- PERFORMANCE OF OR PARTICIPATION IN TNIA PROJECTS

- PARTICIPATION IN WIDE COVERAGE TNIAs

- ACTION TO RESOLVE NON-TRAINING PROBLEMS

Figure 1.6   The role of the line manager

involved. However, the TNIA will be more comprehensive and acceptable if people other than the trainer are involved. Of course, one of the frequent arguments used by trainers for not performing comprehensive TNIAs and the subsequent evaluation, is that they do not have sufficient time or resources. Spreading the load reduces this argument. Consequently the TNIA activities of the trainer will include:

- as the initial practitioner, planning and agreeing the project; obtaining the necessary basic information; agreeing the involvement of others; and preparing the final report
- taking an active role in the TNIA at all stages, particularly where specific expertise may be required – for example, constructing questionnaires, interviewing people to obtain detailed information, producing analyses of collected data
- supporting line management in their TNIA activities – identifying problems, agreeing approaches, supporting interviews, assisting in the formation of job descriptions and specifications
- advising line managers on the suitability of the range of training and development programmes available to help solve the problems identified – the trainer is (or should be) the expert with all the information or the awareness of where to obtain it
- stemming from the TNIA, the trainer and the training department produce appropriate training and development programmes or suggest other programmes
- supporting, where appropriate, the line manager in the implementation of non-training solutions determined by the TNIA – for example, a remedial or developmental coaching programme for members of the department involved (the trainer might coach the line manager in the techniques of coaching, supply some internal training events, advise on or provide aids to support the manager's coaching activities) – these are facilities to be offered, not imposed
- producing, either directly or via the training manager, a final report to the client group describing findings and recommending action

Figure 1.7 summarizes the involvement of the trainer in the TNIA process.

THE TRAINER

■ TAKING INITIAL ACTION TO START THE TNIA PROJECT

■ CARRY OUT SPECIFIC TNIA PROCESS ROLES

■ SUPPORT LINE MANAGERS IN TNIA PROJECTS

■ ADVISE LINE MANAGERS ON T & D PROGRAMMES AVAILABLE

■ INITIATE TRAINING SOLUTION PROGRAMMES

■ SUPPORT LINE MANAGERS IN NON-TRAINING SOLUTIONS

■ PRODUCE OR RECEIVE TNIA REPORTS

Figure 1.7   The role of the trainer

The learner

Finally, although the role of the learners in the programme is to learn, they are involved in the TNIA process – without their comments much of the identification and analysis would not occur. In order to assist in the TNIA they must complete any assessment instruments honestly and fully, and make personal contact with the people conducting a TNIA. They must be made aware of exactly why they are being asked certain things and what they will be used for and with whom. This knowledge will result in significant and helpful comments.

The role of the learner is summarized in Figure 1.8.

This supportive culture will not come about overnight in organizations where it does not already exist, nor will it develop without committed work by, usually, the trainers and their training manager. The claim of lack of time by line managers is often well-founded and the apparent lack of interest by senior management may be caused by ignorance of their role, or perhaps relegation of the process because of a non-understanding of the reason for and value of TNIA. A programme of education should be embarked upon, preferably on all fronts at the same time, to ensure full agreement and commitment.

The TNIA clients

Rarely will a TNIA practitioner embark on a project without some form of client backing or authority for the project. Suspicion of a problem; the decision that a TNIA should go ahead because of the introduction of new work; or action resulting from suspicion that existing training arrangements are not satisfying

THE LEARNER

■   BE AWARE OF THE EVALUATION PROCESS AND BE COMMITTED
TO SUPPORTING IT AT ALL STAGES

■   BE AWARE OF WHY THE VARIOUS STAGES ARE BEING
FOLLOWED AND WHAT WILL HAPPEN TO THE RESULTS

Figure 1.8   The role of the learner

needs, perhaps because of changing employee population or changing work aspects – there will usually be a client or client group that will authorize or request the performance of a TNIA in a particular area.

Identification of the client is fundamental to the practitioner. The client will be the source of your authority, to whom you will refer if you need to clarify doubts and to whom you will address your final TNIA report. The responsibilities outlined in the Training Quintet (see p. 8) will indicate the locations of clients.

Senior management/Board members

Senior management/board members are responsible for steering the organization. They may require TNIAs because they have decided to introduce new tasks, products and operations, or they have become aware of problems in the line work areas and they require specific information about the nature and extent of these problems. Or they may be concerned about the continuing training programmes within the organization and require an audit of the effectiveness and needs of these programmes.

In ideal situations, specific requirements will be detailed by this group and transmitted either directly to the trainers or via the training manager as their link with the practitioner. However, the ideal is rarely achieved and the demand will more usually come to the practitioner as a simple statement that new work is being introduced; there is something wrong in the line operation; there is some concern about the existing training. The practitioner will need to take these as the authority to proceed, in the absence of more specific guidelines, and provided the rather vague advice is sufficient to continue, the TNIA can go ahead. But practitioners should not be afraid to ask (in the most tactful ways):

● exactly what is meant by the request?
● what authority is given to the practitioner?
● how extensively should the TNIA range?
● what evidence is there for the problem existence?
● what resources are available?
● within what time period is the TNIA to be performed?

- is a report required? When is it required? To whom should it be addressed? What form should the report follow – information statement; statement plus recommendations, etc?

Line management

Requests to the training department for TNIA may originate with line managers who have identified, to some extent, that a human performance problem exists in their area of responsibility, or they have been required to undertake new work for which it is apparent that training will be needed. TNIA contracts of this nature will usually be simpler than the wider ones stemming from senior management, but will be equally demanding and will require the same aspects to be confirmed as described above.

Training management

The training manager will probably not be the originating client, but the one with whom you as the practitioner will have direct contact. TNIA requirements coming from the training manager may have originated with senior management or line management, although as part of their responsibility they will be maintaining a continuous audit of the training for which they are responsible. These audits, often as a result of evaluation analyses, may indicate that something is wrong with some aspect of the training function. Although the contact is direct, you must have a full clarification of all matters as described earlier.

The stages of TNIA

Two important events will trigger the need for a training needs identification and analysis in the organization:

- the initiation of an investigation into needs based on suspicion of a problem
- the introduction of a new or revised training event or programme.

The first event will result in a TNIA which can lead to the solution of the problem(s) by either a training or non-training approach: action will be taken to resolve the problem by the various techniques of TNIA and if training is indicated, to lead the people concerned to existing training programmes, or the production of a training programme directly related to the identified problem.

The second event is a natural part of the complete training process and should precede the introduction or modification of any training programme. Figure 1.9 shows the full training process from initial investigations, through TNIA, the production of training programmes, to the final evaluation and audit of the process. The flow chart also indicates the people who should be involved at the various stages – these indications are based on the responsibilities of the role-holders in the Training Quintet described earlier.

Figure 1.10 extracts from Figure 1.9 the elements that are particularly related to TNIA and describes the six stages:

1. The raising of a known or suspected existence of a human performance problem or an organizational decision to introduce new tasks and a clarification of expectations
2. Planning the training needs identification and analysis project approach, methods and techniques.
3. Assessment of the needs of the current situation, including the formulation of job/task descriptions and job specifications.
4. Assessment of the current situation in terms of the knowledge, skills and attitudes of the people involved in the investigation. During this part of the TNIA, any human performance errors or omissions, and dysfunctional behaviours will be identified and analysed.
5. Comparison between stages 1/3 and 4, the expectations of future behaviour and the facts of the current situation will identify what is frequently described as the training gap from which the specific training needs can be identified.
6. From the identified training needs, the training objectives for the programme can be formulated and the content of a training programme described.

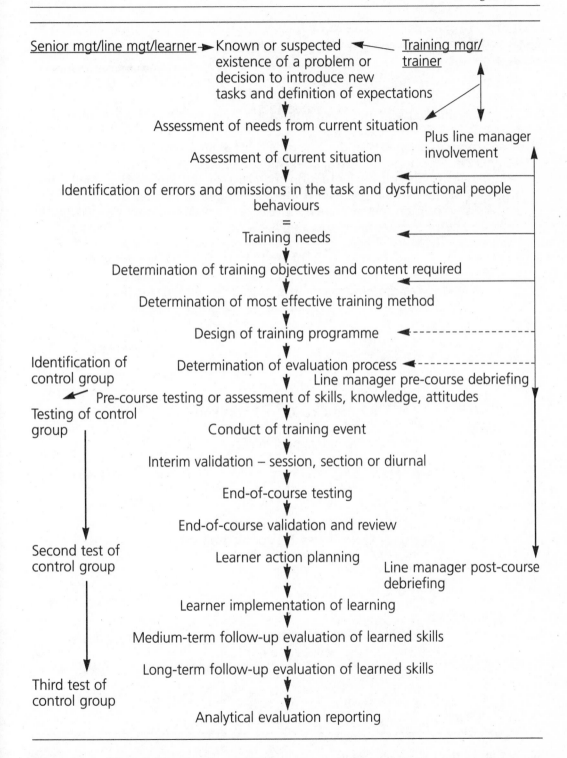

Figure 1.9   The training process

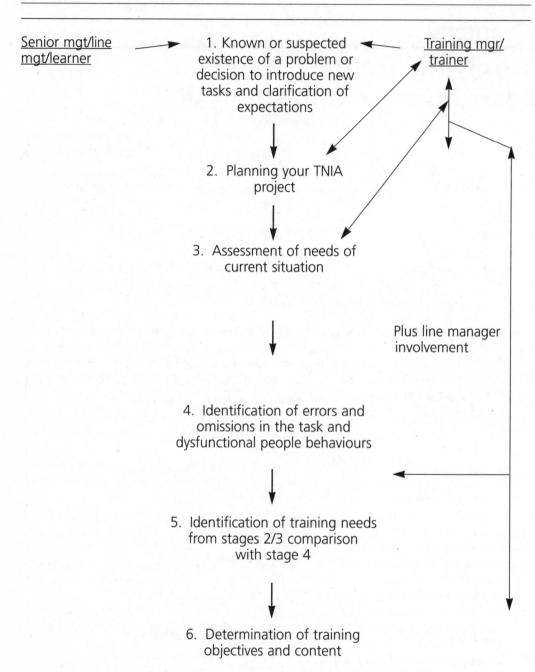

Figure 1.10   The TNIA content of the training process

Chapter 2
Applying Training Needs Identification and Analysis

This chapter:

> suggests some of the practical applications of TNIA
> describes the first three TNIA stages in detail – initial and initiating actions; planning the project; assessing the needs.

Before a training and development programme is developed a training need must be established, otherwise a considerable amount of resource and money can be wasted. Comprehensive surveys and analyses alone can demonstrate that training is indeed required: unfortunately this approach is not always followed. Training can result from other events:

- someone in the senior echelons of an organization decides for a non-defined reason that a certain training course would be a 'good thing' for the employees
- a trainer with an evangelical attitude towards training decides that a particular type of event (perhaps one of which they have just become aware and have espoused) would be good for the organization
- the senior management group feels that the employees of the organization would benefit from 'some form of training' and requires the training department to take immediate action
- the senior management group, having received reports of inadequacies in parts of the organization, feels that training will resolve these problems and requires the training department to take immediate action
- the senior management group, having received reports of apparent inadequacies in parts of the organization, questions these reports and requires a TNIA before a decision on training is made
- the senior management group, from reports and comments received and its own observations, feels that the training and development structure and approach in the organization needs to be considered for updating – a full TNIA is therefore required
- new work is to be introduced into the organization or parts of it, and because of the innovatory nature of the work specific practitioners will need to be trained to perform it effectively

- procedures, programmes, etc. updating existing ones are to be introduced in the organization, so specific practitioners will require updating training
- a number of members of the organization with a strong self-developmental motivation request that they receive training in a range of subjects.

These, and many others, are typical reasons – some relevant, others spurious – for the introduction or extension of training and development programmes. Most should be followed by a disciplined TNIA approach to clarify the facts and to ensure that the training is worthwhile for both the individuals and the organization. The following case studies will demonstrate some of these events.

Case study 1

The following is a type of discussion frequently held between a training officer and a training manager.

TM   I've had a note from the Senior Board that we have to introduce interactive skills training courses as soon as possible.

T   Why?

TM   Because we have been told to do so.

T   Who are they for?

TM   Everybody.

T   Everybody!?

TM   Well, probably not for the senior managers or the clerical and ancillary staff, but certainly for the supervisors, junior and middle managers.

T   But there are hundreds of these. We will need to put on a massive programme to cope.

TM   Right, but I have been told to get on with it.

T   Who is going to run the programmes?

TM   You are. You're my best trainer.

T   But I know nothing about interactive skills training.

TM   Well go on a course as soon as you can and read up about it.

And so on!

A programme of courses was started and because of their location and the nature of their material, the courses were enjoyed by most, though not all, of the participants. After two months the trainer was moved from the post, no further courses were held and nobody ever asked any questions about the events.

Case study 2

A department of an organization with twenty computer operatives used Microsoft Word for Windows. It was decided to upgrade the software to the latest version of the Word program. The practitioner group was called to a meeting during which the updating decision was reported and their views sought. It transpired that five of the operatives had experience of the new version, but the remainder were firmly wedded to the old version. Because of the number requiring upgrading training and the complexity of this upgrading, an IT training firm was contracted for the fifteen unskilled operatives. Follow-up and remedial training was put in the hands of the experienced five who were given a remit to monitor the implementation of the new work and propose remedial action, performing this with the agreement of the department manager.

The exercise was completed swiftly and successfully; two follow-up sessions were run by the experienced operatives; and an evaluation exercise – performed principally by examining the work of the operatives for effectiveness – showed that the updating had been installed with 100 per cent success. The cost and the disruption of the work of the department were minimal because of the comprehensive analysis of what was needed and how it could be best introduced.

This case study is obviously completely the opposite to case 1 both in approach and results.

Case study 3

A large government department was undergoing structural and responsibility changes which would affect all members of staff, but initially the middle and junior management grades. The changes would be operational, procedural and attitudinal and in many ways completely foreign to the established approaches. Training for the new type of work was fairly readily organized and introduced, but it became obvious that a wider training and development approach was necessary because of the greater range of activities involved. The existing training programme for newly-promoted middle managers included a once-for-all two-week course covering an almost impossible range of subjects, and a two-day staff appraisal review course. Nothing was available for senior managers and there was a course similar to the middle-management one for junior managers/supervisors.

The senior management group felt that a) more training and development was needed, b) different approaches were necessary, and c) the training and development approach for the organization should be welded into a programme as comprehensive, logical and essential as possible. However, the group had little real knowledge of requirements or types of approaches. Consequently, rather than issue a requirement to the training department to 'get on with it', it was decided that a full-scale TNIA should be performed, initially among the middle-management group (numbering several hundred) and eventually among other levels of the organization.

A TNIA team was formed and visited as many middle managers as possible within the time and cost scale to identify the range of their requirements. The result was a comprehensive training and development programme which started with a concentrated one-week new manager course, followed by a wide subject range of short modules with the attenders being *selected* rather than *elected*, the selection being based on need. This avoided to a large extent the attendance on the modules of people who were already experienced in the subject or would not use the particular skills within a reasonable period of time. This approach was monitored and evaluated and extended further throughout the organization, a costly exercise but one that introduced effective training and development at a much lower cost than if more haphazard approaches had been used.

These three case studies are a small sample of the varied range of approaches that are used and the particular method must be selected in the light of the organization's needs and resources. The simple message is that TNIA will ensure effectiveness of the resolution of skill and behavioural problems, usually at the lowest cost in terms of money and resources. The opposite approach is to do nothing or introduce something without proper consideration, almost invariably with ineffective results or higher costs than necessary.

The practical implementation of TNIA

The following is only a general indication of the ways in which a TNIA can be implemented in your organization; more detailed descriptions will be found in the works referred to in the 'Further reading' section (pages 239–41). The specific approaches chosen will depend on so many factors: the size of the organization; the size of the problem; the status and level of the people concerned; the resources available to enable a TNIA to be performed; the availability of the people likely to be involved; etc. But whatever the approach, there are two basic requirements to keep in mind:

1. What is the problem or suspected problem or need?
2. Can the problem be resolved by training or some other approach?

If the need is identified as one that training will resolve, part of the TNIA will be to identify the extent of the problem and the existing level of knowledge, skills and attitudes of the people involved. Training is change; change from an existing erroneous or non-existent state to one where the skill is performed in the work environment in the most effective manner. The more closely the existing state is identified, the more effectively will any training programmes be designed and the eventual evaluation made so much easier.

Training and development needs identified in a TNIA can be generally expressed in terms of changes in knowledge, skills or attitudes. Some needs will require support in only one of these areas, others in all three. New entrants to an organization, department or job may require all three aspects – knowledge of the organization and what is required of them; the skills to fulfil those requirements; any cultural, environmental or organizational behavioural attitudes to perform their tasks effectively.

On the other hand, experienced workers changing companies may only need new knowledge about the product in which they will be involved or making; and techniques special to the new company that differ from their existing skills;

specialist training in operating a different model of machine; and so on.

Some training needs will be easier to assess or measure than others. Some will be relatively straightforward – a manufacturing company failing to meet its objectives because its operatives are not fully skilled in using the installed machinery – others will be at the other end of the spectrum where behavioural attitudes may be preventing effective functioning. In the latter case not only will the behavioural dysfunctions need to be identified, but the norms of the behaviour established.

A pattern for identifying training needs

Figure 1.10 in Chapter 1, reproduced here as Figure 2.1, describes the logical path to follow in the identification and analysis of an organization's training or other needs.

The origins of stage 1 have been discussed earlier and may be related to suspected problems only or the specific requirements resulting from the introduction of new or updated tasks.

Stage 2 is the actual start of the process that will end in the statement of a training or other need to resolve a problem, or that a problem does not exist. Stages 3 and 4 will result in an examination of the knowledge, skills and attitudes of the people concerned at that initial period. The process can involve the many methods of data collection.

Stage 5 introduces the analytical component in the comparison between the identified requirements of the job, whether remedial or developmental, and the existing level of knowledge, skill and attitude among the relevant population. This comparison shows either the type of training need to resolve the problem or any other activity necessary.

Stage 6 puts this analysis into practical terms of training programmes or remedial work activities.

Who should perform the TNIA?

Superficially this might appear to be a simple question to answer, but again the most effective responses must depend on the situation and the type of TNIA required.

In many cases a trainer from the training department would appear to be the obvious person to perform the TNIA. He/she will have been trained in observation, analysis of observations and in interviewing to identify detailed aspects of situations. However, resource for this activity may not be readily available and the trainer may have limited or no experience in the area to be investigated. The other group of people who must be considered are the line managers, particularly in the case of existing tasks where the reason for investigation may be remedial. The line manager in charge of people undertaking specific tasks should, at best, have a detailed knowledge of the requirements of the task, or, because every supervisor or manager cannot be expected to be an expert at every aspect of the work they control,

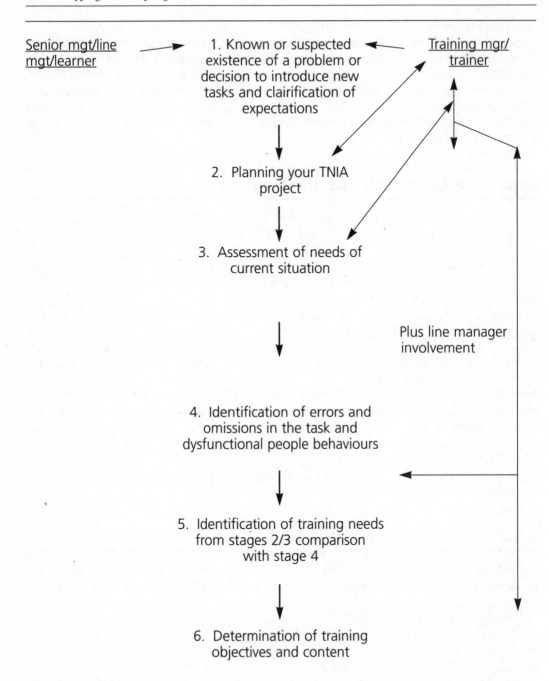

Figure 2.1   A pattern for the identification of training needs

have the means to carry out a detailed analysis.

From the training and development point of view, the ideal will be a co-operative project with the trainer and the line manager working together to produce a realistic and comprehensive TNIA. This has the advantage of involving the line manager in what have been traditionally considered the sacrosanct realms of training, and the trainer in line operations, an area into which the trainer has frequently been discouraged from venturing – training is for trainers; operations are for the line experts!

Line managers will invariably resist requests to perform TNIAs as strongly as many trainers, the arguments against including lack of time and even lack of the necessary skills. The counter arguments to these will include:

● the line manager is in the most favourable position to know the work
● it is in the line manager's interest that the staff are trained (if necessary) in the most effective way and in the areas that the line manager requires
● effectively trained staff, trained as the line manager requires and to the desired extent, will enhance the line manager's operations, this enhancement reflecting on the manager
● the line manager, if capability is the question, can always be trained in the necessary skills
● co-operation between the training department and the line management will reduce the time demands on both and enhance the production of both.

Methods for analysis

The methods and approaches to determine what is required or where inadequacies exist will obviously depend on the type of TNIA. The people and tasks for which a TNIA will be demanded will include:

● new workers coming into an existing work situation
● new workers coming into an existing work situation with some experience that requires updating or change
● completely new work being introduced
● remedial action being seen as necessary
● a need to review new developments
● a need to review existing situations for possible modification.

Most of the above will require similar TNIA approaches, albeit tailored to the particular circumstance. To describe each type of situation would involve a considerable amount of repetition or cross-referencing, so I will describe in detail the steps necessary for conducting a TNIA where remedial action is necessary. Other approaches can be modified relatively easily from this base and some of the more important modifications will be suggested later.

Stage 1: clarifying requirements

Let us assume that the senior manager group has met and has received reports from various sources that inadequacies exist in providing the goods or services relating to the organization. There is no positive evidence about the full nature of these inadequacies, but the group has committed itself to:

> determining the nature of the inadequacies;
> resolving the action to deal with the inadequacies;
> authorizing the action for this resolution whether it be operational activity or training/retraining;

and that to reach a desirable conclusion

> a TNIA should be conducted by the training department with the full co-operation of the relevant line management.

Additional action

A substantial amount of TNIA work is ensuring that information is held or is made available by the use of questioning. Consequently when the requirement described above in stage 1 is received from the senior group, the TNIA performers must be in possession of information relating to the following areas.

Information

- A statement by the client group that any action resulting from either a training or non-training solution will have a significant effect on the value operation of the business. If this cannot be stated, there must be doubt expressed as to whether the project is worth proceeding with.
- All information, reported or suspected, held by the clients – the senior management group.
- All reports relating to the suspected inadequacies.

Aims and objectives

- An indication or more specific information about the areas – environmental or task areas – in which the inadequacies are suspected. The problems raised by the client group may appear to be organization-wide. Resources may be insufficient to cover the complete area: with what type of representative population will the group be satisfied; should certain groups only be targeted; should samples be taken (and be acceptable) from each of the groups involved? The responses to these questions will also give an indication of the importance that the client group is affording to the TNIA. It is more than likely that the client group will not be able to answer such questions or will require you to take the most appropriate decisions – be prepared for this and to be able to make proposals based on your anticipation of the responses.

Within the aims and objectives expressed by the client group there may be undisclosed key areas. You should ensure that these are aired and described before closing your questioning. If at the end of your TNIA these areas have not emerged naturally, your clients may be disappointed or even dismayed that they have not emerged, blaming you for not identifying what, to them, were important aspects. It is so much simpler to ask!

Desired outcomes

● A statement by the client group about the desired situation: acceptable level of performance; percentage increase in efficiency; model of behaviour to which the group subscribes; and so on. This statement reflects, in effect, the aims and objectives of the senior group and the organization and will almost certainly be linked with the organizational mission statement or business plan.

Linked to this will be the question of the final reporting of the TNIA findings. If you are a training officer conducting the TNIA, are you required to report to your training manager who will then report to the client group? Or will you be expected to report directly yourself? Will the final report be required in writing, as an oral presentation, or a written report explained orally in a presentation? If a written report, what type and format will be required? If an oral presentation, what facilities will be available, under what circumstances will the presentation be made, and how long will you be given to make the presentation? Some of the answers to these questions might be held over to a later stage when the results of the TNIA are to hand, but it is frequently much safer/more comfortable to obtain answers at the earliest possible stage.

Providing authority

● The public authority of the senior management group to the TNIA performers to take the necessary action. You might envisage resistance to your approaches in a number of management or operational areas. You must be able to overcome many of these hindrances with arguments relating to the benefits that will ensue, but there may also be times when you will need to quote a strong authority to take certain actions. This of course will be your last line of defence – imposed help rarely achieves the fullest co-operation desirable. Without the full co-operation and co-working of line management, if you are a trainer your encroachment of a traditionally 'no-go' operations area will be treated with suspicion and/or defensiveness. Again the most effective approach will be to overcome this suspicion without recourse to any form of imposition.

Budget issues

● The specific authority to utilize a budget for the TNIA.

Success performance indicators

● What performance indicators will the clients use to assess the success of the outcomes of your TNIA? What outcomes do the clients have at this stage and how flexible are these desired outcomes?

Timescales

● A specific completion date or period of time over which the TNIA should be held. This is another area where you might expect that the client group requires you to suggest a timescale which will be agreed, modified or rejected – be prepared for this to avoid giving an 'off-the-cuff' estimate. Estimates made under these conditions frequently result in deadlines that are eventually found impossible to meet. Your expertise will almost certainly be accepted more readily if you request time to assess a realistic period.

Finally, but most importantly ...

Client expectations

● What are the expectations of the clients?

Although these may appear to be obvious to the client group, it is only too easy for a TNIA to be commissioned without the client having a complete knowledge of what they entail.

Does the client group require a TNIA that covers the problems up to the final stage of identification, or one that not only identifies and confirms the problems that were suspected, but also provides detailed recommendations about how they might be resolved, and by whom?

Having determined the answer to the above question it is strongly recommended that the client group complete or subscribe to a written statement covering the areas suggested. This not only keeps your TNIA objectives clearly in mind; provides an authority document in support of any action you might have to take; but also helps to clarify to the client group what they actually require and are seeking. You might encounter resistance to the production of or subscription to such a written statement, particularly if the TNIA is complex or may take a long time. Assure your client group that they will find it useful in assessing whether you have completed the TNIA in accordance with their original and initial wishes. The human memory is fallible and flexible!

Stage 2: planning your TNIA

Stage 2 follows the clarification, as far as possible, of the suspicions, information and data from stage 1 and is one of the more important aspects of the TNIA process. If it is skimped or ignored, so many problems in the implementation of the TNIA can arise that failure becomes almost a certainty.

The process at this stage is thinking things through – how are you going to implement what has been described as required of you by your client group? Particularly if you are not well acquainted with the areas in which your TNIA is to take place, and even if you are, you will need to ask yourself and others certain questions that will produce the basis for your TNIA. Many of the questions will have been answered in your clarification action in stage 1, but a reminder will reinforce your approach.

1. *What is happening in your organization that has resulted in the need for a TNIA? Some of the reasons might be:*
   - the introduction of new people to the organization or particular sections of it
   - promotions from one level to another, the change requiring the acquisition of new or updated knowledge, skills and/or attitudes
   - the introduction of new procedures, operations or systems or their updating from existing ones
   - restructuring of the organization which might include modification of operations or cultural behaviours
   - the introduction of new products and/or new equipment
   - the introduction of new or additional customers with consequent modification of marketing and sales approaches
   - the introduction of a training and development policy and programme
   - the review of an existing training and development policy and programme.
2. *What are the suspicions or information that have given rise to the need for a TNIA?*
   - falling levels of production or requests for services or repeat services
   - numerous comments about specific inadequacies in appraisal review reports
   - increasing complaints from customers – internal and external – and/or increased loss of customers
   - increasing number of absences; discipline situations; grievances
   - increased labour turnover, particularly in voluntary leaving cases
   - increased appeals to industrial tribunals against treatment received within the organization
   - increased sickness absences in non-epidemic periods
   - increased wastage of materials or products and negative reports from quality control.

3. *Are there any factors outside the control of the organization that might be having an effect on the problems? Such factors could include:*
    ● a faltering economy with particular relationship to the organization in question
    ● new or changed legislation, either industrial or having particular reference to the organization
    ● a changing demand for quality, quantity or product by existing or potential customers
    ● an increase in the numbers or quality of competitors in the same or similar markets
    ● a change in world economy, demand or other influences
    ● problems associated with suppliers of raw materials for production purposes – quality, quantity, timing and so on
    ● changes in interest and exchange rates, both at home and abroad.
4. *What places will have informational and data material available to you for your TNIA activities? Such places will include in the organization:*
    ● production records
    ● activity records
    ● legal records of actions against the organization
    ● personnel records showing the number of disciplinary actions; grievances; labour turnover
    ● financial audits
    ● health and safety records
    ● sales figures and records of marketing activity
    ● management and board reports
    ● staff appraisal review records and analyses
    ● other records and reports held at senior management level relevant to the problems.

Preliminary action planning

With the background data identified and recorded you are now ready to look closely at the way in which you are going, although the final specific plan will depend on your particular problem.

Action planning is an ideal approach to many solutions, and I shall return to this theme in later chapters when the end results of designing and planning are reached, the evaluation of training and development. It is important to complete a written action plan, not simply to introduce yet another piece of paper, but to ensure that:

● there is a written record of intent
● there is a reminder format for your actions
● when the time comes to assess your level of success, you cannot omit an unresolved item by conveniently forgetting it
● interim assessments can be made, action completed recorded and action yet to be taken firmly placed in the mind

● your end achievements can be evaluated against your intentions.

All good action plans start with a statement of intent and your TNIA action plan is no exception! Depending on your specific TNIA, it could read something like:

> This TNIA project will identify whether the problems reported in the xxx operations area are due to a need for training; a failure of previous training and a need for retraining; the introduction of a new training scheme; or failure to carry out known operational procedures, etc.
>
> If the causes are connected with training, recommendations will be made to the clients (yyy) that a training and development programme should be introduced (re-introduced) to satisfy identified needs. Following identification of the needs, a detailed analysis will be made of the causes of the problem and general contents proposed for the training and development programme.
>
> If the causes are connected with non-training reasons, following agreement with the line managers, recommendations will be made for operational change of a relevant nature.
>
> This project will commence on zzz and terminate by aaa. A written report will be submitted to the client group by bbb, initial submission being made through the training manager.

The next stage can be to determine, in advance if possible, any resistance to your TNIA. Although the senior management group and you can see the problems and the need to take a TNIA action to resolve them, the people directly involved in (and perhaps responsible for) these problems will not necessarily be equally motivated and willing to help. Some prior consideration of possible problems will not come amiss.

A force field analysis is useful at this stage. It helps you to identify and consider all the forces that are likely to help or hinder you in your project. This analysis chart will not necessarily be permanent. Some of the forces that at the early stage you might consider as hindering, may in fact turn out to be helpers, and vice versa. Other forces may need to be added as the project progresses, so the initial chart should not be looked upon as written in stone. A typical format is shown in Figure 2.2.

There will normally be many more items on an actual chart and the strength of the helpers–hinderers will vary considerably, but the almost graphical display demonstrates very clearly the extent of the problems. It also highlights the strong hinderers that will have to be addressed and overcome as far as possible and which helpers can be introduced to resolve the hinderer factors.

Project planning

The next logical step would be to produce a project plan defining your approach to the TNIA – methods, people, timings and so on – but this must be delayed here

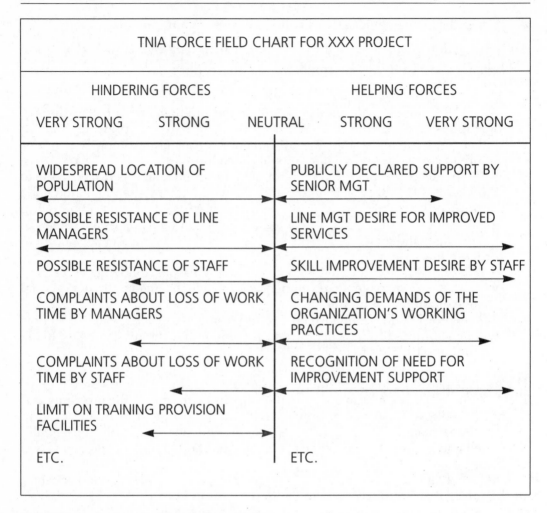

TNIA FORCE FIELD CHART FOR XXX PROJECT

HINDERING FORCES

HELPING FORCES

VERY STRONG   STRONG   NEUTRAL   STRONG   VERY STRONG

WIDESPREAD LOCATION OF POPULATION

PUBLICLY DECLARED SUPPORT BY SENIOR MGT

POSSIBLE RESISTANCE OF LINE MANAGERS

LINE MGT DESIRE FOR IMPROVED SERVICES

POSSIBLE RESISTANCE OF STAFF

SKILL IMPROVEMENT DESIRE BY STAFF

COMPLAINTS ABOUT LOSS OF WORK TIME BY MANAGERS

CHANGING DEMANDS OF THE ORGANIZATION'S WORKING PRACTICES

COMPLAINTS ABOUT LOSS OF WORK TIME BY STAFF

RECOGNITION OF NEED FOR IMPROVEMENT SUPPORT

LIMIT ON TRAINING PROVISION FACILITIES

ETC.

ETC.

Figure 2.2   Action plan force field analysis

to discuss the various methods that can be used before you decide on your modus operandi.

Stage 3: assessing the needs of the current situation

In order to identify if there is anything wrong with a job or person performing a job or task, it is necessary to be fully aware of the details, extent and nature of the job or role, which means assessing and analysing what *should* be happening. In order to do this we need a job analysis, a job or task description and a job or task specification.

Job analyses and descriptions

Job descriptions cover the details of the effective activities that should be found in a particular job – for example, a hotel receptionist, a machine operator in industry, a bricklayer, an accounts clerk and so on. The job analysis *should* not require you to start from square one in the process as there should be an existing range of documents, such as a job description, that define these in the organization concerned. In spite of the wide-ranging value of these documents, they tend to be rarities. They may never have existed, or if they have they were a long time ago and have not been updated as changes occurred.

Without an existing, up-to-date job description the TNIA practitioners will need to build up their own views of the job, supplemented perhaps with other information, such as National Vocational Qualification standards of competence.

Job descriptions are usually fairly short documents outlining the priority duties and responsibilities of the job. Some may go beyond the purely functional aspects of the job and include such information as hours of work, pay structure, lines of communication with bosses, peers and staff and other conditions that are frequently also included in the contract of employment. However, for the purposes of a TNIA we need to concentrate only on the parts of the description that are concerned with the operation of the job or task. If a job description exists, the omission of significant sections may be a first indication of the problems. For example, everybody needs to know the direction and extent of their lines of communication and responsibilities – without this information the job becomes more difficult and frustration and errors can emerge. If the worker does not know to whom they should rightly communicate certain facts or other information that comes their way in the line of duty, this possibly vital information may not be passed on at all. If lines of responsibility are not clear, conflicting demands by several people may confuse the jobholder to the extent that either nothing is done or the most important task is neglected.

A simplified example of a job description for a training officer is shown in Figure 2.3.

When the job description is being used for a TNIA, the duties section will naturally be the most important, although failure in other parts can produce operational problems requiring solution. The example in Figure 2.3 is simplified; the duties should be complete and exhaustive, including an 'occasional duties' section. The terms should be as simple and as unambiguous as possible, thus avoiding misunderstandings with resultant problems in the work.

So your first step as a TNIA practitioner is either to obtain the existing job description and confirm its currency, or take steps to produce one. This latter activity will obviously extend the time required for the TNIA as it will involve detailed contact with the jobholders and their bosses, including observation of the work being performed. Some methods of dealing with this will be covered later.

JOB TITLE	Training officer
FUNCTION	To design, plan, act as trainer or facilitator on, and validate the department's management training and development programmes
LINES OF COMMUNICATION	Upwards – to training manager
	Laterally – to colleague training officers
	Downwards – to course administration staff via administration executive or direct as agreed with that executive
LINES OF RESPONSIBILITY	To – training manager
	For – relevant administration staff as agreed with administration executive
HOURS OF WORK	Non-training periods – 42 hours per week basic including lunch interval and other agreed breaks
	Training periods – duration of agreed training day
DUTIES	1. Designing new training programmes for which objectives will be supplied by the training manager
	2. Planning detailed organization of designed training programmes, including methods, techniques and the use of aids
	3. The production, wherever possible, of training aids to be used in training programmes for which responsible
	4. Recommendations for the purchase of training aids or other training equipment that is not available in the department
	5. Acting as lead trainer or facilitator on programmes for which responsibility has been given; acting as co-trainer or facilitator on programmes for which joint responsibility has been agreed; acting as support trainer or facilitator on programmes whose responsibility rests with another training officer
	6. Validating in accordance with department procedures, training and development programmes for which responsible or co-responsible
	etc.

Figure 2.3   **Example of a simplified job description**

Job and task specifications

By this stage in the investigation you will have gained a significant appreciation of the job and its requirements on the jobholders. However, although the job description is quite full, a much more detailed analysis is required to identify where problems lie. Initial consideration of the description and some observation of the jobholder's performance, perhaps following clues from the jobholder's boss or some of the earlier information, may lead you to need to look in greater depth at certain aspects of the job.

The job specification details in depth the knowledge, skills and attitudes required of the jobholder in every aspect of the job, aspects broadly described in the job description. Figure 2.4 describes one part of the required tasks of a painter and decorator.

In the example shown in Figure 2.4 'attitudes' have not been included; their inclusion will vary from job to job depending on the jobholder's contact with other people and the significance of the interactions.

The more detailed the job specification, the easier it will be to identify possible problem areas, or at least direct you to the areas that need investigation. Unfortunately, even fewer job specifications exist than job descriptions and you may find that you will have to construct them from scratch. Again, depending on the clues given by the jobholder's boss and/or prior information or suspicions, it may be necessary only to produce a task specification for particular parts of the job.

JOB TITLE   Painter and decorator
DETAILED TASKS   Task 3. Paperhanging
         3.1 Task: Selection of paper
         Knowledge requirement: the range of types of wallcovering including relative strengths, textures, environmental suitabilities, etc.
         Skill requirement: the ability to select the most appropriate covering for a range of environments
         3.2 Task: Room measurement
         Knowledge requirement: methods of estimation; unit methods of measurement; imperial and metric systems
         etc.

Figure 2.4   **Example of a job specification**

NVQ competence standards

In recent years lead bodies have produced, on behalf of the National Council for Vocational Qualifications, standards of competence for many of the occupations found in industry and industry sectors. These standards describe consistent levels of performance that are capable of assessment or measurement. They have a wide range of uses although their basic intention is in the award of the National Vocational Qualification for that occupation at one of the relevant levels.

These competence standards can also act as guidelines to employers in recruitment, identification of job requirements, performance appraisal, identification of training, etc. Their link with the process of TNIA is obvious as they describe the details of a job performance without recourse to the vagaries of Job Descriptions and Job Specifications constructed from variable bases. The standards contain for each occupation a Key Purpose, Key Areas and Key Roles – these are the more general statements. Increasing detail follows with the Units of Competence, the Elements of Competence and the Performance Indicators.

Standards have been produced by the Training and Development Lead Body for the various levels of training and development functions. Level 3 of the Training and Development NVQ, the level of the Training Officer, describes the following standards.

Units of Competence

Each Key Role contains a number of Units. For example, the units in key role E2 (Evaluate the effectiveness of training and development programmes) are:

Unit E21   Evaluate training and development programmes
Unit E22   Improve training and development programmes
Unit E23   Evaluate training and development sessions.

Elements of Competence

Even the Units are not sufficiently detailed to enable a realistic assessment of competence in the function to be performed. Consequently each Unit is further described in terms of Elements – statements of the detailed aspects of the function. The Units vary from two to five Elements each. For example, the Elements contained in Unit E21 quoted above are:

Element E211   Select methods for evaluating training and development programmes
Element E212   Collect information to evaluate training and development programmes
Element E213   Analyse information to improve training and development programmes.

You will see that the range of Elements describes the progressive involvement in that particular competence, from selecting methods to analysing the result.

Performance Criteria

The Units and Elements define what are included as functions in the competence standards. The Performance Criteria define what an assessor must look for to determine whether these functions are being carried out satisfactorily – the test of effectiveness – and it is in this particular area that the TNIA practitioner can gain the most use.

Each Element has a number of associated Performance Criteria, ranging from five to ten or more criteria. For example, in Element E211 the nine Performance Criteria for this Element are:

Unit E21　Evaluate training and development programmes
Element E211　Select methods for evaluating training and development
　　　　　　　programmes
Performance criteria:
(a)　the training and development programmes being evaluated are clearly identified and used as the focus for the evaluation process
(b)　the specific objectives and desired outcomes of the training and development programmes are clearly identified
(c)　the purpose, scope and level of evaluation are clearly identified
(d)　methods that are capable of evaluating training and development programmes are clearly identified
(e)　the advantages and disadvantages of each evaluation method are suitably assessed and an appropriate method selected
(f)　evaluation criteria are appropriate to the training and development programme and clearly specified
(g)　evaluation methods are capable of being implemented within the resources available
(h)　all aspects of the evaluation method are clearly identified and agreed with the appropriate people
(i)　a plan for implementing the evaluation is clearly specified.

In addition to the Performance Criteria listed, notes are included in the Element giving guidance on the type of evidence – performance and knowledge – required to satisfy the criteria. For the Performance Criteria described above the Evidence Requirements are:

The performance evidence required is:
identification of training and development programmes being evaluated
specification of evaluation methods and rationale for their selection
specification of evaluation criteria and rationale for their selection
explanation of scope and purpose of evaluation

plan for the implementation of the evaluation
notes of agreement made.

The knowledge evidence required is:
methods of evaluating training and development programmes
range of evaluation criteria available
how to identify criteria for evaluation
employment and equal opportunities legislation and good practice
relevant national and organizational debates concerning learning
relevant national and organizational debates relating to evaluation and
quality improvement.

As the Units, Elements and Performance Criteria describe the occupation in
sufficient detail that the skill of the performer can be assessed, the standards are
ready-made listings of the skills necessary to identify areas that figure in the
TNIA, substituting for job descriptions and specifications that may not exist.

You are now in a position to complete the first part of your TNIA planning
process – the methods by which you will assess the needs of the current situation
– but before you can complete your planning knowledge of the problem,
identification techniques will be required. Chapter 3 describes the techniques
which are linked with the identification of the errors and omissions in the task
performance and the people's dysfunctional behaviours.

Chapter 3
Identifying current training needs

This chapter:

> describes in detail stages 4, 5 and 6 of the TNIA process
> discusses the types of analyses possible in a TNIA
> describes the principal methods of conducting a TNIA
> continues discussion of the project planning process.

Stages 4 and 5: identifying errors and omissions in people skills and identifying training needs

Detailed analyses

Whether or not you use the NVQ standards of competence in your TNIA process you are gong to be involved to some extent in a detailed analysis of the job(s) under investigation. These analyses will be most frequently concerned with skills and attitudes, but occasionally the analysis of the extent of knowledge held by the people involved may be in question.

Knowledge identification and analysis

Determining levels and needs in the knowledge areas is probably the most straightforward of all the analytical approaches. Whether it is with an individual or a group or series of groups, the method will usually consist of simple questioning to find out whether the individuals know and understand the required knowledge. The identification can, in some cases, be observation of the jobholder to confirm that they are following the accepted set of rules or giving accurate and complete information. In other cases, perhaps where the knowledge requirement is more complex or observation is not possible, a test of knowledge and understanding can be set.

Although this approach is relatively straightforward, you will need to set out clearly your objectives for the exercise. Criteria might include:

- What is the range of knowledge to be tested? Is the whole range of the subject to be included or have there been prior indications or suspicions that the lack of knowledge falls in certain areas only?

- What is the depth of knowledge to be tested? Will the answers have to be sufficiently detailed to show or indicate that the jobholder is aware of everything in the subject area and be fully aware, where relevant, of the reasons, etc?

- What questions on which subjects will need to be posed?

- What form will the questions have to take? There is a range of alternative methods of posing questions ranging from simple closed, direct questions requiring answers of straightforward fact; binary choice questions – an alternative of 'yes' or 'no', or a choice between two possible answers, one of which is incorrect; true/false questions in which the relevant answer is sought to a statement rather than a question; multiple choice questions that extend the range of answers over four or five possibilities, again one only of which is correct; short answer questions that demand some form of statement as a textual answer; to the open questions that allow the jobholder to express themselves in whatever way they feel capable or wish to do.

- What are the answers that will be required? The correct answers must be available, checked and confirmed to avoid any error.

- How much variation will be allowed within the answers? This will depend on the type of knowledge sought – some answers will be capable of expression in one way only; others might have several possibilities or subsidiary statements.

- What degree of accuracy is required? Usually an accuracy of 100 per cent to an individual question is required, but the level of the job might dictate whether 100 per cent of the answers have to be 100 per cent correct.

- Who will assess the answers? Will you, as the question poser and TNIA practitioner, do the assessment or will you require a completely neutral person to do so?

Skills assessment

Assessing job, social and attitudinal skills is usually much more difficult than the straightforward knowledge assessment, made doubly so as the practice of skills is the implementation of knowledge. Most skills assessment can only be made by direct observation, frequently supported by interviews, although others can give indications by means of questionnaires. Decide between the following:

- observation of work performed
- interviews with the jobholders to identify the extent of what they perform, both with individuals and small focus groups
- a combination of interview and observation
- questionnaires

- a combination of questionnaires and interview
- nominal group methods including brainstorming
- the Delphi technique
- audits
- diary methods
- critical incident techniques
- mirroring
- psychological testing.

Of the methods listed above, observation, interviews and questionnaires, or a combination of these, are the most commonly used; these will be described in detail with the remainder restricted to a brief description which can be supplemented by reference to more extended sources.

Observation

Where it is feasible and appropriate, observation of the jobholder(s) performing their jobs or tasks is probably the most effective technique to collect data about the practice of the task. This approach is restricted to jobs and tasks that contain readily observable skills and attitude behaviours, usually the more functional types of jobs. General management skills and attitudes, as opposed to specific ones such as negotiations, presentations, interpersonal or social skills, and attitudes generally, though not impossible to observe and assess are much more difficult.

Observers must prepare themselves fully, prior to the assessment, starting with a complete awareness and understanding of the job description and job specification, with any doubtful areas being clarified at that stage. It will help if the observer is familiar with the job, although it could be argued that a fresh mind, armed with the knowledge of what should occur, may be less biased in the assessment. It can also be useful to discuss the job with someone who is well acquainted with the job and who has been assessed as fully skilled. The observer must be fully informed but with a flexible attitude to the task.

Decide at this initial stage on the extent of the observation. The training need question may have arisen about the whole job or, more commonly, only part or parts of it.

The next stage is to meet the jobholder(s) who will be observed as they must be fully aware of the observation and the reasons for it. In an investigatory observation to determine the range of skills required and specifications for the tasks, this openness should present no problems. But in an observation to assess the skill level, it is difficult to hide this fact and divulgence of the imminent observation may have a number of effects:

- The observer may be suspected of motives that have nothing to do with assistance to improve the job and the holder's skills.

- The jobholder, aware of the observation, will perform in a fully acceptable manner – perhaps unlike the usual performance – demonstrating that the initially stated problem is not one of training but of commission of the task. There may be a number of non-training reasons why the jobholder has not been working to standard until the observation occurred.

● Unnaturally perfect performance as a result of the observation may continue for an initial period only. Once the jobholder becomes involved in the task, the presence of the observer may be forgotten and natural reactions occur. Again, if even for an initial period only, the task can be performed perfectly, the immediate conclusion must be that a non-training solution is suggested. Both these situations require further investigation.

These contaminatory effects of known observation raise questions as to whether the observations should be overt or covert. Covert ones will certainly enable observation of natural actions, but if the covert action is discovered all sorts of problems could arise. Some jobs will lend themselves to a covert observation, whereas others will need to have the observer in full sight of, and perhaps close to the jobholder.

Observation preparation

Although flexibility must be the order of the day, the observer will need to be forearmed. Full awareness of the job descriptions and specifications has been mentioned; other preparation might include the production of an outline aide mémoire listing the items for observation, perhaps in the order in which they should be performed, and a description of the items of knowledge of which the jobholder should be aware. Attitudes, where relevant, should also be included in this document. The form of the aide mémoire will usually be based on personal preference and ease of use, but many observers find a 'ticklist' most convenient. Alternatively, separate sheets for knowledge, skills and attitudes might be used, particularly where the pace of operations is not too fast for the observer to work with more than one list.

The observation listings must be comprehensive and accurate: following completion of the outlines, their value should be checked with an authority or expert on the job to be observed. This discussion can also help to determine the order of task performance where this is appropriate to the job.

Observers must be completely objective in their approach and free of value judgements. The observation must be of fact; what happens, not what the observer would like to happen.

Every action, as far as possible, should be recorded. This can be a problem if the task includes several activities in a swift sequence or overlapping. In such situations there will be some omissions or errors, but if time and resource is available the exercise can be repeated to ensure completeness.

Many observers prefer a different approach that avoids the problems of pre-judgement and inflexibility imposed by structured lists. In this case the observer, albeit with some knowledge of the role of the jobholder, starts with a blank sheet and records the actions of the person as they happen. Following the observation, the records are discussed with the job expert and/or compared with the job description and specification and the standards if available.

Case study: the dental receptionist

An example of such an exercise might be the observation of a dental receptionist performing her duties at the desk of a large dental practice. Work of this nature will include knowledge, skills and attitudes as aspects of the complete job and all these must be covered.

The observation might begin during a period when the receptionist is working with dental records – making entries, making clarification queries, filing, etc. The observer will be looking for speed of working, knowledge of what has to be done, understanding of problems and the guidance given to their resolution. It will not be possible to confirm accuracy at this stage for such items as entries and filing, but this can be done following the observation period. Other observable skills will include the receptionist's use of equipment that is part of the job – use and manner on the telephone; keyboard skills with either a typewriter or computer; use of calculators, diaries, etc. If the job includes all these items of equipment, but the observation period does not cover their actual use, other arrangements must be made to observe or receive reports on their use at a subsequent date.

The duties of a dental receptionist normally include considerable use of the telephone, receiving incoming calls from patients or potential patients and making outgoing calls confirming appointments, seeking information, and so on. The observation will include the general manner of the individual; the clarity and tone of the voice; the apparent speed of understanding; the clarity of giving information; and recognized organizational requirements. The last-named aspect might be the procedural instruction of the organization about how to deal with a telephone call – no more than three rings allowed in normal circumstances; the greeting, for example 'X practice; Y speaking; how can I help you?'; the procedure when the caller is asked to wait.

Another duty is the handling of patients who attend the surgery. As with the telephone call, the observer's activity starts as soon as the person enters the reception area:

- Does the receptionist become aware immediately of the patient's entrance?
- Does the receptionist give any visible signal that this has happened?
- Would the patient be aware of the signal given?
- When the patient approaches the reception desk what does the receptionist do – continue working; immediately stop working? What action is taken if a telephone call is happening?
- How does the receptionist greet the patient? (Many of these behavioural and attitudinal skills will be similar to the telephone observations.)
- How does the receptionist address the patient – in a friendly manner; in an interested and helpful manner; using language that the patient would be likely to understand; in an empathic manner demonstrating awareness of the possible feelings of a person entering a dentist's surgery; and so on?

Skills are introduced when the needs of the patient have been obtained – what does the receptionist do to satisfy these needs; how are they effected; how efficiently are arrangements or alternative arrangements made; etc?

Following the observation, the records are compared with the standards model. Any significant variations will indicate confirmation of the problems that initiated the TNIA and the difference between the desired or necessary activity and the observed activity will *suggest* a need to be addressed by either a training or non-training solution – a training programme; a follow-up training programme; at-work discussion; a modification of the job specification; coaching by the head receptionist being some of the possible solutions.

Observation as one of the techniques of identifying training and development needs is summarized in Figure 3.1.

Diagnostic questionnaires

Another common method of determining training and development needs is to use a questionnaire. Although superficially the sending of a questionnaire to a number of people and analysing the responses appears a relatively simple

METHODS	ADVANTAGES	CONSTRAINTS
Observation of the jobholders performing their tasks. Requires full prior briefing and awareness of range of job, obtainable from job descriptions, specifications and standards. Essential that observation is overt, or at least arranged openly, otherwise suspicion cast on operation.	Jobholders are seen in actual working environment and do not require to be taken away from their work. A natural observational environment free from the artificiality of other situations.	Presence of observer might produce spurious and contaminatory effects. Observer needs to be unobtrusive. Time consuming. Not all types of jobs suitable for this approach. Observation must be completely objective.

Figure 3.1   Observation as a TNIA technique

approach, it is in fact fraught with difficulties. The testing of knowledge levels has been mentioned earlier and this can be achieved readily by a test in the form of a questionnaire, but the investigation of skills by questionnaire is much more difficult and subjective.

It is rare that only one questionnaire is sent to one jobholder as it must be accepted that the responses to questionnaires are very personal and are subject to a considerable degree of contamination. In spite of requests to the questionnaire completer, the responses may give the information the completer feels the questioner wants or, rather than being factual, might be a 'text-book' response. Consequently, questionnaires used in TNIAs are usually sent to a significant number of people, say all the jobholders of a particular nature in an organization; all the members of one duty department.

When you are constructing a questionnaire, the first and probably most difficult decision you have to make is 'What questions should I ask?'. Naturally you will be guided to some extent by the job documentation or agreed model, but considerable care must be taken to avoid leading questions or those that will suggest a 'right' response to the completer.

Types of diagnostic questionnaire

A number of variations are possible within the range of questionnaires you might send to the target jobholders, but again remember that the responses will be very personal, possibly slanted by the attitudes of the completer and their intention of responding 'honestly'.

One approach is, from the standards or other documentation, to list the skills involved in the job and ask the jobholder to confirm whether or not they are able to perform these activities. A supplementary list might include other skills on which you might ask the person to comment whether or not they should be part of a job or task specification. 'Dummy' skills might be included in this latter section to confirm that the questionnaire is being completed with consideration.

An alternative approach demands much more work of the jobholder, with the consequence that the responses may not be as comprehensive as necessary. A blank sheet of paper is sent to the jobholder with the request that they consider their job and enter all the knowledge, skills and attitudes they feel are necessary to perform the job satisfactorily. They can also be asked, when they have listed the items, to place them in order of importance and to indicate their individual levels of skill against each of the items.

This 'open' type of questionnaire usually results in further reference to the jobholder. There may be significant omissions that appear on the job standards model or, if the questionnaire is sent to a number of jobholders, some may include (or omit) aspects that have not been considered by others. In such cases you must seek the completers' views on why they have included or excluded certain aspects of the job.

A more 'sophisticated' questionnaire asks the jobholder to rate their skill levels against each of the predetermined skill questions. If honest answers are given to this type of questioning, good indications of training need result. This approach is also particularly useful with a fully validated questionnaire where the individual's responses can be related to a norm.

It must be stressed again that the responses to questionnaires will be highly subjective, being based on the personal views of the completer and can vary considerably, almost to extremes. You can attempt to reduce some of this subjectivity by also sending questionnaires to the jobholders' bosses, colleagues and, if possible and/or desirable, subordinates. In the case of the subordinates, they must be sufficiently aware of what the jobholder should need/be able to do to make their responses relevant. The additional subjectivities of value judgements and relationships can enter into completed questionnaires, not only from subordinates, but also colleagues and bosses.

Provided these dangers are taken into account or avoided, this approach can reach a very wide sample of jobholders and produce a large amount of data which can be analysed. Figure 3.2 summarizes the questionnaire approach.

METHODS	ADVANTAGES	CONSTRAINTS
Sending questionnaires to a sample or complete group of jobholders.	A large number of jobholders can be contacted at the same time. Confidentiality can be contained. Less expensive than some other methods. Large numbers of responses can be compared and analysed.	Return rate can be low unless controlled. The communication is one-way only. Responses can be very subjective and personally-biased. Responses can be contaminated in a variety of ways. People may feel the paper approach is too impersonal.

Figure 3.2   Questionnaires as a TNIA technique

Interviews

The third frequently used method of conducting a TNIA is to interview the jobholders – a similar range of population described in the use of questionnaires. As the interview is generally with an individual, a large number will be extremely costly. However, the direct person-to-person contact ensures that the TNIA is seen to be more human and immediate clarification and extension of the information obtained can take place. The subjective/contaminated responses of the questionnaires can be questioned for validity and the result is more likely to be complete.

Planning the interviews

Although a flexible, unstructured interview can succeed, you are advised to prepare your approach beforehand in substantial detail, although still retaining the means for flexibility. The interview preparation form must not consist of a series of questions in which deviation or modification is not permitted as the aware interviewer can often obtain much more information from the clues given by the interviewee.

TNIA interviews follow the general pattern of basic people interviews. Pre-interview planning will include:

- Confirm in your own mind that an interview is most likely to achieve the required results. Would the same results be obtained by the less expensive questionnaire method?
- Consider and list the information you want to obtain from the interview. Are you seeking confirmation that all actions described in the specification or standards are carried out – fully, following correct procedures – or is the interview to take the opposite direction and determine effectiveness from descriptions of actions by the interviewee?
- Consider in detail your first two or three questions and ensure they will be impactive and will set the scene for the remainder of the event. Writing these first questions down for posing verbatim will help you move into the interview more easily.
- Will the interview be more effective with a single interviewee, or with two or three interviewees? The latter method saves time and resource and ensures that all aspects are covered, something that may not occur with only one person.
- How will you record the information obtained? Will you use a checklist, ticking off the aspects of performance as they are discussed; will there be a space for responses alongside the predetermined set of questions; will you simply record significant information on a sheet as it emerges during the interview?
- Decide or agree the methods by which you will construct a report about your interviews – methods of combining data; format of the report; destination or use of the report.
- Plan sufficient time for the interview. This of course will initially be 'as long as a piece of string', but as your series of interviews progresses you will become more aware of the time required.
- Agree with the potential interviewee(s) a suitable time and place and confirm this arrangement with the jobholders' bosses.
- Inform the interviewee(s) about the purpose of the planned interview and the role you hope they will play in it.
- Suggest that they may – independently – consider their jobs, what they do and how they do it, their stronger and weaker areas, and anything they might wish to say that would improve the job.

Conducting the interview

Planning your general interview approach will not only ease the situation for you – remember that you may be as nervous as the interviewee(s) – but it will save time and avoid needless repetitions. Some 'good practices' include:

- Start the interview by introducing yourself and identifying the members of the interviewee group if there is more than one person.

- Although you may have previously informed the interviewee of the purpose of the interview, usually in writing, repeat these objectives at the start of the interview and determine that the interviewee understands and accepts them. This initial clarification might also give an indication of the interviewee's attitude to the interview and you may need to adjust your approach accordingly.

- Describe the steps or stages you would like the interview to follow, but assure the interviewee that you will be flexible and will be prepared to modify your plan in the light of the interviewee's wishes.

- Confirm with the interviewee that you will be making notes as the interview progresses and the reasons for this notetaking.

- Start the interview proper with simple, straightforward questions seeking information, rather than opinions – asking for a general description of the job is useful in this context as it will be seen to be safe ground and will give the interviewee an opportunity to start talking.

- Always allow a reasonable time for the interviewee to respond. If this waiting time extends too much, ask yourself whether you posed an understandable question. It may be necessary, although you should use this approach sparingly, to ask the interviewee whether they understood the question.

- Generally use open or closed questions, depending on the type of response you are seeking. Avoid leading questions, the type that would give the interviewee an impression of the answer you are seeking, rather than the one they might give more freely.

- Make encouraging 'noises' and positive comments as the interviewee answers. Be sincere about these rather than make it obvious that you are doing so simply because you know you should!

- Do not permit unclear statements made by the interviewee to pass without clarification. Responses are frequently given in this way to test *your* listening or understanding capabilities!

- Avoid making judgmental statements and always challenge any made by the interviewee.

- In a group interview, give everyone the opportunity to make their points.

- At the end, summarize the interview although not in too much detail; reiterate what is going to happen to the information; ask if the interviewee(s) have any questions or anything further to add; thank them for their co-operation in providing the information.

Figure 3.3 summarizes the interview technique.

Telephone interviewing

It has been noted above that interviewing can be expensive because of the numbers necessary to ensure a comprehensive coverage. This will be particularly so in an organization with establishments scattered throughout the country, and internationally. Questionnaires will be less expensive, but we have seen some of the constraints of this method and the more effective results with interviews.

METHODS	ADVANTAGES	CONSTRAINTS
Conducting interviews with jobholders or group of similar jobholders – often described as a focus group. The purpose is to gather information and/or confirm job effectiveness and comprehensiveness.	Information is obtained in a direct manner that can be clarified or challenged immediately if necessary. The personal contact gives the jobholder a feeling of being of real value and use. Jobholder contacts are made that can be useful in follow-up situations or eventual training. Non-verbal signals can be seen and their support of the verbal messages confirmed. Group interviews ensure complete coverage.	A large number of interviews takes time. The declared aspect of confidentiality may not be accepted and there may be suspicions of the interviewer as a 'bosses' spy'. The interviewer may find it difficult to avoid personal judgements and interpretations. There may be difficulties of interview arrangement. Group interviews can be difficult to manage or control.

Figure 3.3   Interviewing as a TNIA technique

One method of reducing the costs of TNIA interviews, especially in the case of multi-establishment visits, is to conduct the (initial) interviews by telephone. These are often not as effective as face-to-face interviews. Many people find telephone communication a rather constraining medium and, of course, important non-verbal signals cannot be observed, but they can reduce costs and, if necessary, some contacts can be followed up by shorter face-to-face interviews.

The planning and conduct of the telephone interview will follow a similar pattern to the face-to-face interview. However, to save time and allay any feelings of suspicion, you may need to be more expansive in your pre-interview written contact.

One comment that really should not have to be made, but is a factor that is frequently overlooked, is that an appointment for the telephone interview should be made in exactly the same way as for the face-to-face interview and the interviewee should have time off from work to take the extended telephone call.

Combined techniques

There may be some discussion about whether telephone calls are in fact less expensive than face-to-face interviews. Analysis of telephone costs versus travelling and subsistence of the interviewer will give this answer, but of course costs are not everything. You could compromise by using a questionnaire in conjunction with face-to-face or telephone interviews. The questionnaire may pose straightforward questions about which there is likely to be little or no controversy, and may be followed up if necessary by an interview.

Nominal group methods

Nominal group methods are in effect brainstorming sessions, which are often useful at an initial stage in a TNIA to obtain a wide understanding and also to recognize some signals that may indicate follow-up action in the form of questionnaires or interviews.

The planning activities include:

- making a decision on the subject area to be brainstormed
- selecting the nominal group to take part.

The meeting can be conducted roughly along normal brainstorming lines in which the group is told of the purpose of the meeting and the methods to be employed. One method is to follow free brainstorming methods, setting as the subject something like 'Identify the main factors involved in carrying out such-and-such a job or task'.

A more controlled alternative form of the meeting would be as follows:

1. Ask each participant to write down on a small piece of paper their individual response to a question posed by you, for example: 'What is the most important factor that stops your job and its performance being as effective as it could be?'
2. Collect the sheets of paper and enter on a poster or whiteboard *all* the comments made, making a note against those items that are repeated by more than one jobholder.
3. Repeat the first activity to give the participants the opportunity to add comments that might have been triggered by the initial ones, or those that they had forgotten to mention on the first occasion.
4. Add further items to the list and, if necessary, repeat the individual annotation stages.
5. When all responses appear to have been made ask the group, again as individuals, to write down on a sheet of paper the rankings of items they feel

should have some priority. Depending on the objectives of the exercise all items might be ranked, or perhaps the top ten items only and the lowest ten (or some other appropriate number).

6. The priorities are added to the posted list. Ask the group to discuss the rankings, particularly those where there is significant divergence, making special notes of any significant minority views.

Following the nominal group meeting, make a summary and analysis of the group views and maintain good relations by sending a copy to the participating members with an invitation to comment as they wish. The result should be a comprehensive analysis of the area investigated. Other variations of the technique are possible: for example, more discussion is encouraged during the meeting; a summary is produced at the meeting and discussed; comments are made by the participating group on further steps that should be taken. The aim is to produce a free atmosphere in which all can participate and which will enable a maximum amount of opinion and information to emerge.

Figure 3.4 summarizes the nominal group methods.

The other methods listed on page 40–41 are used less frequently. Information about these methods is available in the resources listing at the end of the book.

METHODS	ADVANTAGES	CONSTRAINTS
Bringing together a group of jobholders to brainstorm subjects of TNIA decided by the trainer and the group. A range of methods is available within the general approach.	Less expensive than interviews and more personal than questionnaires. Brings together a group of like people who can supplement each other's views with those of the group. Permits the views of large numbers of people to emerge with a minimum expense of time and money. A comfortable environment for individual disclosure. Group responses may cover the area more comprehensively than individual ones.	Difficulties of bringing a group together at one time. May be viewed as a 'training' rather than a work-based exercise. May be difficult to control with discussion arising on non-essential topics. Strong individuals may dominate the discussions, although the use of individual, written views helps to avoid this.

Figure 3.4   Nominal group methods as a TNIA technique

Project planning

Discussion of the production of a TNIA project plan was deferred from Chapter 2 to identify the various methods that could be used in stages 3 and 4. We can now return to completing the project plan.

The completed plan will answer the following questions:

1. Which group(s) of people will be included in the TNIA?
2. How many people will be involved? Everybody? A limited sample? A statistical sample?
3. Which information base will be used to obtain data on the job and task requirements? Job description? Job and task specification? Competence standards? Interview, observation, questionnaires, combined methods, etc? Other sources of information?
4. Which methods will be used to identify the current levels of knowledge, skills and attitudes of the people involved in the TNIA? Interviews, observation of performance, questionnaires, nominal group methods, other assessment methods?
5. Obtain authority required to have contact with the staff of line managers and agree line manager action through a meeting with the relevant people.
6. At the same time as above, agree co-operative measures with the line managers involved.
7. When will the TNIA commence and over what period will it run? Is there any latitude in these timings?
8. By which date should the recommendation report be completed and to whom and by when should the report be submitted?
9. Any other action necessary?

Outcome analysis

At the end of the TNIA a mass of information, data and views will be held which are then used to provide solutions to the problems that caused the TNIA to be performed. The TNIA:

> pinpoints the problem(s)
> identifies the size of the problem
> identifies the scale of the need
> indicates the type of solution
> provides training objectives.

Whichever method of identification of requirements and practice is used, at the end of the survey you must analyse the information in preparation for the next stage. List the job and task needs and compare them with the actual practices. If there is a difference, there is a solution which will be either a training or non-training requirement.

From a number of possible approaches choose the one that you, the analyst, is most comfortable with. Any method should be capable of directly comparing the two lists of job standards, desired and real, although a straightforward text listing can become very cumbersome and inflexible, unless the problem is simple.

In complex issues an effective method is to display the data in a way sometimes referred to as storyboarding, dynamic classification charting or card-groups. You will need three items:

- the analysis of the job or task produced from a job description, job specification, standards of competence or other identifications of need, the hard data perhaps supplemented by soft data of behaviour, attitudes and personal qualities
- the analysis of how the job or task is actually performed, obtained by the methods described above
- a number of index cards on which the above-named analyses are entered – the requirement analysis can be entered on the cards in, say, green and the analysis of actual performance in red – each item of the job or task is allocated a card.

If the cards from each set are compared with each other, differences, divergences and variations will readily become apparent. The result, where the TNIA has shown that a problem exists, will be a number of green cards for which there is no red parallel – a need. Further investigation will show whether this is a training or non-training need.

Figure 3.5 suggests a checklist of solutions to identified problems, although obviously this list will not be exhaustive.

It may sometimes be difficult to identify non-training problem reasons, although this is not part of the brief of someone performing a TNIA. However, it is a natural extension of the TNIA and a line manager will welcome support and assistance in the identification. The problems are usually the result of dysfunctional behaviour and the flowchart in Figure 3.6 suggests some of the causes.

Moving on

At this stage you should have collected all the relevant information, both to the job needs and the person ability levels; this data has been analysed; a training or non-training solution has been identified, and a project report for the TNIA has been completed and submitted to the relevant client. Let us assume that the problem(s) have been identified as requiring training solutions and your recommendations have been accepted.

Stage 6: determining training objectives and content

The next stage links the TNIA process with the start of the design and preparation of the requisite training programme. The designers must be given the full information about the identified operational shortfalls which are producing training needs. This is the final stage in the TNIA part of the process, although

IDENTIFIED NEED	POSSIBLE SOLUTION PROCESS
The introduction of new systems, procedures etc. to improve the work process.	The introduction of a new or revisionary training programme concentrating on the new items being introduced.
Revised or modified knowledge, skills and/or attitudes.	The introduction of modified or newly constructed training programmes that concentrate on the revisionary areas identified.
Although all jobholders possess the requisite knowledge and skills, the problems are caused by dysfunctional behaviour.	Introduction, or modification if one already exists, of an interpersonal skills training programme.
Although the jobholders possess the requisite skills, knowledge and attitudes, and have received training in all their job and task aspects, they are not performing as trained.	Further training, provided the original training was validated as effective, is unnecessary. Action should be taken at the workplace to ensure implementation of the tasks and their requirements by perhaps stricter control and monitoring by the manager or individual or group coaching at work.
There are no problems of omission or commission (training or non-training), but the problems are caused by unnecessarily difficult or complicated procedures.	Non-training solution of modifying working practices.
There are no problems of omission or commission, except those caused by insufficient staffing.	Non-training solution of consideration of the engagement of additional staff.
There are 'problems' caused by identifiable reasons, but they are insignificant, rare and cause little or no difficulties.	Do nothing.

Figure 3.5   Checklist of possible solutions to some identified problems

there will be reference to it later in the training programme production.

The identified training needs can either be passed to the programme designers in the form that resulted from the TNIA described above, i.e. in terms of shortfall or remedial aspects determined or, preferably, the person who has conducted the

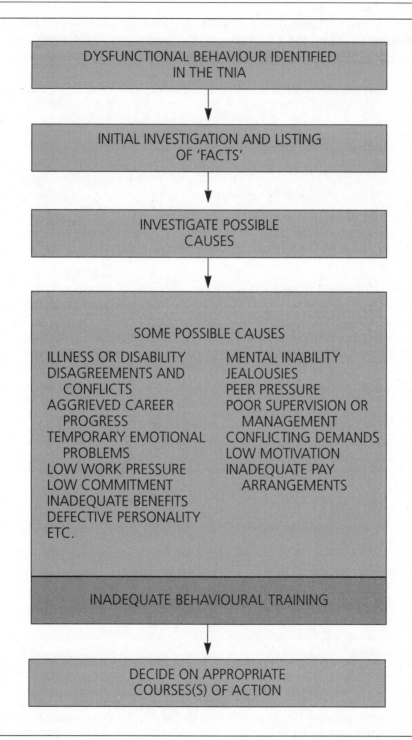

Figure 3.6   Causes of dysfunctional behaviour

TNIA would work with the designer on a formulation of aims and objectives for the programme based on the TNIA results. Of course, the TNIA completer and the programme designer may be the same person!

Part Two

Planning and designing training and development programmes

Chapter 4

Designing the training and development programme

This chapter:

    identifies the learning qualities, styles and preferences of learners
    suggests a communication model and an alternative learning model
    applies the learning models to practical situations
    identifies and describes the barriers to training and learning.

Part One described the start of the planning and design process of a training programme – the detailed training needs identification and analysis, which must be the forerunner to every new programme or important modification. At the end of that stage the needs of the organization or the people in part of that body were firmly identified in the movement through the TNIA process from the original suspicions or requirements. These identifications were intended to provide the basic solutions to the 'problems' raised, whether training or non-training solutions. From this point we shall assume that the identified need requires the development of a training and development programme. The TNIA produces as a minimum for this development the overall aims for the training plus an indication, according to the depth of the TNIA, of more specific objectives.

Part Two describes the design and preparation of training programmes to meet the identified needs – see the shaded area of Figure 4.1 – an apparently small area that in reality includes a substantial amount and variety of work. The first line of the area is the link with the TNIA in which a start was made on the formulation of the aims and objectives for the training and development. These aims and objectives are now translated into actionable plans.

The shaded area covers a wide variety of aspects and requirements that will be described in this Part. They include:

- individual qualities of the learners
- nature of the learning required
- resources available
- venues
- use of training aids
- direct or open or interactive learning
- control of the learning process.

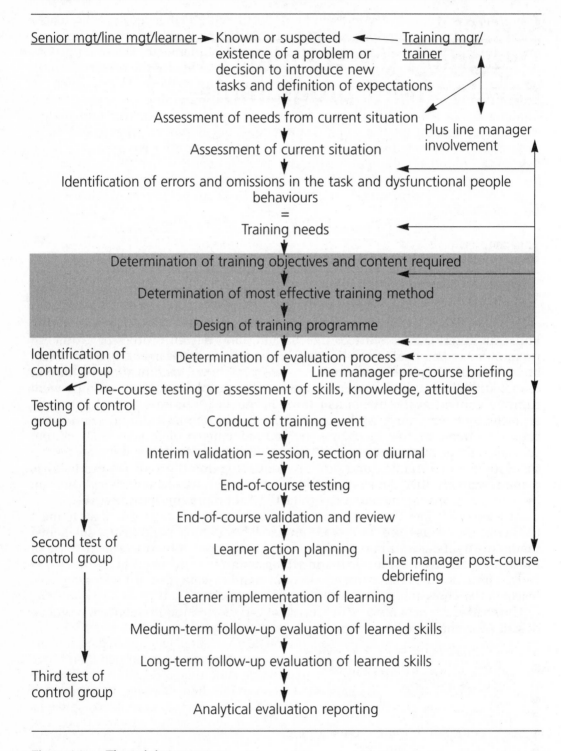

Figure 4.1   The training process

These subjects will be considered in more detail, with further resource references given for more advanced practice. Note the use of the word 'learner' rather than one of the many alternatives – trainee, participant, student, etc. The sole purpose of any training and development programme is to provide for the person learning opportunities that can be implemented on their return to work. This satisfies the description of a training programme as the vehicle providing the means for an implementable behaviour change, behaviour including aspects of knowledge, skills, attitudes and relationships. Training and development programmes have progressed a long way in recent years from the academic approaches in which the learners were indeed 'students'; from the didactic events which they attended to be *trained* – hence 'trainees'; and, although perhaps a pedantic differentiation, a 'participant' is one who attends and takes part, but does not necessarily learn from the participation.

Individual learner qualities

At one time (not so very long ago in many cases, and in fact still quite common) the almost universal reaction to the identification of a training need was 'Let's put on a course'. 'Course' was translated as a series of lectures, roughly approximating the identified needs but also reflecting the performance preferences of the trainers or lecturers. Rarely were the learning preferences or attitudes of the learners considered – in fact rarely were they known – and it was assumed that because they needed to do so, the people concerned would benefit from the course irrespective of its nature. Fortunately this attitude was gradually replaced by the trainer's awareness that different forms of training events could produce more effective learning. The charted pattern of violent change from didactic, lecture-based courses; to free-for-all, almost totally experiential events; then to more balanced programmes containing mixtures of input sessions, discussions, activities, projects, video and computer interactions, is well known. This does not necessarily mean that the balanced programme is achieved easily or always successfully.

Alongside this revolution in the nature of the training programme developed an awareness of the differing nature of learners as individuals or groups of individuals. Following the personality type studies of psychological gurus such as Jung, David Kolb became the architect of modern concepts of the way people learn. In the 1960s and 1970s he developed what became known as *Kolb's Learning Cycle* from which developed a model of learning styles and preferences.

The Learning Cycle (see Figure 4.2) proposes that the process of learning in most cases starts with the learner experiencing an event, a feeling, an emotion etc.

In order to learn from this *experience* it is necessary to let it happen then move on, as so many of us tend to do. The experience should be reflected on in terms of what happened, when they happened, who made them happen, what resulted from these actions, etc. From this *reflecting* the next stage is to make conclusions about the experience – what was good and bad about it and why, what worked and what didn't (and why). As a result of *concluding* in this way and identifying what you have learned, *planning* can take place about how you might behave in a

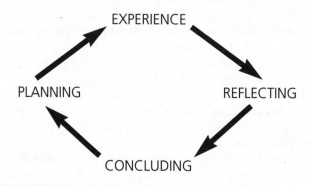

Figure 4.2　Kolb's Learning Cycle

future situation of this nature and certainly how you intend to use the learning. Unfortunately in most group situations, the *reflecting, concluding and planning* stages are likely to be ignored. Well-balanced learning events should ensure that there is encouragement and give time to the learners to take full account of all the stages.

In some ways the model can be considered to be too simplistic, as it gives the impression that *all* learning must commence with an experience, and that it is a simple progressive cycle from experience to planning. In practice learning does not follow the cycle in a neat progression; it often commences at a different point in the cycle; and although the cycle describes effective learning, many people do not take advantage of all the stages, because they have different approaches or preferences towards learning and doing. Although learning can begin with an experience, and the learning stages can follow from that event, it can begin at an earlier stage. Figure 4.3 suggests an alternative model in which the learning does not follow a simple progression, but moves to and from different parts of the cycle.

In this alternative experiential learning model, the process begins with the realization that you should learn or that a potential learning situation exists. This need is reflected on before considering what action can be taken – this consideration is then agreed either with yourself or a third party. In this situation there are events, principally reflective, occurring before the experience.

The central sector of the Figure 4.3 model then follows Kolb's model which suggests experiencing, reflecting on the experience and concluding from it. It may then be necessary to reconsider the position and approach as a result of errors and omissions in the original path, before planning for a repetition of the experience, trying a new experience to extend the learning, or implementing the learning. The various stages can therefore be visited and revisited within a single experience before final learning is achieved.

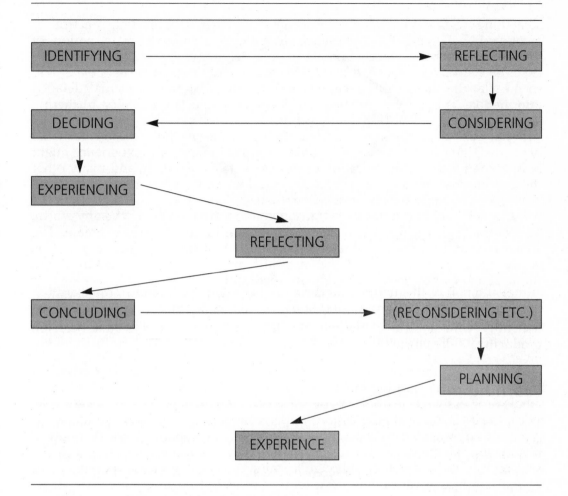

Figure 4.3   An alternative learning model

Learning styles

Whereabouts in the learning cycle you begin, or to what extent the complete model is used, depends on your own preferences for learning. Kolb's research which produced his Learning Style Inventory, developed from the Learning Cycle, proposed specific learning preferences among people. It was carried out in the United States and somewhat similar studies were conducted in the United Kingdom by Peter Honey and Alan Mumford. These two management development consultants and psychologists followed a much more pragmatic path than that of Kolb and the result, the learning style questionnaire, is a more practical instrument for general and training use.

The Honey/Mumford model is also based on the classic Learning Cycle. Its basis, like Kolb's, is that the Learning Cycle represents the ideal, fully effective approach to learning. It 'starts' with the learner doing something, experiencing something, feeling something – an incident whether it be factual, practical or emotional. Following the experience, learning is reinforced by a period of reflection on what has been observed and what can be recalled about the experience – *what* happened, *how* it happened, *who* did it, *what* the result was, and so on – all the observable incidents which can be stored as factual detailed information. This activity requires the learner to stop any other or furthering action in order to 'catalogue' the reflections.

In the third stage, the information is analysed in terms of the reasons for what happened, the reasons behind it, alternative ways in which the experience might have taken place, an identification of the most effective option, and many other theoretical considerations based on what was done and what was seen to be done. This is the stage of the theorist or conceptualizer.

But conceptualization has to be translated into action if it is to have any worth. This is the fourth stage, when the pragmatist attitude becomes supreme. The watchword of this person is 'if it isn't practical, then it isn't worth anything'. This is the area and the time when the historical considerations are translated into future action by people who care about practicalities.

The cycle then returns to the experience, which may be a repeat of the original incorporating the lessons learned in the previous stages. The cycle recommences, hopefully with a shorter lifetime, the lessons learned on the first occasion producing a fully effective event.

Learning preferences

The learner having progressed through these stages has learned something at all stages and the personal learning process for that event is complete. This, of course, is the ideal. In practice most people have a preference for one or more of the learning stages, and if these preferences are strong and overpowering, they will hinder complete learning.

For example, a learner who becomes 'locked in' to the active, doing stage is less likely to stop and reflect (or even to consider and reflect before starting) or analyse and consequently will repeat the original mistakes or even make new ones. The reflector who is so enamoured with considering what has happened will let life pass by with others making decisions, taking action and so on. The locked-in theorist will become so interested in the convolutions of the internal intricacies that nothing will be done. The pragmatist at the end of the cycle might destroy or ignore all that has preceded because if it is not a practical event it must be of no value or interest.

Naturally, not everybody has one preference only. The ideal is a balance of all stage preferences, but in practice most people have one or two strong preferences with the others either weak or just appearing.

Figure 4.4 describes the learning style preferences of the *Activist*, the *Reflector*, the *Theorist* and the *Pragmatist* and demonstrates their direct relationship to the Learning Cycle.

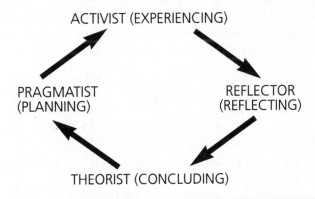

ACTIVIST (EXPERIENCING)

PRAGMATIST
(PLANNING)

REFLECTOR
(REFLECTING)

THEORIST (CONCLUDING)

Figure 4.4   The learning styles of Honey and Mumford

Sensory learning

Learning preferences are controlled not only by the styles outlined by Honey and Mumford; the reactions of learners to and their ability to learn from sensory effects – hearing, seeing, touching, smelling, visualizing, doing, and so on – have an additional helping or hindering factor. Balanced learning programmes must take these reactions into account.

Sensory learning includes four preferences that rely on the *sense of sight*:

- *Learning by reading.* This learning preference can be translated into reading information, skill techniques or procedural written material. It can be difficult for many and is fraught with problems caused by the level of intellect, understanding capabilities and other considerations such as language, particularly where a number of races and cultures might be involved. Reflectors and theorists are usually more at home in this medium. There is little doubt that when the words are accompanied by pictures of some form, the effect of the words is strengthened. However, this is not an easy or cheap addition to the pages of most books that are dominated by text.

- *Learning by seeing.* Many people have to see something before they can understand and, as a result, learn. The sight might be the object itself, a model, or even a graphic visual aid or computer graphic. Seeing the object of learning avoids the necessity of the learners' attempts at visualizing. Use of these objects can be easily introduced in most, if not all, learning events.

- *Learning by visualization.* This is a difficult approach that requires the learners, from verbal or written descriptions to visualize an object, event or concept. It is often used in conjunction with a sight of the item after a visualizing description has been made to prepare the learners.

- *Learning by writing.* Whether it is the art of copying from an existing text;

interpreting, analysing and summarizing an extended text; or making notes from a verbal presentation, many people find the act of writing it down helps their learning, retention and recall.

The *sense of hearing* can have a significant effect on:

- *Learning by listening.* Those who find it difficult to learn via the written word, either because of difficulties of understanding or an inherent problem with that medium, will frequently understand and learn more from the spoken word. This type of learning usually takes place in an environment where questioning and discussion can take place, thus helping the learning process.

Although more limited in some ways, the *sense of touch* cannot be ignored in encouraging effective learning and in particular, if it is considered in terms of *doing*, it can then become the most important method.

- *Learning by touching.* Touching has a more limited, but significant, application in the learning of certain skills, particularly those where a few minutes of hands-on experience is worth hours of description. In the training environment the opportunity to 'have a go' can save many problems if the first practice is in the real world of work – try to describe the feel of a snake's skin if neither you nor the learner has previously held a snake. In some cases, an operation can succeed or fail as the result of the 'heavy-handedness' of the operator – an event very reliant on the sense of touch.

- *Learning by doing.* This approach is considered by many as the ultimate in learning processes, usually preceded by other forms such as verbal descriptions, graphical representations, and so on. The learners are given the opportunity, usually under supervision or observation, to perform an act, whether it is practically operational, procedural or one requiring the performance of task or people skills.

The final senses, *smell and taste*, are perhaps even more limited in application, but in specific forms of training must be considered as an aid to learning. If the training of a gas meter reader ignores the opportunity to smell escaping gas, it is not as effective as it should be, particularly if the learners have lived in an all-electric environment and have never smelled domestic gas. Similarly, learner-perfume practitioners have a need for the effective use of this sense.

A communication model

Learning in a training and development programme is substantially dependent on communication between the trainer and the learners and among the learners themselves. In any communication there is a sender and a receiver and all communication would be effective if these were the only factors. Unfortunately this is not so. Figure 4.5 demonstrates graphically what happens when a sender (the trainer) attempts to communicate with a receiver (listener, learner).

The figure shows a number of barriers between the sending of the message and its reception. These barriers can be erected by either the sender or the receiver.

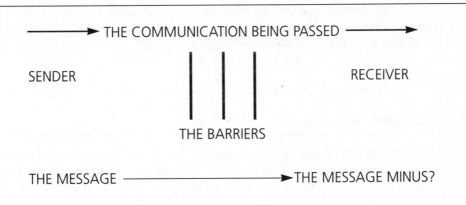

Figure 4.5   The group communication model

One sender and one receiver can erect certain barriers; another sender and receiver a different set of barriers. And, of course, one common sender can find different barriers with different receivers, demanding recognition of the barriers in each case. The sender can be the person erecting the barriers to the successful passage of the communication, and unfortunately may not be aware of these problems. We have seen earlier how differing styles of presenters can produce various barriers.

The problem is exacerbated when the receivers are a group of individuals. Many of them may have the same barriers, but it is likely that each individual will also have his or her own set!

To be an effective presenter you must recognize your own barriers and those of the audience members and, by being aware of them at the design stage, attempt to avoid them. It is easier to overcome your own barriers, once recognized, but much more difficult with those of the learners.

Application to learning

The models and concepts of learning are not merely interesting theories, but have a direct application to our training and development activities. A balanced learning programme *must* contain elements that will try to satisfy all the learners with their different approaches and preferences. A balanced programme of this nature will include some input of new material with time for the reflectors and theorists to consider it; the activists must be motivated by practical activities, but again must be encouraged to reflect and consider/conclude. Finally, the pragmatic nature of whatever is presented must be made clear for the pragmatists who will be interested only in something that they can implement without difficulty.

The construction of this comprehensive and balanced programme will be difficult, and will be hindered by the content, time available and so on, but unless the learning population is of one preference only – an unusual event – there must be a realistic attempt to achieve at least some balance. Paraphrasing a famous quote: 'You can only please (satisfy) some of the people some of the time, some of the people all of the time or all of the people some of the time, but not all the people all the time!'.

The purpose of training

Training and development programmes have been referred to on several occasions so far as instruments by which change is effected. The elements of change must be included in the design of a programme and the direction of this

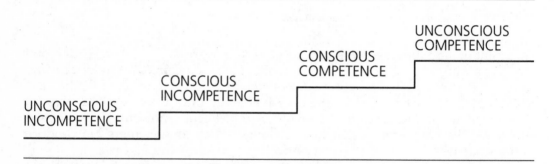

Figure 4.6   The competence stepladder

change can be compared with a stepladder – in effect, a competence stepladder.

People performing a task or role may be doing so without complete competence, but are unaware of their deficiencies. By a variety of mechanisms they may be made aware and so ascend the step to the area of conscious incompetence in which they know that they are not fully capable – material ripe for development. As a result of taking some learning action, they become capable and competent in the process, but have to perform it consciously and deliberately. For example, Learner drivers have to think about co-ordinating gears and clutch, clutch pedal and gear leaver, all actions that the experienced driver does without thinking. Full implementation, practice and performance at work raises the level to the top step of unconscious competence where learning has been achieved and the task is performed effectively without too much thought. A problem is that all too easily unconscious competence can slip back to unconscious incompetence! So many similarities with car driving can be seen here!

Learning programmes set out to achieve this change, at least to the borderline between conscious and unconscious competence.

Barriers to learning

One of the first lessons that a trainer must learn, when designing programmes which include a large number of personally presented input sessions, is that the learners will not hang onto their every word as if the trainer was the fount of all knowledge. As suggested earlier, there will be so many barriers that it is always a source of amazement that anybody ever learns anything! Remember these barriers when the programme is being designed. They may include the following.

Language and speech

Vocabulary

Programme designers must use a vocabulary that the learners can understand, otherwise the trainer might as well be talking in a foreign language.

Jargon

Jargon quickly becomes the shorthand talk within an organization. This is very well if the learners are part of the organization and know the jargon. If not, it will not only be not understood, but it will annoy and inhibit learning.

Ambiguity

When the inputs are being planned, the briefs and how they are used must say what is meant, not simply what it is intended to say. Extra care is required when multi-cultural learners are involved in view of the different meanings that can be afforded to some words and sayings.

Woolly and/or rambling speech

Remember KISS (Keep It Short and Simple).

Unusual words and phrases

The presentation must be planned in a straightforward manner. Is it the best/only/correct/most appropriate word or phrase or is it being used simply for effect? Is the learning group likely to understand it?

Psychological barriers

The psychology or, simply, the attitude of the learners, is an important part in their acceptance of the learning material and can be affected by a variety of factors.

Pressures

All sorts of pressures are bearing on a learning group detracting and distracting them from learning to the desirable extent – work, health, domestic, money, learning difficulties, social, etc. Many of these will be hidden agenda and will be difficult to envisage or prepare for by the programme planners.

Mood

In certain moods, learning will not be a priority for the programme participants, so the designer must ensure that the optimum programme is presented to try to overcome any negative reactions.

Forced resistance

Not every learner attends an event voluntarily and in such cases learning will be resisted. If these circumstances cannot be avoided, material must be built into the programme to try to overcome the resistance.

Shyness

The learner has overcome the first shyness barrier by attending. Follow up this development by giving the learners the motivation to involve themselves in the programme.

Aggression

Some learners will display an aggressive manner, often due to enforced attendance and techniques must be included in the programme to lessen this attitude as quickly as possible.

Resistance to learning and change/The know-it-all/Too old to learn or change

Almost all trainers will, at some time, encounter participants who are resistant to the learning programme. The reasons for this are many, including enforced attendance; impending retirement; failure to see the reason for the training; resistance to change and the 'know-it-all' attitude. Barriers of this nature can only be breached by offering interesting, useful and involving programmes – a recipe for an effective training and development programme – and demonstrating that the learning will be useful whatever the circumstances. Experienced trainers will possess techniques for reducing some of these barriers, but often may need help from the programme itself.

Status differences

Learning programmes can be severely disrupted because the learners are at different status levels in the organization and they allow this to have an effect on their learning capability. Higher status participants may not wish to comment or act in front of junior colleagues, and vice versa, for a variety of status-based reasons. If this is a potential problem, the programme design must identify the most suitable learning population on each occasion, thus avoiding any conflict.

The environment

Noise/Heat/Cold/Ventilation/Space available/Interruptions/Work intrusion

These are all potential barriers to a training programme and should certainly form a significant part of the planning and preparation of the event. Although there will be occasions when a negative factor cannot be avoided, most potential problems can be forecast and resolved before the event.

Restricted time

Time is a factor that must be taken into account when the programme is being designed. It is not uncommon for the designer to be told that three days are available and a programme should be designed to 'fit this time'. This is the wrong way to approach the design of a programme. The TNIA will have identified what is required of a training programme and the calculation then should be 'how long is necessary to include the TNIA requirements?'. Unfortunately this is not always possible, and the result must be a compromise between what is needed and what is available. Other factors are the level of the learners and their capacity to learn a particular competence in a dictated period of time; and the complexity of the material. The designer, supported by the practitioner trainer, must be prepared to argue with the time allocators about what is realistically necessary and should be allowed.

The trainers

The allocation of trainers to particular programmes is a factor that is frequently out of the hands of the programme designer and planner, and is commonly dependent on availability. This allocation frequently results in unsuitable trainers being selected – either they are unskilled in the particular nature of the programme or simply they lack training experience. The 'humanness' of trainers running programmes can obviously create additional barriers to learning.

The unskilled trainer

An unskilled trainer, in spite of advice, might use methods and techniques which are not the most effective for encouraging learning. Of course, the trainer may not yet have gained sufficient experience to have an extensive training toolkit. If there is sufficient time, these failings can be corrected by trainer training in the additional skills required.

The unskilled speaker

Perhaps more difficult to remedy, particularly in a short interval, is the trainer who lacks practice in presentation of material. This might be evident in the introduction of activities, rather than the more demanding input sessions. Too many hesitations, verbal noises (ers), distracting mannerisms, etc. will be noted by the learners and will easily distract from their learning. Most people can be trained to become *more effective* speakers, albeit not completely expert; this can take time, and practice in safe conditions is essential.

Accents

Where is the training programme to be held? Who will the learners be? How strong a regional accent has the trainer selected to run the programme? At one time regional accents were not acceptable in many areas of public speaking, but this has to a large extent been discounted and their use is often encouraged. However, if the accent is too strong it may not be understandable and thus hinder the learning. Do you recall the television series *When the Boat Comes In* in which the 'geordie' accent was frequently very strong? My wife turned away from this excellent programme because there was so much she could not understand.

Dialect words must not be used as they might not be widely understood. Advice to the trainer on the use of language should avoid this barrier.

Manner

A trainer's manner is a much more difficult trait for the designer to take into account or take action to resolve as it is often integral to their personality. However, overt manner and behaviours – aggressive, patronizing, abrasive, self-centred, exaggerating, obviously lying, over-casual and negatively critical – once identified can usually be modified even if only for the period required.

Prejudices

- a trainer's prejudices on race, sex, age, disability can emerge without the trainer realizing
- judgemental views that try to enforce the trainer's attitudes on the learners
- ignoring or rejecting out of hand the views of the learners because they do not fit in with those of the trainer
- over-direction to the trainer's viewpoint, however well intentioned
- non-acceptance by the trainer of learners' rights to have a say in their learning

The above prejudices held by trainers can have a strong negative effect on learning in a programme that the designer has tried hard to develop effectively. Sometimes these prejudices are so strong that the trainer finds it difficult to keep them hidden. It would be disastrous if the content and the objectives of a programme conflicted violently with the views of the trainer who might be considered initially responsible for its progress.

Lack of knowledge

All the efforts of the programme designer can be wasted if the trainer lacks knowledge of the subject. This is not as rare an event as you might think: an organization's training department is told to mount a particular type of programme, but none of the available trainers have knowledge of the subject. Learners will have sympathy or empathy with a trainer who lacks training or presentation skills, but lack of knowledge of the subject will rarely be countenanced. The designer must be sure that the trainer is familiar with the subject or take the necessary steps to develop this.

These barriers may not be present when the designer is planning the programme, but their existence must be considered if success is to be achieved. Many of them appear trivial, but can have the maximum detrimental effect on a situation. It may be that the designer does not have the means or the opportunity to resolve any of the problems identified, which must be recognized as a potential hazard to the level of success of the programme.

The learning attention span

A general barrier to learning that is common to almost every learning situation is that however well motivated and skilled the trainer, learners will have a limited attention span at any one time. This will vary depending on such factors as the motivation of the learners, the enthusiasm of the trainer, the skills of the trainer, and the other barriers described above. Research has suggested that in input sessions or lectures presented by a trainer in the traditional role, attention starts to fade after about 10 to 15 minutes and continues reducing until there is little remaining beyond 30 to 40 minutes. In the shorter sessions some attention will re-emerge towards the end, which can unfortunately be attributed to the learners' realization that the session is drawing to a close and perhaps lunch is the next item on the programme.

This factor will have a strong influence on the designer's construction of the learning programme. There will certainly be a number of inputs during the programme, not all of which can be contained within the 20-minute period. However, the 20-minute period relates to one stretch over which attention will be reasonable. At, or before this point, a change in the session can be introduced: a break, even though this adds to the total time for the session; a discussion, rather than the trainer's singular input; an activity related to the material covered so far; an appropriate video or computer program insertion; and so on – in fact any other type of activity rather than continuance of the input, although the change must be relevant to the session and not appear to be simply an add-on.

From the content of this chapter you will have realized that, without even considering the content and style of the programme, there are many pitfalls that must be taken into account by the designer at an early stage in the planning process. Some more positive steps will be described in the next chapter.

Chapter 5
Training Objectives

This chapter:

discusses the training objectives that will develop from the TNIA
advises on the method of writing objectives effectively
describes an objectives action process
suggests practical application of objectives.

The TNIA sets out the general aims and objectives for the proposed training. It is the task of the designer and planner to translate these general aims and objectives into the specific programme. The purpose of a training objective in particular is to state as clearly and unambiguously as possible, what the programme intends to achieve and what the learners will be expected to know or do by the end of it. A training objective should specify:

- what the learners will be able to know or do at the end of the programme in a different manner from that at the start of the programme – that is to say, the change intended – outcomes
- how they will demonstrate the extent of this learning – conditions
- the standards they will need to achieve to confirm their new competence levels – standards
- any time constraints that will be imposed to achieve the objectives – conditions.

A frequently used mnemonic for objectives is **SMART**:

Specific – as specific as possible, using active words that will be described later
Measurable – knowledge and skills are more easily quantifiable and measurable; 'people' skills and attitudes, less easily so, but there are usually some ways in which they can be assessed, certainly compared with the level at the start of the training.
Achievable – there is little sense in setting an objective if it cannot be achieved at that time, in that time and in that place or is too big to be achievable
Relevant – some activities may be favourites of the designers or trainers and the learners, but are they relevant to the programme, particularly if there are

time problems? Remember, some apparently irrelevant activities have a relevant use in lightening the learning, giving the learners time to assimilate what has just happened, increasing the attention span, and so on

Time bound – this can refer either to the length of time in which a learner should complete an activity etc., or the statement of the achievement of the objectives: 'By the end of the training programme, the learners will ...'.

The aims are a more general statement of intent from which the objectives are detailed; for example, the aim of a particular programme might be 'to develop the organization's communication systems' whereas the objectives following this aim would state details as indicated above.

These objectives must be *written* to avoid mental manipulation if they are constructed and retained in the mind only. It is only too easy if the objectives are not in black and white to excuse a failing by saying, 'Well, we didn't really have that as a firm objective'. If it is recorded, success or failure can be evaluated unequivocally.

Objectives in the form described above are generally referred to as the training or learning *terminal* objectives, for obvious reasons. However, the terminal objectives can be broken down into enabling and lesson objectives – the two last-named are important for the detailed construction of individual sessions or other activities. The *enabling* objective describes what the learner will need to do to achieve the terminal objective, and the *lesson* objectives further define what has to be included so that the learners can achieve the terminal objectives once the programme has been successfully completed. Figure 5.1 is a simplified example of how these objectives relate to each other. At the design stage the designer will be more concerned with the terminal objectives, but if the other sub-objectives are kept in mind the designer will avoid eventual difficulties.

Obviously the final objective statement will be more detailed than this and will interact with the session briefs and plans; however, effective objectives described in maximum detail will prove invaluable when the sessions have to be written.

Aims	Improve training programme effectiveness
Terminal objective	The learner will be able to present a 20-minute input session using training aids
Enabling objective	Give a 20-minute training input session
Lesson objective	Develop a good knowledge of, and be able to adjust, the session brief to take account of the barriers to learning

Figure 5.1   Relationship of terminal objectives

The advantages of objectives

The comments above indicate that a significant amount of time will be taken up in writing effective objectives, but there are distinct advantages in investing in this time:

- The appropriate amount of training is given. In many training and development programme cases the content may seem more appropriate to a 'Rolls Royce' as opposed to 'Mini' approach that the subject deserves, or by which it would be best served.
- Irrelevant and unnecessary content is avoided, so that the time taken for the programme is not excessive.
- Irrelevant and unnecessary content is avoided, so that the learning messages are clear to the learners.
- Guidelines are provided for the design and planning of the programme as a whole and its more detailed constituent parts.
- Comprehensive advice is given to the trainers about what is expected of them and the programme.
- They provide the base by which the programme is validated for success or otherwise – without identified objectives at the start of the programme, validation at its end is worthless, as it is not measuring any change.
- Written objectives provide quantitative material on which any investigation for possible revision can be based.

The disadvantages of objectives

The use of objectives is not universally accepted, although in my view the arguments against them are not sufficient to negate their use. Some of these arguments include:

- Trainers find their rigorous approach too difficult to accept within their practitioner style.
- Objectives make training programmes inflexible by constraining the trainers to the objectives material alone.
- Designers and trainers find that the *writing down* of objectives restricts flexibility.
- Objectives require the categoric demonstration of outcomes. Practitioners claim that some forms of learning are not capable of quantitative demonstration and evaluation and that, as a result, the more subjective forms of 'soft' training must be excluded.
- Too much time can be expended in formulating objectives and writing them down.
- Training objectives are seen as behaviourally anchored outcome measures and exclude the programme's theory and knowledge content.

The proponents of these comments are obviously sincere in their arguments. However, investigation has revealed that many of the dissenters are in education or higher education rather than training and development. In the former, theory and the acquisition of knowledge is more common than in the latter which is usually concerned with practical applications. But programmes, whether educational or training, that are concerned with knowledge are still open to validation – there is little value in attempting them if it cannot be shown that knowledge has been achieved – and as validation is dependent on the statement of the starting position (objective needs) it follows that objectives are in fact set (or perhaps implied).

Certainly in most training and development cases, practical application is the end result and objectives are essential in its assessment. It may be that the lesser criticisms of inflexibility etc. are a defence against lack of skill.

Writing training objectives

As suggested earlier, the writing down of objectives is as important as their construction and these written objectives must be comprehensive and unambiguous. Mentally-held objectives are open to manipulation, misinterpretation and challenge of ambiguity: written objectives should be free from manipulation because of their objectivity, but the written word is rarely free from misinterpretation and ambiguity. The use of correct words is important and the use of action verbs in the written objectives will help to avoid problems. Even the knowledge area can be defined by action verbs. Figure 5.2 lists the relevant action verbs in the writing of objectives. It is not necessarily complete and possible additions should be challenged by asking what would be the result of the action. The broad learning areas of knowledge, skills and attitudes are broken down into more specific elements.

Many of the verbs in the list will need to be and usually are combined. For example, many of the knowledge verbs are usually the first indications of movement towards a practical, actionable objective: 'Having *recognized* the various factors, *list* and *analyse* the most important, *combine* them with the list provided and *determine* a total action plan'.

An 'objectives' action plan

We have already considered a number of aspects relating to the formulation of training objectives and identified some of the problems that might arise. The process of completing objectives for a training and development programme is summarized in Figure 5.3.

Prioritization

Item 3 in the figure introduces the prioritization of the objectives. This is particularly important when the TNIA has identified a large number of need objectives, but the constraints on training programmes suggests that not every one of these objectives might be met.

LEARNING AREA	ACTION VERB		
KNOWLEDGE	Define	Write	Underline
	State	Recall	Select
	Recognize	Be aware of	
COMPREHENSION	Identify	Illustrate	Explain
	Justify	Represent	Judge
	Select	Name	Label
	Indicate	Formulate	Classify
	Perceive		
APPLICATION	Predict	Choose	Construct
	List	Reproduce	Select
	Find	Compute	Assess
	Show	Use	Explain
	Perform	Demonstrate	
ANALYSIS	Analyse	Select	Justify
	Identify	Separate	Resolve
	Conclude	Compare	Break down
	Criticize	Contrast	Differentiate
SYNTHESIS	Combine	Argue	Select
	Restate	Discuss	Relate
	Summarize	Organize	Generalize
	Précis	Derive	Conclude
EVALUATION	Judge	Support	Identify
	Evaluate	Validate	Defend
	Avoid	Determine	Attack
	Recognize	Criticize	Choose
ATTITUDE	Prefer	Recognize	Be motivated to
	Relate to	Accept	Be committed to
	Be aware of		Identify with

Figure 5.2   Action verbs for written training objectives

The priorities can be determined by posing a number of questions to both senior and line management and, if possible, the learners. These questions should include:

● What is the minimum amount of knowledge, skill and attitude needed by the

1. Identify the objectives from the TNIA

2. Clarify and select the actionable objectives

3. Establish priorities

4. Check for feasibility

5. Put into a logical flow

Figure 5.3   Objectives process checklist

learners to enable them to carry out the task to a satisfactory level?
● Which other items would be desirable in addition to the basic needs?
● Which items would it be helpful, but not essential, for the learners to know and be able to do?

Training practitioners will recognize these levels of need as the three priority decisions that are made in connection with the training material to include in their beliefs – Must, Should and Could Knows.

Feasibility

The following questions relate to the feasibility of the objectives:

● Is the learner target population small enough to be covered in the time allocated?
● Is the learner target population capable of learning what is required within the time allocated?
● Are all the objectives identified as essential included within the time constraints linked with the prioritization of objectives?
● Must all the objectives be covered in detail, or might some be left for follow-up training or for mentoring/coaching by the line manager?
● Must skills be learned to the highest level, or is a satisfactory 'can do' level all that is required?

Checking the objectives

When you have followed the objectives process checklist and have written them down, it is necessary to check the objectives for errors and omissions (see Figure 5.4.).

The practical use of objectives

The obvious use of objectives – as the basis for designing a training programme, following on from the TNIA – has been described, but they have other practical uses as learning instruments within a programme itself.

1. Read the objective.	Go to 2
2. Can you say in precise and active terms what the learner is expected to know or do?	If yes, go to 4 If no, go to 3
3. The objective is defective and must be re-written. It must state clearly what is expected of the learner in terms of behaviour that can be observed and measured. Rewrite.	Go to 1
4. From reading the objective, do you know precisely what standard of performance you expect from the learner?	If yes, go to 6 If no, go to 5
5. The objective does not enable you to decide how much or how well the learner will have learned. If a level of acceptable performance is stated it enables you to make accurate judgements. Rewrite.	Go to 1
6. Does the objective state under what conditions the learner will carry out the required activity? Is there a time constraint? Where will the activity be performed, etc?	If yes, go to 8 If no, go to 7
7. Verify that these conditions do not affect the learner's level of acceptable performance. If you think they do, the objective must be rewritten.	If rewriting, go to 1
8. The objective appears to be satisfactory.	

Figure 5.4   Checking a training objective

Prior to a programme

The objectives can be introduced into the pre-event activity of a programme in a number of ways. In most cases they will have been finalized by the TNIA practitioner – usually the trainer, who might then use them to design the programme. Although the potential learners have been involved to lesser or greater degrees (if at all) in the TNIA, their input has been as a contribution to the final objectives. It is rare that any further reference is made to them, but this would reflect good practice. Two practical approaches are suggested.

1.   Before the final objectives are used to construct a training programme, copies of them should be sent to, at least, the people who took part in and contributed to the TNIA. This serves a number of purposes, not least in that it paves the way for a return to these contributors or their further use on another occasion. In so many cases of training activities the learners complain that they never hear anything further – not a good foundation for their future co-operation. Copies of the objectives can also be sent to the wider population who might be affected by a training programme based on them. In both cases the recipients should be asked for their reactions to the objectives in the context of the proposed training programme. This serves two purposes: it gives recipients an opportunity to comment (favourably or otherwise) on the objectives as they affect them; it is an opportunity to correct any misinterpretations or misstatements.

2.   When learners are invited to take part in a training programme, the invitation should include a clear statement of the objectives for the event, whether it is a training course or some form of open learning. This will give them the opportunity to confirm or otherwise the suitability of the programme, possibly at the time of the pre-programme discussion with the learner's line manager. It also ensures that the learner has as much information as possible prior to the programme, a move that certainly helps to encourage motivation and co-operation.

At the start of the programme

The objectives can have further uses at the start of the programme. Let us assume that the programme starts with a training course. At this stage, the objectives can be used in at least five ways:

1.   It is very common that pre-programme training material is not read, or only very superficially, by the learners. Whether you suspect this or not, it is always useful to start your programme with a re-statement of the objectives, perhaps clarifying them as necessary.

2.   Present, or re-present, the objectives and seek the views of the learners: (a) about the objectives, their relevance, the learners' understanding of them, and so on; and (b) whether they wish to suggest any further objectives at this stage.

3. Display the programme objectives as part of an introductory session. Ask the learners to introduce themselves in one of the many variations, but including comments about (a) the programme objectives and (b) their personal objectives, preferably linking these to the programme ones. In this way 'objectives' start to become more person-related than ethereal factors.

4. The objectives, programme and personal, can be used as or linked with programme evaluation measures. Seek the learners' views on how they will know at the end of the programme whether the objectives have been achieved or not.

5. Using the objectives directly with the training programme underlines the fact that all the stages of the training/learning cycle are linked, particularly the early part of TNIA and objectives, and the evaluation of the programme. Objectives in effect state the overall deficiencies in the skills of the learning group, but within that group individual skills can vary considerably. As we shall see later, start-of-programme tests or other assessments identify the individual level of skills. The process will be repeated at the end of the programme to validate change resulting from the training. This assessment will depend on the nature of the programme – knowledge, skills or attitudes.

   Knowledge will normally be assessed by written tests; skill assessment will depend on the type of skill – practical, technical or operational skills are the simplest with direct observation of the learner performing the task; people skills require a rather more subjective assessment, frequently based on a concept or model, of the learners performing training exercises; behaviours can be assessed by an observational method such as behaviour analysis.

   Learners may find it useful to assess their own skills or attitudes by means of a self-awareness questionnaire. This can be the first part of the three-test validation instrument, the complete use of which will be described later. The assessment asks learners to rate themselves on a scale of 1 to 10. Figure 5.5 demonstrates an example of this type of questionnaire, the questions being taken from the objectives for a training programme on interpersonal skills.

During and at the end of the programme

At the end of the training programme validation and evaluation measures are used to check the satisfaction of the objectives against the learning by the participants. Consequently approaches and methods will be covered later in Chapter 11. But this important linkage and association must be kept in mind in view of the integrated and comprehensive nature of the training process.

SELF-REPORTING AWARENESS QUESTIONNAIRE

Please ring a score in each item which represents your present level of skill

		HIGH	LOW
1	Being aware of my own behaviour	10 9 8 7 6 5 4 3 2 1	
2	Being aware of the behaviour of others	10 9 8 7 6 5 4 3 2 1	
3	Being aware of the reactions of others to my behaviour	10 9 8 7 6 5 4 3 2 1	
4	Being aware of my reaction to the behaviour of others	10 9 8 7 6 5 4 3 2 1	
5	Being aware of how much I talk	10 9 8 7 6 5 4 3 2 1	
6	Being aware of how much I support others	10 9 8 7 6 5 4 3 2 1	
7	Being aware of how much I build on the ideas of others	10 9 8 7 6 5 4 3 2 1	
8	Sensing the feelings of others	10 9 8 7 6 5 4 3 2 1	
9	Being aware of how much I interrupt others	10 9 8 7 6 5 4 3 2 1	
10	Being aware of how much I really listen to others	10 9 8 7 6 5 4 3 2 1	
11	Telling others what my feelings are	10 9 8 7 6 5 4 3 2 1	
12	Being aware of what behaviour modification I need to do	10 9 8 7 6 5 4 3 2 1	
13	Knowing how to modify my behaviour	10 9 8 7 6 5 4 3 2 1	
14	Being aware of how much I bring out the views of others	10 9 8 7 6 5 4 3 2 1	

Figure 5.5   **Interpersonal skills self-reporting awareness questionnaire**

Chapter 6

On-the-job training

This chapter:

> describes the initial considerations in the design of on-the-job training and development
> describes the detailed steps in designing the content of a programme
> describes the training approaches available.

Decisions on the design of a training and development programme will follow from your considerations of the training needs identified and the various aspects of learning described in Chapter 4.

Operational design

The initial stages in the design of the programme for on-the-job training and development are summarized in Figure 6.1.

---

1. List the agreed objectives for the training programme.

2. Consider the learning population and how they will affect the programme design.

3. List the ways in which each objective might best be met.

4. Decide whether the learning will be best achieved by an on-the-job or off-the-job programme form.

Figure 6.1   **The initial stages in designing an on-the-job training programme**

List the agreed objectives

How to identify the required objectives for the training programme and their practical application was described in Chapter 5. At the first stage in the design process the objectives are listed as the start of a blueprint. They need not be listed in any particular order, although some logical order may have emerged from the investigation of the job or task – probably that in which the details of the task were observed or emerged from some other TNIA process. That order will not necessarily be followed in the training programme.

The learning population

The learning population is an important consideration in the design of the programme.

● How many people will be covered by the programme? This will obviously have an effect on how many events must be arranged.

● What will be the age range of the learners and who might be involved? New entrants, young, inexperienced will require a different approach from existing, older, experienced people and advice must be given to the planners accordingly.

● What will their learning preferences be? If you can determine this before the programme you are in a favourable position to give advice to the planners about the type of learning approaches required. However, this is a rare event and you are advised to accept the fact that the learners will represent the distribution of learning preferences that have been identified within the population as a whole. Honey and Mumford (see p. 63) demonstrated that most people had a strong preference for one or two of the learning styles, and only a small percentage had preferences over the full range. As a result they tended to be locked into these one or two preferences and resisted learning in the others. For example, some people had a very strong preference for either the Activist, Reflector, Theorist *or* Pragmatist approaches to learning almost to the exclusion of the other approaches. Many had 'twinned' preferences – Reflector and Theorist, or Activist and Pragmatist. Some had multiple preferences – Reflector, Theorist and Pragmatist.

This type of information can lead to three approaches:

(a)   If the learning preferences of a particular group are known, the training can be planned to concentrate on these preferences. For example, a group of Theorists will probably react more favourably to a programme that includes a number of inputs or lectures presenting models or concepts for them to consider and discuss in depth. Activists will react most favourably to taking part in a large number of activities with even relatively passive input time being at a minimum. Similarly with Reflectors or Pragmatists.

(b)   Similarly, where the learning preferences of a particular group are known, it might be decided to widen these preferences and undo the locks that have been binding them to singular preferences. Reflectors would be given time to reflect, but would need to take part in an Activist or Pragmatist type of activity on which to reflect. Similarly Theorists would also need to take part in activities, although time would be given for them, following reflection, to consider in reasonable depth what the activity demonstrated and to discuss this with the expert. The Pragmatists might be exposed to non-work related activities or work that does not have a direct relationship to them to show that significant lessons can be learned from this type of activity.

(c) It is more common for programme designers to have no previous knowledge of the learners and their preferences. The safest and most logical approach in such circumstances is to produce a balanced plan in which all the learning preferences are satisfied for at least some of the time. In such programmes an additional learning objective might be 'to widen the learning preferences and skills of the learners by exposing them and learning from the variety of learning situations and activities'.

If the programme designers have no knowledge of the learners' preferences there may be time at the start of the planning process to identify them, e.g. by using the Honey and Mumford *Learning Styles Questionnaire*. The planners can then introduce modifications to take these preferences into account.

- With what level of knowledge will the learners be starting their programmes? To a certain extent there should be data about this as a result of the TNIA – it will probably show, except in the case of completely new work, a range of levels. This will obviously produce problems for the practitioner trainer in terms of the level at which to pitch the training. Too low and the more skilled participants will lose interest; too high and the lower skill level learners will not learn and may cease trying. Although most training programmes have to cope with the mixed range, every attempt should be made in your liaison with the line manager part of the Training Quintet (see p. 8) to select learners for training events on the basis of level.

- The location of the potential learners will affect the design and perhaps the number of individual events to be included in the programme. An organization with a large number of potential learners located nationally and/or internationally will have to be consulted on whether the training should be provided centrally, possibly as an off-the-job event or on a temporary secondment. These will involve additional costs of bringing the learners to the centre.

- Problems, problems, problems! One of the complaints made about training provision by both learners and their line managers is that the appropriate training event is not available when it is needed. From the trainers' aspect they complain that when they have training events available, they are unable to fill them because line managers can/will not release the learners at the time! On-the-job learning should be able to solve many of these problems.

Material design

There are of course other design requirements, including questions of what material is to be contained in the programmes (see Figure 6.2).

---

1. Decide on the nature of the training approaches – one-to-one, mentoring, coaching, etc.

2. Plan the order of events to meet the programme's and individuals' objectives.

3. Prepare an outline plan for the programme detailed from the previous items.

4. Discuss the proposed plan with the people who will be involved and, if possible, the learning population and their line managers.

5. Complete a final, agreed programme plan from which detailed plans can be produced.

Figure 6.2   Checklist for designing the content of an on-the-job training programme

A competences approach to programme material

A useful tool when deciding what to include in a training programme has developed in recent years in the form of the competences standards used as the basis for National Vocational Qualifications. Consistent standards of competence have been produced for many occupations – standards that are detailed and describe the activities in the occupation that determine the outcomes of the job. This powerful tool was demonstrated in Chapter 2 as an instrument in determining training needs. Its use can be extended in the formulation of a training programme. If the TNIA has identified an area or areas of the job that are not being performed effectively, the standards can identify the details. This identification provides the basic planning for a training programme, including at least the practical skills to which can be added further needs of knowledge, attitudes, relationships and other personal qualities.

Types of training approach

The first, and probably the most important, decision concerns the type of training approach that will be used to satisfy the agreed objectives for a particular group of learners. Subsequent decisions will follow on naturally from this initial decision.

On-the-job approaches

One-to-one instruction

One-to-one instruction used to be referred to, in derogatory terms, as 'Sitting with Nellie'. The 'Nellie' approach was where a new entrant sat alongside an existing skilled operative and was told to watch them carefully. After a period of observation they were given their own machine and told to 'get on with it'!

The introduction of realistic training programmes retained the 'Nellie' method, but in a much improved form in recognition that training on-the-job, where possible, can often be more effective than the 'artificiality' of training courses.

One-to-one instruction, usually introduced into practical standards, can be summarized as:

1. Identify a person skilled in the processes to be learned.

2. Confirm that this skilled person is also skilled in instruction and training. If not, make arrangements for training in these techniques.

3. With the learner seated beside the operative or other worker (e.g. clerical work at a desk and/or computer), the 'instructor' follows a Tell, Show, Do approach. First the operation is explained, with relevant aids, to the learner; the instructor then shows the learner how the process works, ensuring as far as possible that there is understanding; finally the learner practises the process under the supervision of 'Nellie'.

4. Feedback on the learner's performance is given and, if necessary, the 'Do' part is repeated until the learner has reached an agreed satisfactory level.

5. The learner, within a training area or under the continuous supervision of 'Nellie', is allocated production work to perform until they are ready to progress to full production work.

This type of on-the-job training is most frequently used with practical tasks such as machine operating, but it can be adopted for other forms of occupational training – clerical procedures, reception duties, office machine working, computer programming, ancillary medical or dental duties, and so on. The approach works most effectively with operations of a relatively routine and repetitive nature, although the same principles can be applied to higher level complexities of training.

Coaching

Coaching is a training and/or developmental approach in which the learner follows a learning process at work, usually with the involvement of the manager or supervisor, but using real work projects. This learning at work is different from traditional training methods. It is achieved by the use of actual work, as opposed to the more artificial nature of training course activities.

The uses of coaching

Coaching is a multi-purpose training and development approach and its uses can include:

- *Remedial training.* In many cases a TNIA will demonstrate that, although the learners may, at some time, have received training in the skills required to perform their work, they may have forgotten, misinterpreted or implemented it erroneously so that the required level of performance is not being achieved.

- *New or extended duties of work.* Learners are required to extend their skills as a result of having to undertake new work or increase the range of their current work. These increased skills can be achieved by the learners attending training courses, but at the expense of resource time and the possible failings of a training course as opposed to learning from 'real' work.

- *Career development.* Skilled and efficient workers may be on the point of promotion to higher duties or may need job enhancement to stretch their abilities and ensure career development or continued job satisfaction. Coaching can offer a very effective method of introducing the learners to these more demanding tasks. Higher-grade work is delegated to the learners, giving them the authority to carry out the work that would normally be held by their boss, but the boss would retain the final responsibility for the results of the task.

- *Training consolidation.* In many cases, attendance at a training course is not an end in itself and requires substantial follow-up when the learner returns to work. Training course material is often very general, deliberately so to give a base for a range of situations in which the skills have to be implemented. Back at work, the more general training skill may need to be translated or interpreted to the particular work situation; real-life practice in the skills will certainly be necessary; at-work training in additional parts of the skill might be needed; and so on. If the training is to be worthwhile in a work practice, the supervisor or manager must accept this continuing need and their responsibility to support it, and start coaching projects and assignments to achieve this. Good training is often deemed to have failed when the real cause is the lack of opportunity, encouragement or support to put the training into practice.

- *Complete training events.* A coaching approach might be the alternative to sending learners on expensive training courses, provided sufficient skill exists in the work area to cover the material effectively, particularly when it is linked with real job tasks. Both approaches will have to be considered so that a cost- and value-effective choice can be made. Coaching can be considered a form of one-to-one, on-the-job instruction when the 'instructor' is either a member of the work staff or a trainer brought to the workplace to support the coaching/training.

There is no guarantee that coaching, of whatever nature, is less costly than a training course, particularly where several people require the learning, and in some ways coaching is more expensive in resource time than a course. However, the benefit of the learning taking place at work and the value of real work tasks being undertaken must be significant factors in the cost/value balance. Many learners find that good coaching has more impact on them than a training course that they may see as divorced from the working situation.

Coaching practice

Coaching techniques are similar to those of many other forms of training and development. In summary these will be:

1. Identify the individuals requiring training and development for one of the reasons described above.
2. Confirm that coaching will be the best and/or most cost/value effective form of satisfying the training needs.
3. Discuss with the learners what is needed and agree with them that a coaching process should be followed.
4. Agree with them the terminal objectives for the coaching and the most effective ways of achieving them.
5. Construct an agreed coaching plan that will be supported by both of you as the manager and the learners.
6. Agree starting and finishing dates for the process.
7. Agree interim progress discussions and also the final discussion on completion of the project at which, it is hoped, the results of the project will be accepted.
8. Review with the learners the learning resulting from the event and discuss future action.

The coach must offer full support to the learners and above all must not 'look over their shoulder' all the time, but remembering that this is basically a training exercise and that they still retain the final responsibility for the success of the task.

Project management

Project management is an approach that follows on naturally from coaching and usually relates to the development of experienced people who need to have their skills and capabilities widened. In the natural development of learners, as their skill in certain functions is achieved, they need to increase the number and range of their skills; or well experienced persons might need to be extended or tested by performing tasks with which they have had no previous experience but will need if they are to progress in their careers.

The management of projects as a training and development approach has a similar procedure to that of coaching, and will include:

1. identifying the learners and their particular developmental needs
2. identifying suitable projects that the learners can manage
3. discussing and agreeing the project management activities and their objectives with the learners

4.   discussing methods and approaches with the delegated project managers and advising as necessary
5.   agreeing levels of authority and responsibility, but with the manager retaining the final responsibility for the success of the project
6.   agreeing starting and finishing dates; interim review dates; and a final review and reporting date at the end of the project
7.   discussing the learning achieved by the event and agreeing future action.

Mentoring

Whereas coaching is usually applied to operative and similar tasks, mentoring is an approach that has application in higher level and/or more complex situations. There are a number of different ways in which mentoring is applied, but usually one experienced person will act, often over an extended period, as the mentor, supporter, adviser, event arranger, etc. to the learner.

One example of mentoring might be with a newly-appointed management trainee. Following more formal induction and management training courses, a departmental manager or series of managers might be appointed in a progressive plan as mentors to the trainee. The mentor and the trainee would have a close association during which the trainee might 'shadow' the mentor for some time; undertake some of the mentor's tasks (under supervision); complete projects – artificial and real – set up by the mentor; attend training events on the advice of the mentor; discuss a range of topics with the mentor; and have review meetings with the mentor at which the preceding actions are discussed with particular reference to the learning achieved, and also further action is agreed.

Mentors must, of course, be highly motivated, not only to the organization and its work, but also to the active support of learners. Their mentoring will, at times, make considerable inroads into their time and resourcefulness, but one of the reported pay-offs for mentors is the satisfaction of seeing their learners progressing upwards in the organization, knowing that they had a significant role in helping this progression.

Open learning

Open learning is one of the generic descriptions given to a range of approaches, the core of which is that the learning takes place at work, or in association with the workplace and, basically, is self-instruction without the presence of a trainer, instructor or 'Nellie'.

Self-instruction at its simplest is attempted learning from a text – a book or manual relating to the learning. The next stage is to follow a correspondence course in which the text reading and learning follows a guided programme, the work is checked and the results fed back to the learner. Further, there is a specially designed self-instruction text, usually known as a programmed text, which instructs the learner about a particular area of knowledge or skill before it is put into practice.

More complex open learning 'packages' can include text-based approaches supplemented by audio, video, interactive video, or computer material and programs. Or the 'package' can consist of one or more of these without written text-based material. Almost any mixture of approaches can be used with the open learning packages, including, of course, coaching, mentoring and training courses.

Open or distance learning was hailed as the perfect answer to people attending training courses, thus reducing costs and increasing the effectiveness of the learning. The rapid demise of direct training courses were forecast as a result. However, experience has shown that open learning can be very effective in certain instances, but in others cannot replace training courses. In skill learning, although the theories models and concepts can be presented in one of the open learning formats, the learners still need to practise the new skills, preferably in a safe environment such as that provided by a training course, before using them in a live, work situation.

The open learning method is one approach that can be used to satisfy the needs identified in the TNIA and the design and planning of such approaches has many similarities with those needed for training and development courses. However, additional authoring skills are necessary if the package is to be effective. Open learning must also have the active support of the learners' managers who should give the learners time and other resources to make full use of the package.

Self-learning can be a difficult and lonely process, demanding considerable motivation and determination to complete the learning. In many cases, the effectiveness of an open or distance learning package is enhanced if it is supported by an 'expert' whom the learner can contact to question and discuss when problems arise. This may be the case when a package is used within an organization with, for example, a resource centre staffed by people who can fulfil these requirements. Support of this nature is less likely when programmes are bought in from commercial open-learning package suppliers direct to the learner.

Audio material

When audio material is included in an open learning package or as a stand-alone learning device, it usually replaces a written text. The audio tape can contain a lecture or other form of input, followed by activity suggestions to practise the learning material. It is less commonly used now, having been replaced to a large extend by video tapes, but audio cassettes have an advantage that the cassette player is much more portable than the video recorder and can be used almost anywhere. Learners can listen to tapes while driving to and from work, particularly useful if they are help up in traffic jams. Audio tapes are simple and relatively cheap to produce and a wide range of subjects is available, including tapes of subject expert speakers at seminars and conferences, either as a reminder of what you heard or if you were unable to attend the event. Apart from the advised practice activities, audio tapes are essentially knowledge learning instruments and consequently must be supported by other approaches.

Video material

The widespread availability of video-taped training material revolutionized the use of the more traditional media of films as well as audio tapes. Video material can be hired or purchased in a wide range of subjects from commercial sources such as Video Arts, Melrose, the BBC and Fenman Training and are produced for a variety of purposes. Many of them use the video in conjunction with other approaches such as a live training session. These uses will be discussed later (see Chapter 9) when specific training session construction is being considered.

In some cases a video programme is used as the self-instruction training vehicle, although if dependence is placed solely on the video, similar problems to the open learning restrictions of learning alone arise.

Otherwise, videos can be linked with, for example, a discussion leader who would lead a discussion following the viewing of the video.

Although the approach has been attempted, it is doubtful whether a complete learning programme can be successful from a video or series of videos alone, except perhaps in very restricted subject coverage, but used intelligently and supported by other learning vehicles, they can be powerful training techniques.

Interactive video materials

One of the criticisms levelled at the use of training videos in a self-instruction, do-it-alone mode is that the learner cannot talk to the video as to a live trainer. The video tries to put over a particular message, model or concept – if the learner does not understand parts, disagrees with, or otherwise wants to discuss the material, they cannot do this with the video and the event can be very frustrating.

Interactive video attempts to compensate for this difficulty, although until technology advances considerably, the interactivity will be very one-sided. A typical interactive video, as opposed to a more traditional 'straight-through' video, asks the viewer at stages to answer a question or suggest what should happen next. The response is keyed in a variety of ways and the viewer is told whether they are right or wrong – if the latter they might be invited to try again. This involves the viewer in the process to a much greater extent than passively watching the video alone.

However, the arguments against the interactive video as an effective learning vehicle are the same as for the straight-through video. If the viewer, having responded to the programme's questions and having received feedback, disagrees with the video producer's concepts or model, there is nothing they can do about it. The situation is improved only if the video is viewed with an expert who is able to discuss the material or the disagreements. Otherwise the learner is expected to accept the correctness of the video material (or reject it and stop watching the video!).

Computer materials

An increasing number of situations are becoming suitable for and capable of training through a computer program. Usually this consists of a computer program package, or as part of a multi-media package – text, video, questionnaires, projects and activities – relating to a specific subject or range of related subjects. It is almost always a self-learning package rather than part of a training event, although most packages can be modified and inserted into parts of the training event.

The advantages of the CBT package include:

- the learners take part in an active form of learning
- study can be at the learners' own pace
- understanding checks can be built in easily
- the learning can be at the learners' place of work or even at home
- time and resources are used effectively.

The disadvantages are few and include:

- the learning requires a high motivation and commitment by the learner
- managerial, trainer or other expert support should be readily available, although this is not always possible
- some feelings of isolation may be felt with the learner sitting alone in front of a computer screen
- some people have an aversion to, even a fear of working with a computer, although this is a decreasing problem with their increasing availability.

Learning packages, usually on CD-ROM, are available in an increasingly wide range of subjects from commercial sources at very reasonable costs, particularly when you can consider that they can be used on more than one occasion. It is also possible for a custom-written program to be made, either within your organization if you have an expert computer program writer, or by external professional houses.

CBT packages are relatively simple to use.

1. Issue the package to the learner and give instructions on its operation, although these are often an integral and logical part of the program itself.
2. Allow the learner to work through the package at their own rate, taking part in the required activities or projects.
3. If difficulties, misunderstandings or non-understandings arise, reference is made to the supporting manager, trainer or other expert, and/or regular interim reviews are held.
4. Arrange for reviews during and at the end of the program, with implementation being contracted on an action plan, agreed with the learner's manager, and the learning put into practice.

The use of the computer as a learning aid in training and development can also be linked with other operations, principal among which is interactive video already described and the computer programs themselves are often interactive (within the constraints mentioned earlier). More and more interactivity is developing, particularly through CD-I (interactive compact disc). Multi-media computers make the use of CD-I simple and extend the programs of non-CD computer much beyond simple-visible text or graphics. Sound and animated motion are common; interactivity through questioning etc. is more alive than with the video, although many of the constraints still exist. Computer voice control is developing rapidly and will soon be commonplace, but the time when an intelligent, free conversation may be had with the computer is still some way off.

Few, if any, of the training and development methods described in this chapter are effective stand-alone techniques, nor indeed is a training course if run along the traditional 'talk and chalk' lines. So many different techniques are available, many of which complement and supplement each other, and the best training and development programmes are those that intermix a number of the approaches, even self-instruction packages which link with direct training courses. Chapter 7 discusses the use of these non-course programmes with the various approaches for training courses.

Chapter 7
Off-the-job training

This chapter:

  describes the method of designing off-the-job training
  discusses the range of training formats
  considers trainer power and the centring of training
  describes the principal methods in off-the-job training and development
  describes methods of sequencing programme material
  suggests the format for a design blueprint.

The previous chapter considered some of the on-the-job methods for satisfying the training and development needs identified in a TNIA. There is no doubt that these methods have increased in number and effectiveness in recent years, but more learners attend some form of off-the-job training event for these purposes than any other.

Operational design

Figure 6.1 suggested an initial approach for designing an on-the-job training programme; Figure 7.1 does the same for off-the-job training.

Objectives and the learning population

Objectives and the learning population were considered fully in Chapter 6. Additional comments related to off-the-job training are made here.

● How many people will need to be covered by the programme? This will obviously affect how many events or courses must be included in a programme.

● The age range of the learning groups can affect the design or practice of the events. A group of young active learners will probably react differently from a group of older, less active, and perhaps more considerate people. However, beware of making assumptions about age or sex differences and their learning

1. List the agreed objectives for the training programme.

2. Consider the learning population and how they will affect the programme design.

3. List the ways in which each objective might best be met.

4. Decide whether the learning will be best achieved by an on-the-job or off-the-job programme form.

5. Consider the possible accommodation and how it will affect the course design and practice.

6. Confirm whether you are restricted to a certain period of time or whether the programme will be allowed the full time required for effective completion.

7. Confirm from previous information when the programme is required to start and finish.

8. Consider material design.

Figure 7.1   The initial stages in designing an off-the-job training programme

processes. In practice, you are most likely to be presented with a completely heterogeneous group. Follow the overall principle of training design: make the programme as varied as possible to ensure that it will appeal to all the participants at all stages. But remember, you can satisfy some of the people some of the time, but not all the people all the time (sometimes not even some of the people some of the time).

● Learning styles should be taken into account as far as possible (see Chapter 6) but again if the groups are heterogeneous (similar to the population as a whole), try to make the programme as attractive and useful to all by varying approaches.

● As with on-the-job training, the location of the learning groups will affect your planning. When the learners are distributed nationally or internationally, the decision has to be made as to whether the training should be provided centrally, involving the additional costs of bringing the learners to the centre, or whether the trainers should be the ones who should travel to the learners, perhaps to convenient selected centres.

● One of the problems described in on-the-job training concerned the availability of the training programme. Off-the-job training presents more of a problem when either a suitable training course is not available when needed (either by individuals or groups) or the learners cannot be released at that time. Unless these problems can be accepted, you should seek other ways of satisfying the needs, e.g. open learning packages or other on-the-job approaches.

Training accommodation

If the organization has a training centre or college and it is easy to bring learners to this centre, then the possible problems are those that can be dealt with by the administration departments. It is assumed that the centre possesses all the necessary types of accommodation to avoid problems of design that might arise.

But if training accommodation has to be found elsewhere, design must consider any effects that restrictions imposed in these locations may place on the programme. For example, if the programme includes a considerable amount of experiential activity requiring the provision of large areas of space or a substantial number of rooms, a suitable location must be sought or the programme modified to take account of the constraints.

Time constraints

The effect of time constraints on the design of training programmes is one of the main factors in the design process.

The constraint might be imposed without consideration of the needs demonstrated by the TNIA – 'You have x days in which to run a training event' – which places substantial restrictions on the design of the programme. Irrespective of the total needs identified, decisions must be made about which of the needs must be included in the programme. The earlier prioritization of the objectives will help in this instance, whether it is based on importance of the subject or on the widespread nature of the deficiencies. Whichever base for the constraint exists, the designer with senior manager support (for example, the training manager or senior line managers) must try to reverse such a decision.

Alternatively the designer, taking into account the identified needs and their minimum priorities, must propose and fight for a length of time that would be sufficient to mount an effective programme.

In many cases, if the designers or their representatives are effective negotiators, a compromise will result – not quite sufficient time to make the training programme fully effective, but not so constrained as to make it almost a non-event.

Starting and finishing dates

The designer should give consideration to the starting and finishing dates of the programme. Time is always at a premium and if the demand for the provision of training has originated at a senior level, it was usually wanted yesterday! There is a good argument for the training manager to be involved in senior management decisions at an early stage, thus avoiding a dictat demanding unreasonable or impossible action.

The design of a complete training programme, including the planning of individual events and sessions, is very time-consuming and sufficient time is almost invariably not afforded (or so the designers often claim!). But undoubtedly there is a lot of work and, consequently, time involved. It is usually not a continuous process on which the designer is able to work without interruption. Some researchers suggest that planning for a single session needs between six and ten times the period allocated to the session itself. This time will vary depending on the complexity of the subject, the availability of material, the experience of the trainer, the availability or production time of training aids, and so on.

Sometimes the remit includes dates by which the programme must start and be completed. Bearing in mind the comments above, if this requirement is unreasonable it should be challenged in the most appropriate way. The strongest argument must be that if the request is in fact unreasonable but is complied with, the resulting programme will be less than effective and as a result the organization's money will not have been wisely spent. The result of an improvement of business must always be behind the provision of training and development.

Advantages and disadvantages of off-the-job training

Advantages of direct training events include:

- groups of people with similar needs can be brought together for learning events
- a wide variety of learning methods, including many of those discussed in Chapter 6
- they are generally cost-effective in training a large number of people with a common need
- views, opinions and information can be shared with the other people in the group who can bring a wide range of experience or knowledge to the discussions
- new concepts and techniques can be presented to a large number of people in the shortest possible time
- opportunities for the learners to clarify aspects of the learning that they do not understand or on which they require additional information.

Every technique and approach, in addition to having advantages usually has disadvantages or problems; group training events are no exception. These include:

- the different learning speeds of individuals who are usually forced to progress at a compromise rate
- the different learning preferences of individuals or groups cannot always be taken into account
- not all the learners will be starting at the same knowledge or skill level and there is a risk that those starting at the lowest levels, if account is not taken of this, will be lost from the start

- not all the learners will have similar motivation levels and, in fact, some may be resisting learning because they did not want to come.

Material design

The main steps involved in designing the content of a training programme are summarized in Figure 7.2.

---

1. Decide on the nature of the training approaches.

2. Plan the sequence of the sessions to meet the programme objectives.

3. Prepare an outline plan for the programme detailed from the previous items.

4. Discuss the proposed plan with the training practitioners, the training administration group and, if possible, the learning population and their line managers.

5. Complete a final, agreed programme plan from which detailed sessions plans can be produced.

6. Pass the agreed, final plan to the training practitioners who will be responsible for the individual sessions of the training programme.

Figure 7.2   Checklist for designing the content of a training programme

Training formats

An early decision that must be made in the design of a training programme is the format and nature of the programme.

Training courses

The most common group events in training and development, collectively known as training courses, can vary enormously. They can be organized internally for the staff of an organization; publicly for completely mixed groups; or – an increasing approach particularly welcomed by small businesses – a mixed group organized either by an external agency or by one of the participating companies. Those companies may not have sufficient staff to hold courses or prefer not to (or cannot afford to) send people to public courses.

Training courses can last from half a day to several weeks, or programmes may cover a year or more. One recent programme in which I was involved arranged a one-day event once a month over twelve months. The learning group can be a mix of groups of peers, hierarchical levels, stranger, cousin or home groups. The course can be structured, unstructured or semi-structured with either a formal or informal atmosphere. The style of the trainers can be tutors (i.e. teachers), trainers with a range of adult learning techniques to offer, or facilitators (i.e. helping agents).

The training course concentrates on a range of skills to provide learning opportunities or, in a modular form, on specific skills. The format is invariably a series of training sessions, including any of the wide range of learning methods available.

Workshops

One type of group training activity is a workshop. Unfortunately this is a term that is widely misused. Straightforward training courses, and even single activities, have been described as workshops. They are definitely learning events and, like unstructured group training courses, involve substantial participation by the learners. The workshop can concentrate on a single topic or a number of related topics or themes. The chief difference from a training course is that there are very few 'expert' speakers or even formal training sessions. Inputs are usually short and are simply introductions to the topics, either arranged by the facilitator (trainer) or requested by the learning group. The workshop participants, who usually come from the same or similar disciplines, often decide themselves (with the guidance and support of the facilitator) how the workshop will be run and what will be the terminal objectives. The emphasis is on doing, either in the production of objectives or plans to operate on return to work, or the practical production of materials, methods etc. A workshop of several designers is a useful method of designing a new training and development programme. Consequently the participants return to work with actual work problems solved, training programmes designed, training materials produced or designed, or with new methods of approaching their problems.

Conferences

Conferences are not always recognized by the organizers and/or the participants as training events. An accepted aim for a conference, consisting of people from the same or similar professions, or with similar interests or simply from the same organization, is that participants go away with a greater awareness than when they arrived, even if this might be only what the chief executive expects of them in the coming year. The format of conferences can vary, but is commonly a series of talks/lectures by company members or external speakers, sometimes linked with more informal, small group discussions or breakouts. Only too frequently the organization's annual conference has been seen as an occasion for a variety of social events rather than a learning occasion. Indeed it has been known for a company to organize a conference simply as a 'thank you' to their staff for a year's good work.

Seminars

In many ways seminars are the better types of conferences, on smaller scales and require a greater degree of involvement from the participants. A seminar may often, though not uniquely, concentrate on a single theme rather than a range of topics. The format is usually a sequence of speakers who are experts on their parts of the subject theme, and subsequent syndicate or small group activities. These are followed by plenary sessions at which the small group considerations are aired and discussed. A seminar is often described as a 'symposium' and it is difficult, if not impossible, to differentiate them. The purpose of both is the dissemination of information, refined or new, and consequently must be part of a learning process, usually at a professional level.

Group training strategies

The centring of training – trainer power and authority

Trainers are usually in a position to exert power and authority over the learners for which they are responsible. This power can be used appropriately to determine the centring of training, but it can also be misused with the result that the training becomes ineffective.

Power emerges in a number of ways and can be determined by either the behaviour of the trainers themselves or the situations in which the training is being held, or both. Occasionally the employing organization or client may require a particular form of power use by the trainer. In such cases the trainer must decide about acceptance of these roles and how they will be used in the programme.

Types of trainer power

Power position

The trainer who is placed in charge of a group of learners automatically has power and authority. This position is generally recognized and accepted, in the initial stages at least by the learners who are often seeking this type of lead because of their uncertainties in the early stages of a training event.

However, care must be taken that the role is not overdone and the trainer must continue to be aware of its effect and be ready to vary the approach as circumstances require.

Expertise power

The trainer has been given responsibility for a programme of training, should have a good knowledge of the subject and be an expert in the techniques of training. To some extent, learners also expect their trainer to be a subject expert. This view is dangerous for the trainer whose credibility can so easily be lost, particularly if the 'expert' view was fostered, but eventually the mask slips and the learners realize that the trainer is not all that was represented.

Environmental power

The trainer has considerable power, again at least in the early stages of a programme, to control the environment for the learners. The place, time etc. has been determined by the trainer who also has power over such aspects as the timing of events and the duration of the training programme. This power and authority must obviously be used in the most effective way for the benefit, not only of the trainer, but perhaps more so for the learners and the programme.

Personal power

Personal power is the most ephemeral of all and usually has to be earned by the trainer (and can so easily be lost). It is often described as 'charisma', but this may be a dangerous assumption. Even charisma can wear thin and mere mortals are advised to concentrate on knowledge, technical skill and feeling for people to maintain their position in the group.

Relational power

A more fragile source of power depends on the relationship that trainers build up between themselves and the learners, and which often needs to be fostered in out-of-training hours. It can so easily be misunderstood by both the trainer and the learner – the trainers having the mistaken impression that their 'socializing' in the bar will add to their authority the following day, and the learners perhaps being suspicious of an extreme change of behaviour out of the training room.

Power centring

Power centring combines the power preferences of the trainer and the needs of the methods employed in the training event and represents an important area in training and development programme decision making. The range of approaches can be expressed in a simple diagram (Figure 7.3) which demonstrates the increasing risk to the trainer where there is an increased sharing of responsibility with the learners.

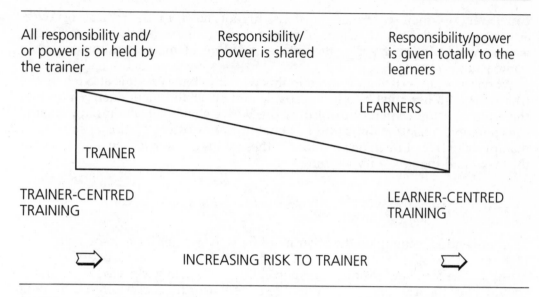

All responsibility and/ or power is or held by the trainer

Responsibility/ power is shared

Responsibility/power is given totally to the learners

TRAINER-CENTRED TRAINING

LEARNER-CENTRED TRAINING

INCREASING RISK TO TRAINER

Figure 7.3   The sharing of power

Trainer-centred training

At one time there was no question about where training was centred; training courses were designed, planned and produced by trainers, who made all the decisions of content and practice. The universal development of people demanding to be involved in a variety of events was not lost on training and development and has necessitated the decision about whether the training should be trainer-centred or led, or learner-centred or led.

Trainer-centred training involves the decision by the trainer about the content of the event, in both broad and detailed terms; a defined series of training course events – lectures, discussions, activities and other approaches – all aimed at achieving the predetermined training objectives. The timing, pace, sequencing and so on are all decided and controlled by the trainer. This gives the impression of an autocratic, harsh approach, ignoring the needs of the learners, and in a number of cases this is true. But certain events must be controlled in this manner, for a number of reasons: very constrained time, the introduction of completely new material of which the learners have no experience, and similar requirements.

In spite of an increasing desire and need among learners to be more involved in the event, many of them, particularly those from an organization with similar attitudes, feel more comfortable in such a directive event. The counter argument is that these learners will react more favourably to other approaches because they are released from organizational constraints with which they may not be in tune. This comfort may be a reducing factor as some participants may hide behind the trainer control and take a passive stance in the event. Many trainers also feel more comfortable in this type of environment because the material and its use are completely in their control, and they do not need to be radical or over-adventurous in their approaches. However, many trainers feel that this approach is too constricting and prefer the greater freedom of methods found in other approaches.

When the event is trainer-centred in this way, it follows that it is also led by the trainer. The trainer must be a fully capable and effective practitioner, not only in the matter of the content, but also in the wider skills of pace, timing, tactics, interpersonal relationships and behavioural control (dare I say kind manipulation!). Failure in one or more of these skills can jeopardize the success of the event and the necessary learning.

Learner-centred training

Learner-centred training on the other hand frees the trainer from enforced control of the event and gives the learners a much greater degree of control over their own learning. The fact that the onus of responsibility for learning is placed more on the shoulders of the learners can be a double-edged sword. Learner-centred training can range from the learners being given the responsibility for aspects such as setting the pace of learning, the sequence of topics, the way in which learning will be best achieved, to the extreme of the learners being given complete control of the event within perhaps the total time constraints.

In learner-centred and learner-led training the trainer takes a back seat and becomes more a resource, or perhaps a facilitator, available as required by the learners. This learning culture does not absolve the trainer completely from responsibility for the event and in some cases the trainer-facilitator must be prepared to take control if the event appears to be in real danger. Consequently the demands on the trainer's skills are substantial, not only in terms of training and facilitating skill, but also in decision making. The trainer must have a wide knowledge of resources as the learners might ask for virtually anything to help them learn. This lack of direction, uncertainty and possibility of difficult demands can frighten many trainers as it is the opposite of the 'safe' approach of the trainer-led culture.

Senior managers, clients or other training sponsors frequently prefer the trainer-centred approach as they can relate more easily to this, and suspect learner-centred approaches as events where games are played. It must be part of the trainer's brief to modify these views if the learner-centred approach is judged to be the most appropriate in the circumstances.

Not all learners prefer events for which they are given responsibility, direction and control. This is a traditional response, most of the learning events that they have previously attended being of the more usual trainer-centred and led courses.

The decision to introduce a learner-centred approach will depend on many circumstances, not only those just described, but also on the nature of the training material and the learning group. If the learning is developmental, for an experienced group the 'teaching' approach would probably not be welcomed, and experienced learners will have definite views on the responsibility for their own learning. Training practitioners are a group that has decided views on the learning approach which they themselves favour and usually prefer a much freer type of event – over-direction can too often appear to be patronizing.

In so many learning events the answer is not a black and white one and a compromise is the most appropriate approach. For example, in interpersonal skills events that I run, because the learners usually come from traditional cultures, launching straight into learner-centred approaches would be most traumatic, apart from eating into the very restricted time available. Consequently, the very early stages are trainer-centred, the learners being 'warned' that they will soon become responsible for much of the learning. It is a fine decision about when to move to the freer approach and varies considerably from group to group. Even when the change has been made, it need not be consistent; the group may reach developmental stages where it requires 'expert' direction rather than flounder.

In the previous chapter, the combination of different methods of on-the-job techniques was suggested as being appropriate in many cases. The same principle can apply here – before a more learner-centred programme, the learners might be required to undertake pre-event work, such as reading, working through open learning packages, viewing videos or computer programs, so they have a base on which to form their learner approach when they attend the group event.

This might be considered to be the most difficult strategic decision for the programme designer, but effective training demands creative approaches rather than the easy option of the trainer-centred and led method.

Structured or unstructured events

The above discussion leads to a further decision about the form of the event. Trainer-centred events tend to be structured, many highly structured as a result of substantial pre-planning of how they should proceed. This is one extreme of inflexibility. Modified trainer-centred events contain varying degrees of flexibility moving to the other extreme of the completely learner-centred event. One example of this is the structured programme which at the design stage contains a specific series of events, timed and detailed in their content. However, in many cases the trainer is not aware of the levels of knowledge and skill of the learners in the group until they are gathered at the start. Where completely new material is to be introduced this presents no problems, but commonly the range of knowledge and skill can be varied, both within and between events. The trainer must then be able to assess the level of the learners and adjust the content accordingly. Some material may need to be extended, reduced, omitted and further material may need to be added. If the design brief is absolutely inflexible, or the trainer is unable to cope with the flexibility required, the event may fail miserably.

These possibilities argue for trainers with wide training skills and knowledge, are flexible in their attitudes and have a wide knowledge of resources on which they can call if necessary. These trainer factors must certainly be taken into account when the programme is being designed.

Group training methods

Much of the decision making on the nature of the training method will fall on the training practitioner responsible for individual sessions, but the programme designer must have a good grasp of what is available so that a comprehensive assessment of the programme and what it can and should contain can be made. The time constraints are an important consideration. It may be desirable to include x experiential activities within the programme, but because of the time required for them, their number must be limited to those that will carry the most significance.

Group training methods include:

- trainer presentations/lectures/input sessions (or similar activities)
- discussions
- demonstrations
- question and answer sessions
- case studies and simulations
- role plays
- activities – including icebreakers, games and group tasking
- videos
- computer-assisted training (CAT) or computer-based training (CBT).

These methods are described briefly here so that the programme designer understands what might be included in a programme. In Chapter 8 they and other methods of session construction are discussed in greater detail.

Trainer presentations

The presentation session, in one form or another, represents the most common group training programme event, although in many cases it is not the most appropriate. In their basic form they are 'tell' events, traditionally described as 'lectures'. The trainer or other expert speaker talks to (or at) the passive audience who is expected to note the many words of wisdom and learn from them.

There are of course situations in which this training method, presented in an effective and appropriate manner, is correct, but as it is probably the easiest type of approach, it may be used on too many inappropriate occasions. The presentation of completely new material or, for example, the results of personal research represent examples that would be best presented in this manner, at least in the initial stages.

Discussions

Discussions are common and very useful learning techniques, either as part of a presentation session or as a stand-alone, whether they have been planned (essential in a constrained programme) or have occurred naturally. They involve the learners actively, particularly useful when the event is relatively passive; give everybody the opportunity to speak (provided they are effectively led); and enable a wide sharing of information and views.

Discussions can be planned to take place during a trainer presentation to obtain the views of the group members, as a trigger for a subject for attention or even a break from the process of the session. Planned inclusions must be taken into account in the design of the programme and the time that can be afforded to them.

Unplanned discussions can arise in any session, and in view of their obvious importance to the learners, the programme designer may find it valuable to anticipate them and allow time for them in various sessions.

Demonstrations

Demonstrations are practical methods of either showing the learners a piece of equipment, or operation and how it works. Obviously much will depend on the size and availability of the piece of equipment, etc. The demonstration will usually be linked with a trainer presentation and form part of the introduction to a session, or in a progressive manner as the session develops.

Demonstrations such as people skills are much more difficult and indeed may present dangers. If the trainers demonstrate, for example, a negotiation, there is the danger that the learners will see this as patronizing – this is the way you must do it – or, if it fails in some way, the credibility of the approach becomes suspect in the minds of the learners. A video that represents a neutral demonstration of skill, and which may in fact lead to criticism by the learners, is much safer and more useful.

Question and answer sessions

Question and answer sessions may be deliberately included in parts of the programme though rarely as sessions of their own, or may occur naturally, but are one of the techniques that must be handled with care.

Case studies and simulations

Case studies are problem-solving activities, although usually more complex than the average problem-solving activity that follows a trainer presentation on a particular kind of technique. They can be long or short, simple or complex, and within a programme can either form part of a presentation session, follow such a session, or be the length of the programme which is built around the case study.

A simulation is an extended case study in which the learning group becomes a simulated company, or group of companies competing with each other, behaving as company managers. All the necessary background information is provided initially but, particularly if a computer is available, additional database and spreadsheet data is given for which the group has to search, having identified that it needs further information.

Both case studies and simulations can form complete training courses in which all the training objectives and learning points have been included. The conclusion of the activity is its review, and if more than one group is involved in competition, a comparison of the respective results. Once again, the designer must be prepared to allocate a substantial amount of time to this feedback and review period as a considerable amount of learning can be achieved during this part of the activity. Closed-circuit TV may have been used and this will add to the time required in the feedback.

Role plays

Role plays are one of the most widely used activities in training courses and provide learners with the opportunity to practise, in simulated conditions that are close to real life, the learning they have achieved. Usually the role plays are those related to interviews, following trainer presentations and other activities about the techniques of interviewing in particular situations – counselling, grievance, discipline, appraisal, selection, termination and so on.

The value of role plays, if conducted carefully, is that learners can practise newly learned techniques in a safe environment and have feedback – the latter is rare in real life, but is essential to let the learner know how well they are succeeding.

Activities

The favourite and much used supplements to the input session of many trainers are activities. They can be group activities or exercises in which the learners practise as a group the learned techniques; are required to solve problems; demonstrate behaviours that can be observed and for which feedback can be given; provide vehicles for learners to practise the various forms of observation and subsequent feedback; and so on.

The extent and complexity of the activities are constrained only by the time they need, the resources required and the creativity of the designer, but perhaps more than in most aspects of programme design the designers must be careful not to let their enthusiasm for activities run away with them.

Activities can be used in the introductory part of the programme to make the start interesting – many of them would be described as icebreakers as this would be their objective; during the programme as interest revivers; and at the end as final practices of all the lessons learned during the programme. The latter type of activity also acts as a validation of the learning from observation of the skills used that did not exist at the start of the programme.

Videos

Videos in training can be stand-alone parts of a programme, or can be supportive aids for other types of sessions; and even, with some live support, can be complete restricted programmes themselves. Most videos last from 15 minutes to about an hour, the majority of 20 to 30 minutes. Consequently their inclusion in the design of a training programme does not in itself add too much time, but remember to allow time also for review and discussion.

The pace of interactive videos is controlled by the learners with the staged posing of questions by the video and the response of the learners who choose the best answers. Decisions on the place, their use and the time required for videos will be made in the design of the specific sessions, but decisions must also be made at the initial programme design stage about whether they will add to the effectiveness programme; is time available for their inclusion; and are they the best medium to progress the training and learning. The relevant equipment must be obtained and the skill of the trainers in operating the equipment checked.

Computer-assisted training (CAT)

Computers can be used in a number of ways in training programmes, including:

- interactive programs similar to interactive videos but with the greater flexibility of the computer, usually with the use of CD-I (interactive compact discs) – CAT
- small programs inserted in other types of training activities – CAT
- complete training programs related to specific subjects, e.g. updating to a new version of a software application either as the full training programme or integral parts of a larger programme – CBT
- complete training programs on the use of computers and applications – CBT.

The inclusion of a computer program, its nature and its timing will depend on the training and development programme itself, and comments similar to those made about the use of video and interactive video programs.

Sequencing of programme material

Following the selection of the training methods that should be included in a programme, taking into account their relevancy to the subject and the time required, the next stage is to determine the sequence of the sessions. Depending on the type of material and its complexity, most programmes follow a series of classical sequences, such as the one below:

- *Known to the unknown* – the initial introduction of known material easing the learners into the situation and giving them confidence to progress.
- *Simple to complex* – it is a recipe for failure if at the start of a programme the learners are given a mass of highly complex material before they have settled down, accepted the training situation and are prepared to learn.

- *Logical stepping in a process* – remember the simple–complex considerations.
- *Interesting material to more serious needs* – the sequences naturally suggested might need to be amended to introduce material that will attract the interest of the learners at the start so that they will be prepared to continue to learn, a necessary consideration when designing a programme of very 'heavy' or complex material.

Other factors might have an influence on the sequencing of training programme material:

- *Random sequencing.* Not all subjects require logical or other sequencing, permitting a planning that might depend on the availability of particular trainers or guest expert speakers, the length of time required for the various sessions to ensure that the material is contained effectively, etc.

- *Dependency.* Some training, particularly in skill aspects of operational tasks, in spite of other considerations, requires the pattern of sessions to follow the progression of learning and reliance on the previous session. One danger in this approach of which the designer must be aware is that this method is dependent on the slowest learner – movement cannot be achieved until this slowest learner has understood the preceding material. One way of avoiding this potential problem is to build in to the programme the opportunity for these slower learners to have accelerated learning to the norm point by individual, special learning techniques.

- *Knowledge to doing.* This approach can be amalgamated with other forms of sequencing as it involves giving the learners the knowledge that allows them to perform the skill, e.g. by means of a practice activity. It is particularly useful when it is known that the learners have no previous knowledge of the material involved.

- *Doing to knowledge to doing.* This is a reverse of the previous method and uses a practical activity to initiate the learning process. The learners are given an activity to perform that contains the learning points for that part of the programme, but is not too complex that the activity cannot be performed at all. It may be necessary to take the learning points in stages, even though this would not be the normal case. The errors or failures are identified and their significance for the learning group assessed. This will indicate the training activities, particularly trainer presentations of skill knowledge, models or theories that are then followed by further practice to confirm that the learning has been achieved. This approach can be particularly useful where the learners are known to have some previous knowledge or experience.

Training and development programmes are not (or should not be) written on stone as fixed and inflexible plans. So many factors can exist about which the designer, or even the trainer until the programme is under way, will or can know nothing. The range of knowledge and skill level of individual learners has been mentioned several times and this factor can have an important effect on the progress of the programme. The design must not be so set that it cannot be modified on the spot by the trainer because of such factors, otherwise the remainder of the programme could fail. Individual sessions, although linking in a logical sequence with preceding and following ones, should be capable of omission if circumstances at the time demand this. Similarly, if during the event trainers identify a significant need for additional material, there should be leeway built into the design to allow for this, perhaps omitting other material to make way for it.

These comments suggest that although design is important, it is not the final arbiter of what should happen on a live programme when so many other factors might demand flexibility to ensure effectiveness. If the designer and the trainer are one and the same person, it is a decided advantage, particularly if that person is also an experienced practitioner. But good design can assist considerably a separate trainer and one who may not be too experienced and needs substantial guidelines.

A design blueprint

Blueprints guide producers of objects: a blueprint can be produced for the training programme and gives the 'big picture' to the trainers who are to present the programme, in addition to giving the designer the self-assurance that everything has been considered.

A training programme written blueprint should contain:

1. A statement of the aims and objectives of the programme, expressed in measurable terms, supplemented by information about timings to be followed.
2. Any information about the potential or specific learning population, their likely existing knowledge and skills, and differences in status and organizational level that may affect the practice of the programme.
3. A checklist of the types of recommended training methods so that the relevant trainers can ensure they are skilled in these methods.
4. Guidance on the flexibility that will be allowed in the programme for the trainers to use training methods appropriate to the various sessions, and the flexibility allowed generally within the programme.
5. A detailed programme design showing the proposed sessions and their aims (specific session objectives might best be determined by the trainer practitioner responsible for the session).
6. Discussion of the foregoing aspects of the blueprint with the trainers involved and agreement of the content, in particular including the flexibilities.
7. Agreement for reviews with all designers and trainers concerned following the first conducted event to consider its achievement of success or otherwise and any validation information obtained.
8. Discussion of the agreed arrangements with the training administration, and the requirements of the programme.

Part Three

Planning and designing training sessions

Chapter 8
Planning the training sessions – I

This chapter:

    describes step-by-step planning of individual sessions
    describes in detail sufficient for session planning the methods introduced in
    Chapter 7 plus approaches more relevant to session rather than programme
    planning.

Chapter 7 considered the training programme as a whole, providing
information about which training programme methods could be used. At the
end of the chapter a design blueprint was suggested. With this blueprint to hand
the individual sessions that make up the agreed programme can be planned and
designed. Figure 6.2 suggested a step-by-step plan for the complete programme
– a similar checklist can be constructed for individual sessions (see Figure 8.1).

Session objectives

Training objectives were discussed in detail in Chapter 5 and during the design
of the full programme, when it was suggested that in addition to producing
objectives for the programme, outline objectives at the least for each session
within the programme should be produced. Specific and detailed objectives
must now be formulated and stated in writing for each session. Construction of
these objectives will follow the guidelines described in Chapter 5, but session
designers will benefit from remembering the **SMART** approach to objective
construction:

    Specific – as specific as possible, using active verbs, ensuring ease of
    understanding, and avoiding ambiguity and a lack of clarity.
    Measurable – the objective and the results of its practice should be
    expressed in measurable terms. This will not always be possible to the
    fullest extent, but even subjective measurement is acceptable when it is
    consistent and when quantifiable measurement is not possible.
    Achievable – restrict the objective to what is required and achievable within
    the time available for the session. A useful criterion to keep in mind is not

117

1. Confirm and list the agreed objectives for each session.

2. Investigate the relevant training approaches for each session and list these for decision, including the levels of trainer- and learner-centring and power.

3. Identify the material that could be included in the session and decide on the training method.

4. Decide on the content priorities of the material and plan the sequencing.

5. Produce a session guide.

6. Produce a planning script.

7. Produce a session plan.

8. Produce a session brief and plan the session activity.

9. Plan and arrange for the operation or production of evaluation approaches and methods.

Figure 8.1   Checklist for designing training and development programme sessions

to produce 'Rolls-Royce' training when 'Mini' training only is required.
Relevant – the objective must be completely relevant to the session and favourite, but non-relevant, topics should be excluded.
Time bound – referring to the session as a whole or to constituent parts contributing to the total objective.

As in the case of the programme objectives, you are strongly recommended to commit the objectives to paper, not only so that they cannot be manipulated, but also so that they can be used in the other ways described (see Chapter 5).

Training approaches

In Chapter 7, a number of training approaches were suggested as options for the programme.
   The fuller range of group training methods that can be considered for session construction includes:

*   trainer presentations/lectures/input sessions (or similar activities)
*   buzz groups
*   syndicates
*   discussions

- demonstrations
- question and answer sessions
- case studies and simulations
- role plays
- activities – including icebreakers, games and group tasking
- videos
- computer-assisted training (CAT) or computer-based training (CBT)
- brainstorming.

Many of these approaches and techniques can be combined to make a more varied and interesting session and, as suggested on several occasions, a multi-method approach of this nature produces more effective learning events than single-method approaches. This is particularly so in the case of trainer presentations.

Trainer presentations

Trainer presentations are 'tell' events in which the trainer gives what can sometimes be described as a lecture, or less didactically, an input session. By their very nature they are passive events as far as the audience is concerned and the concept is that they will learn by listening and taking in the words of this expert speaker! In many ways it is the easiest form of training as the trainer has complete control of content, manner of expression and timing, but there is considerable doubt about the extent to which it contributes to real learning.

Very few learning events include 'bare' presentations, i.e. consisting solely of the speaker talking for the whole period with no variations included. A more effective trainer presentation or input session can be achieved by the inclusion of appropriate training aids, breaks in the monologue with the use of buzz groups, discussions, videos, computer program inserts, and activities. On some rare occasions the straight lecture will be most appropriate – usually when there is no opportunity to use other approaches – but even the most didactic lecture is usually relieved to some extent by the use of overhead transparency slides or 35mm slides.

Planning for input sessions must take into account the communication barriers described in Chapter 4 (see Figure 4.5) and the learning attention span, although the latter can be improved by the additional use of the other techniques mentioned above.

For design purposes, if there is to be a multi-style approach, the 20–30-minute maximum need not be adhered to, although any one session should desirably last no longer than 45 minutes to one hour. The exact length will depend on the nature of the various component parts of the session, the complexity of the subject and the likely motivation of the learners. Initial design might suggest the following pattern:

a brief introduction to the subject	up to 5 minutes
input by the trainer, oral presentation supported by visual aids	up to 15 minutes

an activity related to the subject to give the learners the opportunity to practise what has been learned	15 to 20 minutes
a feedback session on the activity	about 15 minutes
a summary of the session and the lessons learned	up to 10 minutes
Total time for the session	about 65 minutes

This example is one in which time for the constituent parts has been cut to the bone and considers a relatively simple subject content. Note that even so, the approximate time required is over one hour. Effective training takes time and it is better to reduce the amount of learning material to ensure its effectiveness than to try to cram too much into a constrained period.

Buzz groups

One of the effective interrupting techniques during input sessions is when the trainer, having reached a pre-planned point, preferably before the decreasing attention watershed, poses a question to the learning group, or having made a statement, asks them to consider this. Often it is not convenient or desirable for the group to leave the room to do this so the technique known as 'buzz group' is introduced. The learning group is asked to break up into smaller groups – say, in a group of 12 learners, into four groups of three – by moving their chairs into these subgroups and discuss as repeated. The 'buzz' becomes evident as up to 12 voices can be heard in the room!

Usually groups are asked to buzz for short periods of 5 or 10 minutes and if the event takes place early in the course when individuals may not be keen to speak out in public, you can suggest that a spokesperson is elected from each group. When the full group is reconvened, the spokespersons then give, neutrally, the subgroups' views or responses.

Buzz groups by their nature are informal events, or at least superficially, and can be introduced at almost any stage in a session or programme. Numbers are not material to a great extent, although when large numbers are involved the grouping can become difficult. Learning events nowadays rarely consist of more than 20 participants, usually and preferably much less than this, but if the group is larger the subgroups can be increased in size or number.

Syndicates

A syndicate in a training event is an extension of a buzz group and is sometimes referred to as a task subgroup or a breakout group. A learning group, either during or at the end of a trainer presentation, is divided into smaller subgroups and given a task to complete. The syndicates are allocated separate rooms where they can work in private before returning at the end of the allotted time to the main group for what is referred to as a plenary or review/feedback session.

The task given to the syndicate can be a problem-solving, decision-making task; a views and opinions gathering exercise; or a management or other skill exercise, game or activity. A time in which to complete the task is usually specified and, in meeting or leadership training events, a group leader is selected or the group is asked to elect a leader.

One of the benefits of syndicate working is that they can be observed so that behavioural and operational feedback can be given to the learners. Where there are a number of groups, continuous observation presents difficulties for the trainer, but observers may be selected from the learning group or the syndicates can be advised to, in addition to performing the task, take notice of how they as a group approach the task; the behaviours and skills they use; the skill of the leader; and so on.

When the syndicates return to the full group, a review and feedback session is held during which the observations of the observers (if any) are given to the participants, followed by a general discussion on the activity and the lessons learned. Recall of the events during the syndicates, often a problem, is helped by preceding the review session with the learner leaders and members completing questionnaires designed to identify events during the activity. The recalled information is then used in the ensuing discussion.

Plenary sessions are often lengthy affairs, particularly when a number of syndicates and observers are involved. One method of reducing the time for this event is for each syndicate's observer to review simultaneously the activity with their syndicate members at the end of the syndicate work. When specific feedback has been given a much shorter plenary session can be held to discuss common problems and points that emerged in each group.

Discussions

Discussions have as similarly wide a use as syndicates, and of course syndicates can be used as discussion groups. Basically they are another way of reducing the bare, not very effective input sessions and involve the open or syndicated discussion of topics relevant to the learning event.

Discussions are either pre-planned or spontaneous and held as separate session events or as integral parts of sessions. Pre-planned discussions can be separate sessions in which the learners are asked to discuss, usually in small groups, the appropriate topic. The objective of the session is simply to allow the learners to air their views, or can aim to have a specific terminal result or decision. This type of discussion may be part of an input session, at a pre-planned time, with the topic obviously being directly related to that of the session.

More informal, spontaneous discussions may also be held. During an input session a comment or disclosure might be made by a learner or learners, that the trainer feels should be followed up immediately. A discussion is then started with commonly the trainer, who should be a skilled discussion leader, conducting it to a natural conclusion. In certain circumstances, e.g. discussion-leading or meeting management programmes, the learners are invited to take over the discussion themselves, using the skills they have just learned.

In terms of time control, discussions may be unknown quantities – the subject matter for one group may be an uninteresting or a strange topic, whereas with another group it may be of riveting interest and substantial knowledge. These opposite aspects will affect the interest in and depth of the discussions, and consequently the time needed.

Inexperienced trainers or those inexperienced in discussion leading, tend to shy away from including discussions in their session plans because of these unknown quantities and their uncertainty about their ability to control the situation.

Discussions that are planned as specific events during, or as, a session require more preparation than they are usually afforded and should be viewed by the planner almost as substantial as input sessions. Discussions can incur a number of pitfalls which are usually the result of the discussion being unplanned or badly planned. Even spontaneous discussions will normally be controlled, albeit covertly, by the trainer who must be skilled in discussion leading or controlling. Discussions form part of almost every activity in a training course and consequently trainers should include these skills in their 'training toolkit'.

The planning process for a discussion to be held as part of, or as, a session will include the following steps:

1. Decide whether a discussion at a particular point in a session or as a session itself is the most appropriate form of learning aid in those circumstances.

2. If the discussion is to be included in a session, you must decide exactly where you are going to introduce it and how you will move into it from another part of the session activity.

3. Decide on a specific subject related to the session or programme – one that will interest the learners sufficiently to encourage them to discuss; make sure that the discussion will last for the time that you allocate.

4. Following on from the last point, allocate a period of time within which the discussion should be completed.

5. Decide how you will launch the discussion:
   (a) by reference to previous material in the session or an earlier one
   (b) by making a provocative statement
   (c) by showing a visual aid containing a statement or statement graphic
   (d) by simply announcing that a discussion would be valuable at this stage.

6. Decide on and write down your opening statement – starting a discussion is often the most difficult part and being confident about your own input will encourage and support the learners to continue.

7. Decide on the role you will take – the observer once the discussion has started; the discussion leader; a member of the discussion group with a learner leader appointed. Whichever role is decided, and it may be useful to ask the group which role they would want you to take, your aim is to be

as neutral as possible, making contributions yourself only when unavoidable. Your personal views should be minimal.

8. Decide your strategy regarding unclear or incomplete statements made by the learners. Will you let them pass in the hope that eventually the learners themselves will take them up or, if this is not evident, will you take the initiative and challenge them?

9. Whether you are to lead the discussion or be a participating member, it is still your responsibility that the discussion should be effective and complete. In order to help you to do this you should, when planning the discussion, produce a discussion brief for yourself. This can take the form of a 'shopping list' in which all the possible aspects of the subject are listed and can be ticked off as they are discussed. Alternatively a 'pros and cons list' can be used: this consists of two columns, one listing the arguments in favour of the subject, the other the arguments against. Again the items can be ticked off as they are covered. In both cases, use your list to identify items that you might want to insert into the discussion if it starts to falter or if it is obvious that the item is not going to be covered in spite of its importance.

10. Finally, you might wish to consider other introductory activities. If discussion leading itself is part of the learning, you might set up a small group in which you lead a bad discussion, and in which the learning points emerge and are noted by the discussion participants and the rest of the group. This 'bad' discussion then leads to a full discussion event on discussions, discussion leading and the effective aspects of discussions.

Demonstrations

As described in Chapter 7, demonstrations are mainly found in sessions that are concerned with the knowledge and or skills of operating some object, piece of machinery or equipment, or a procedure, e.g. using a computer. As we saw in the 'Nellie' approach, which depends heavily on demonstration, they are part of the 'Tell, Show, Do' instructing technique. In a group situation a typical demonstration practice would be for the trainer to describe, perhaps with overhead project transparencies, the object, its use and its operation. This description would then, wherever possible, be backed up by the object being shown to the group and operated in the correct manner by the trainer. In some cases, for example large pieces of machinery or other immovable objects, the trainer may have to take the group to where the object is located; otherwise, drawings and preferably photographs will need to be used. The final stage is for the learners themselves to practise using the object, initially under close supervision by the trainer or supporting skilled operators.

Demonstrations may form part of other training approaches, particularly input sessions during which several might be included.

Question and answer sessions

Anyone who has been in a situation where they were asking questions will realize that this is a difficult and dangerous approach. If questions are asked in an inappropriate way, the required level of response is not received; unintentional emotions may be raised; a series of questions may be seen as interrogation; and so on. But in so many training situations it is essential that questions are posed to obtain information, views, opinions and feelings and the skilled trainer must be capable of using them effectively.

The trainer who is inexperienced in eliciting information from a group falls into the '*closed question* trap' and wonders why simple answers of 'yes' or 'no' are received, or straightforward information when detailed descriptions were sought. In most cases, unless of course closed answers are required, questions should be as *open* as possible. For example, rather than asking 'Did you find that part of the activity difficult?' to which the response would almost certainly be either 'Yes' or 'No', a more effective format would be 'How difficult did you find that part of the activity?'. The response to this second type of question would produce much information and would give you a good indication of (a) the skills level of the learners and (b) the value of the activity, which is what you are seeking.

Other questions to avoid, unless they are appropriate in certain circumstances, include *leading questions* which might suggest to susceptible learners that you want the answer contained in the question, and *multiple questions* where learners have difficulty in knowing which question to answer.

Other 'question and answer' traps are when the trainer tries to obtain the views of all the learners in a group and questions each of them. Questioning starts at one point in the group and the trainer has the intention of moving along the line so that everybody is approached. However, the original line of questioning may be sidetracked or a discussion might arise halfway round the group. As a result, one or more members may not be questioned and they think that you are not interested in their views – so from that point on they do not give their views easily or voluntarily.

If you intend to ask everybody in the group, make sure that you do. Often it is more effective, when seeking group views, to pose the question to the group as a whole rather than to each individual.

On many occasions a trainer may have posed a question, only to be faced by silence. There may be two principal reasons for this non-response. When people are asked something, depending on the complexity of the question they have to think for some time before risking a response – the silence may mean just this. However, if the silence continues for a period that seems excessive, the question may not have been understood. A re-worded question will help understanding and hence response.

If you are planning to use the question and answer technique in part of your sessions, consider the form and wording of the questions and so avoid the problems discussed above. Many questions arise spontaneously without any pre-planning, so as a trainer you must be as skilled as possible in questioning techniques (you will even then make mistakes!).

Case studies and simulations

Case studies

Case studies and simulations were described briefly in Chapter 7. They can be significant aids to learning either as complete learning events or, more usually, as activities linked to other parts of the training. In the latter case, they often follow an input session or series of linked sessions, as a real-life case study or as an artificially-constructed study, and give the learners a chance to practise what they have learned. They can be similar to syndicate problem-solving activities in that the learners are given a statement of information containing a problem that they are required to solve. However, the cases are usually longer and more complex and contain several problems. Case studies of this complex nature are more suitable for inclusion at the end of a training event, for example on group leadership, the study requiring the learners to practise all the aspects of leadership that have been covered and may have been practised individually in syndicate groups. A case study of this nature can require a substantial period of time to perform and even longer for the following review and feedback session. When you are planning such a session it is safer to allow extra time rather than eventually discover that there is insufficient time to satisfy both your and the learners' review objectives.

Simulations

Simulations are usually studies involving the allocation of real-life roles: the use of computers and the completion of reports, holding meetings and numerous cases of problem solving and decision making. Individuals are given, or select from within their group, the roles of managing director or chief executive, financial director, sales and marketing director, production director, personnel and training director and so on. The group is given a time in which to solve a number of problems or otherwise exist as a company with the objective of making a profit over a sum given to them at the start. Many variations of this type of simulation are possible and the time taken can also vary. Consequently, simulations will normally have been considered during the programme planning phase and may represent a complete learning programme.

If the simulation is one part of a learning programme, the trainer(s) responsible for that simulation must ensure that:

- copies of the initial briefing are available for the learners and that these give the maximum amount of information and advice within the constraints of the learning event
- all materials, equipment, reports etc. are immediately available to the learners when needed
- computers will be available if necessary and that they are loaded with the suitable software applications

- database and spreadsheet information is available in the computer programmes
- simulation roles have been identified where these are to be involved
- there is sufficient time for the simulation to achieve the desired results
- there is sufficient time to review the simulation.

A substantial amount of the planning time for a case study or simulation is taken up in writing the case for modifying an existing one to suit the particular circumstances. This might involve visits to line locations to observe functions and interview jobholders, in addition to collecting and collating reports, critical incident reviews etc. This information must be written in its various forms – written briefs, reports, minutes etc. and computer program data – so that everything necessary for the effective performance of the activity is available to the learners. Loss of training credibility and loss of trainer credibility and status may result if the learners ask for vital information during the activity, and this is not available because of inadequate preparation.

Preparation must include the printing and recording of the information and data referred to above and, if observers are to be used, observational aid instruments for these learners. Many cases and simulations require a number of rooms and a variety of equipment – typewriters, paper, computers, calculators etc. – and plans must be made for these to be available.

The pre-allocation of required time is most difficult, particularly if the case is being used for the first time. A dummy run with a guinea-pig group can be most worthwhile, not only to iron out problems, but to assess the time required. As with the majority of training and development events, a review and feedback session must be planned. A case or simulation which extends over a significant period must be reflected in the time available for review, particularly if the case was complex. CCTV can be used extensively as in the activities described earlier, but again with the caveat that they are expensive in the use of time.

One approach that has been used successfully is to delay the review session, although not for too long, and ask the participants to spend the intervening time in reflecting on the event, identifying incidents on which they want to comment, and planning what they want to say. The review can be, say, the following week – half a day or even a day, depending on the complexity of the case, being allocated to the event.

Role plays

Role plays, like simulations and case studies are important, linked parts of a training programme. Substantial planning is necessary to ensure that the role plays are as close to real life as possible and that they reflect closely the learning commenced in the preceding sessions. Role plays are usually associated with interview training, one learner taking the part of the interviewer, the other the part of the interviewee, but roles can be allocated in syndicate groups, case studies and simulations.

Although role play should be as realistic as possible, it is sometimes necessary to construct 'artificial' cases to ensure that all the learning points are covered. They may be developed from real-life cases that have occurred in the learners' organizations (names and places are changed to protect the originators) or the learners are asked to provide details of cases of which they are aware or in which they have been involved. The latter case is particularly valuable as it gives an individual the opportunity, having learned new techniques, to 'repeat' the interview, avoiding the mistakes of the original. The case 'owner' may also act as the interviewee, thus giving a view from the other side of the fence.

Variations

There are a number of planned variations possible with role plays, depending on the circumstances within the programme. The reverse role application has been mentioned above where the original interviewer becomes the interviewee. There is a technique known as 'ghosting' or 'doubling' in which, at stages during an interview, or if the interviewer seems to be losing the way, the trainer or another learner stands behind the interviewer and carries on the interview for a period until the original interviewer is ready to continue. 'Empty-chair' role playing is where the problem-owner starts by describing the problem to an empty chair opposite them, discussing all aspects of the problem and raising solutions. Many people find it easier and more valuable to talk the problem out with an empty chair than with another person. Alternatively the person with the problem switches chairs and hence roles, first as the problem-owner then as the interviewee or devil's advocate.

Review and feedback

As with most learning activities that supplement input sessions, extensive time is required, time that the designer must build into the programme, in addition to the feedback session following the role play. When people skills are being learned such activities as role plays must be included, otherwise the first 'practice' interview that the learner conducts is in real life back at work – and rather than take the chance on what are really more effective techniques, the learner falls back on the 'safe' approaches they have always used, however ineffective. The designer must also decide whether a training group is to be divided into smaller groups to practise the role plays, or whether role plays should take place in front of the rest of the group (for example, in presentation skills training). The former saves time with multiple events taking place simultaneously, but the latter, although more expensive in time, offers a wider range of review feedback.

The different forms of role playing described above require extensive pre-planning to ensure success, although sometimes when the trainer realizes the skills of the learners, decisions can be made during the sessions about the use of other than straightforward approaches. Even then, the trainers should know what alternatives are available, how they are used and the possible problems involved.

Observing role plays

Planning for role plays includes observation, an important part of these activities. The options, many of which will depend on the time available, include:

- role plays by two learners in front of the whole group, observation for eventual feedback being made by
  - the trainer
  - the learning group
  - the learning group and the trainer
- role plays by the full learning group simultaneously
  - in pairs with no observers, reliance being placed on the learners to note their own processes
  - in triads, the third member acting as the observer and eventual giver of feedback to the role players
- either of the above approaches, but using CCTV to record the interview, the CCTV being supplemented on occasions by an observer.

Whichever form of role playing and observation is taken, in addition to time planning for the role plays themselves, there must also be significant periods planned for the review and feedback sessions following the events. The most effective and time-saving approach is for the review to take place immediately following the event, the interviewer and interviewee's observer giving the feedback and conducting a review discussion with them. Again this can be occurring simultaneously with every role play event that has been taking place, the trainer(s) moving round the groups to ensure that all is going well. At the end of the reviews, the full group reconvenes for a plenary session at which a discussion takes place on the points that have arisen in the subgroup reviews. If these reviews are to be worthwhile, an appropriate amount of time must be allowed in the session preparation.

Action summary

Planning and preparation for role-playing sessions can be summarized as requiring:

- consideration of the type of group – pairs, triads, whole group etc.
- consideration of the type of role playing – straightforward, reverse, ghosting, empty chair etc.
- preparation of role briefs for the participants – these should be sufficiently detailed to enable the role player to understand the role and the situation, but not too detailed to confuse or require over-concentration on the situation rather than on the skills required
- consideration of the use of observers and how feedback reviews will be held.

Activities

'Activities' is the term I use for a range of practical training events that are variously described as 'games' or 'exercises' and have uses ranging from buzz group discussions and syndicate events to problem-solving, ice-breaker events, group introduction events, and even the more specific case studies and simulations. Many activities are linked with a preceding input session, giving learners the opportunity to practise what they have learned in the safe atmosphere of the training course. This practice, in addition to increasing their skills, gives them the opportunity to assess the learning issues prior to deciding whether to implement them at work.

Activities require time periods ranging from 5 minutes to several hours, and the session planning must identify the most effective activity for the objectives involved that can be completed in the least time.

Activity restraints

A number of trainers do not use activities as much as would be useful to their programmes and the learners, for the following reasons:

● activities lead the programme format away from the 'safe' atmosphere of the lecture or other trainer presentation

● the trainer has not run activities and may be hesitant about using them
● the feedback and review session can be daunting for trainers with little or no experience in this
● the designer or trainer is not aware of relevant and suitable activities
● there is concern about the time necessary for the activity and its review
● the trainer is afraid that the learners may not 'play the game' or treat it simply as a game.

Many of these concerns can be resolved relatively easily. The final 'fear' in the list above is common, but in my experience it rarely happens, or only in the very early stages. As the activity progresses the learners soon settle down and become immersed in the task. A useful learning experience for the trainer, before including an activity in a programme, is to take part in the activity and thus gain firsthand experience of how it is viewed. Even activities that appear to be childish games, if presented well can become serious and valuable learning experiences. I have seen more than one group of senior managers crawling around the training room floor with Lego bricks, completely immersed in building a mast and not seeing anything unusual or childish in this.

Once trainers become activity users, they will soon realize that activities are as 'safe' if not safer learning events than input sessions. Provided the activity is set up efficiently and all the requirements are satisfied, the event is in the hands of the learners themselves, the trainer acting in perhaps an observer's role only or as the timekeeper (even this can be delegated to the activity group).

Lack of experience certainly introduces some concern as does any change to the unknown, but if this is holding the trainer back experience can be gained by working with another trainer who is using activities until the trainee feels sufficiently confident to run the activity alone, perhaps initially under supervision. Similarly confidence can be built in observation and feedback, and attendance at a training event in these skills will give additional support.

I have used activities to such an extent in my training career and have researched them so extensively that I have the reverse problem to the trainer who doesn't know where to obtain a suitable activity – there are so many activities that it is a problem searching the mass for the activity I want! At one time the number of training activities was quite limited and new trainers inherited sets from their predecessors, continuing their use. Trainers with creative minds have either modified existing activities or created new ones, usually because of the learner demands for organization/task/role relationship. This creation of activities has become part of the publishing industry and published collections now offer more than 4000 activities. This presents the problem of how to choose from so many activities:

● Which and how many collections should you obtain?
● How can you find easily the type of activity you seek?
● Which parallel activity should you use?

Many of the earlier collections contained general activities with a wide range of application. More specifically directed collections are now available – activities for time management, counselling, discipline interviewing, team building and so on. This has eased the problem, but it cannot be completely resolved until a full descriptive index of all published activities has been prepared – an almost impossible task. Publishers such as Gower, Kogan Page, McGraw-Hill and Fenman Training offer collections of this nature and the index of training resources (p. 233) gives information on some of these.

The collections also offer a solution to some of the other concerns raised:

● full descriptions of the activity are given indicating the relevant situations in which to use them, and in many cases suggesting a range of alternative situations
● in most cases the time and resources necessary for the activity are detailed
● full guidance is given on how to set up, introduce and run the activity
● guidelines are given in many cases about how to review the activity, detailing many of the relevant questions to ask.

The use of activities satisfies many effective programme needs by providing the first stage in the learning cycle – the experience of an event. If this is followed by the other learning stages of reflecting, considering and planning for future action, the full learning process has been covered and the training is much more likely to succeed. Most learners enjoy taking part in activities and as enjoyment of training is a criterion that helps towards its success, their inclusion is a helping factor towards objective achievement.

Action summary

Because 'activities' have many practical similarities to the role plays described earlier in this chapter, planning action can follow the same stages (see p. 128).

This chapter has described the traditional aspects of a training and development session that are available for inclusion in the session planning stage. Further supplementary or free-standing activities can be included, many resulting from the speedy progress of technology. These are described in the following chapter in addition to other considerations for the session planning stage.

Chapter 9
Planning the training sessions – II

This chapter:

> continues a discussion of the training approaches that might be used in the sessions forming the programme
> describes the steps in compiling a programme
> describes the principal methods of constructing planning scripts and session briefs.

Training approaches

Videos as complete programmes

Videos used alone can be complete training programmes, although they are usually limited to a reasonably detailed consideration of a single topic. This might be time management, counselling interviewing, the use of questions, advanced tips for trainers, delegation etc. – the range is extensive and the video will be selected because of its particular topic. It is difficult to envisage whole training programme being conducted completely with a series of videos, although some video producers have offered these. More usually the single video is used as a mini training session. Often these sessions are held during a lunch break, before the start of daily business (for example, for the first hour on a Monday morning in a retail establishment), or the suspension of part of the business for an hour at some time during the day.

Too frequently the video is used on these, and unfortunately on other, training occasions by a 'trainer' who brings the group together, tells them that they are going to see a video on a particular subject, then shows the video. At the end of the video, the 'trainer' may ask if the viewers enjoyed it and after this 'discussion' they return to work. In most cases, if questions were asked about the video, its content and its lessons even several hours after this 'training' session, little would be seen to have been remembered. Not surprising!

This ineffective approach can be much improved by planning the session with a small increase only in the use of time and with more realistic training:

- give a more effective introduction, including:
  - comments on why the video is being presented
  - a brief summary of the video content
  - guidance on what the viewers should be looking for
- show the video – this might be straight through, particularly when time is limited, but can be interrupted for action that will be described later in this section
- issue a questionnaire on the learning points of the video
- lead a discussion on the information the learners have extracted from the video, what views and opinions they have on this information, and how they might apply the learning in their work.

By following this practice the video becomes more meaningful to the learners and maximum value is obtained from it.

Interactive video and CD-I

The arguments against videos in training and development, particularly when they are unsupported by subject experts, include that they transmit only their own message and if the viewer disagrees with this message, apart from accepting it, the only recourse is to switch off! The approach described above avoids this problem as the short-session video is usually supported by a trainer or other subject expert, but for most of the time the audience/viewers are passive.

More recent developments have attempted to increase the activity of learners/viewers, by linking the video to a special video player/computer, and the more recently by use of the CD-I, a compact disc which contains much more material than a video cassette.

The interactive video (IV) and the CD-I are intended to be used mainly as self-instruction aids, although they can be incorporated into training programmes and sessions. The key difference from the traditional video is that at stages during the presentation the process is suspended and the viewer is asked a set of questions. These may give a multiple choice response, possibly concerning what should happen next or a summary of the learning to that point. CD-I equipment can include similar interactivity, but also a large amount of other material such as additional video clips, lesson plans, questionnaires etc., including material that can be printed out.

Unless the IV or CD-I are supported by an expert, the learner must either accept or reject, without question, the model, concept, statements and attitudes expressed in the medium.

Video-supported training

More traditional approaches to training sessions can be aided by standard videos, but IV and CD-I can be accommodated. There is a variety of methods by which the video can be used during a training session, including:

- as an introduction to the subject at the start of the session
- as a summary at the end
- as an interim review of the learning material at a critical stage in the session
- presenting a model or concept in which the session presenter is not an expert
- as a trigger for discussion.

The first four in the list above are self-explanatory and represent the traditional use of session videos. Videos replaced 35mm films because of their ease of use, flexibility and durability, but they also introduced an additional element. The video can, with little detrimental physical effects, be stopped at any stage and on any number of occasions, thus facilitating the introduction of a discussion or questioning – 'How do you think that situation was handled?'; 'In what other ways could that situation have been handled?'; 'What do you think is going to happen next?'; 'What should happen next?'. Of course, during the planning stages, you must familiarize yourself with the video in order to identify the stages at which you might ask the questions, make notes about what you are going to ask, and record the tape counter positions.

The planning and use of videos as triggers to questions and discussions has been made easier by some commercial video producers, particularly Fenman Training, who have produced specific 'trigger' videos. The concept of the triggers is not new, but their commercial availability make planning and use so much easier and do away with the need for you to produce your own. Each trigger video contains a number of cameos showing short scenes linked to the subject of the video. For example, a trigger video on the subject of discipline interviews might contain cameos showing the interviewer receiving the interviewee; the manner of the interviewer introducing the discipline matter; the offer or non-offer to the interviewee for their comments; and so on.

Their value is increased when they are linked to a full video on the subject which would then be followed by the trigger to produce discussion.

Commercial triggers are not yet available for every training situation, but amateur trigger videos can be produced quite easily, using organizational situations with staff as the 'actors'. The result may not be as professional as the commercial videos, but if the need for a trigger exists, they are better than nothing at all.

Naturally the use of videos, whether 'straight', 'interrupted' or in 'trigger' form must be planned carefully, not forgetting the time necessary for discussion – which is usually extensive.

Computer-assisted training (CAT)/computer-based training (CBT)

The development and more extensive availability of computers has increased their use in training and development programmes. Computer-based training (CBT) has been described in Chapter 7 when the planning of complete programmes was discussed, as CBT programs are usually specific-subject software. They are used as self-instruction packages, group training aids or training programmes at work over the internal network.

But the computer is also useful during sessions, in the same way that we saw with videos, IV and CD-I. Special short programs can be written specifically for a session and used in the same way as with videos – stand-alone, interrupted, introducers and summarizers, and triggers. In many ways the same material on the video is more effective on the computer, because of the increased flexibility of the computer. Programs can be written or manipulated to pause at particular points or introduce other programs and, if necessary, each learner can have their own monitor with the program being networked within the group – this principle of the language laboratories is a very successful, interactive approach.

The arguments used against videos as an unsupported medium apply equally to a computer program, but these problems can be alleviated by the presence or availability of the subject expert.

Brainstorming

A rather different technique that can be planned for inclusion in a training session is the use of brainstorming. This is a method of generating a large number of ideas for a subject or possible solutions to a problem.

The process is simple, but requires planning before the session to ensure the most effective use of time. A chairperson is selected for the brainstorming meeting – in order that all the learning group might take part, this role can be taken by the trainer. A 'scribe' is also required to write down on flipchart sheets the ideas that may come rapidly from the group. If there is another trainer, they might take on this role, or someone from the administration section might be enrolled. The rules for both these roles are strictly defined.

The chairperson is an arbitrary controller whose objectives are to:

● introduce the subjects for brainstorming
● keep the members on the subject
● control the meeting by stopping discussion or comments on the ideas or suggestions made
● encourage contributions from all members
● summarize the contributions, with the help of the scribe, at stages during the brainstorm and at the end
● keep the meeting to time, either a predetermined time for the brainstorm, or when it becomes apparent that there are no more contributions.

The scribe writes down the suggestions made by the members, ensuring that every contribution is recorded and that, as far as possible, the proposer's words are used; and reads out the list of contributions when the chairperson requires an interim or final summary. The requirement for a scribe is the ability to write fast!

The members are there to take part fully in the brainstorm, to put forward ideas or suggestions, and not to restrict themselves to the traditional, logical approaches, but to let their minds freewheel and produce creative solutions. The chairperson can help this last-named process by putting forward some rather wild ideas, and so encouraging the members to do the same. A wild idea often triggers a more workable idea in another member, or the apparently wild idea turns out to be one of the best solutions.

Apart from planning the subject for brainstorm, session planning will include the time to be allocated to it and any subsequent action. The brainstorm ends with a list of ideas about the subject introduced. The next stage is an assessment of these ideas and the learning group might then become the assessment group. The ideas need to be identified as:

- completely unworkable
- too wild to be accepted
- have been tried previously and are not appropriate for the current situation
- wild but might bear investigation
- immediately applicable.

If the learning group is also to be the assessing group this decision is made at the planning stage and time is allocated to the session.

Compiling a session

With the training methods now in mind you are ready to start compiling your sessions. First ask yourself the following questions:

1. What do the learners need to learn from the session (their objectives)?
2. What do you feel should be included in the session (your objectives)?
3. What are the priorities in the material you have for the session?
4. How much time do you have available for the session?
5. What will be the most appropriate training approach for the session?
6. What sequence should the session follow?
7. What training aids do you need for the session?
8. Should you produce a session plan and what form should it take?
9. What form of brief are you going to use?

1. What do the learners need to learn from the session (their objectives)?

This question links with the TNIA as it reflects the views and skills of the learning group when the TNIA was being produced. However, individuals will have their own objectives. You might seek the learners' views on their individual objectives, before the programme and take them into account as far as possible, or you might seek their views at the beginning of the programme or of each session.

2. What do you feel should be included in the session (your objectives)

This aspect of the planning has already been considered and decided following the TNIA.

3. What are the priorities in the material you have for the session?

Within the objectives for the session will be priorities, dictated by the amount of time available, the desirability of including certain material (for a variety of reasons), the culture of the organization or the express statement of the senior management, line management or other sponsors.

You will have a degree of choice on the priorities usually because of the time element only, the other reasons probably being beyond your influence. This is not to say that you should accept without question the dictates made by others; they may not be aware of the effectiveness of other aspects.

If time is a restricting factor in achieving your session objectives, you will need to build into your session guide an indication of the priority of the various sections so that you can include or exclude material as the session progresses. There are three simple priority indicators: *Must Knows; Should Knows; Could Knows.*

The *Must Knows* are items which if they were not included would cause the session to be an immediate failure; these are absolutely essential items and form the largest part of the session. The *Should Knows* relate to items that, although not essential, would help the learners considerably in the material relating to the session. However, if there is insufficient time, some or all of them can be omitted, although the session may not be completely effective without them. The *Could Knows* are information items that, if omitted, would not affect the learning of the group, although they would be interesting and could be useful, albeit not essential. These are the first items to be omitted if the timing is limited.

4. How much time do you have available for the session?

The question of the time that you have available for individual sessions will be linked necessarily with the time available for the complete programme and for the priorities within it. You may have a particular interest in a session and want it included, but examination might show that other sessions have more priority, resulting in either a restriction or rejection of the session in question. The programme designer will probably, having the full picture in mind, allocate timings to each session, and you, as the session designer will have to plan around this. Again, the initial decisions are not set in stone, and if you feel that you can justify additional time for particular sessions you should argue your case, bearing in mind that if one session is increased in length it will almost certainly mean the reduction of another. An effective balancing act can produce success.

If the time allocated is absolute, then you must plan the material in conjunction with the session objectives and the agreed priorities described in 3 above. This planning must be as exact as possible. If you carry on beyond the agreed time, you are restricting the time for the next session, or throwing the whole programme out of kilter.

5. *What will be the most appropriate training approach for the session?*

With some ideas about what needs to be included, what you would like to include and what can be included, you can now decide on the most appropriate and effective training session approach. Reference to the first part of this chapter and to the previous chapter, should suggest this approach. You will then need to gather together all the material relevant to that approach and plan your session around it. Figure 9.1 summarizes these approaches and strategies, in terms of the type of strategy, its objectives – knowledge (K), skills (S) or attitudes (A), and the most important areas of effectiveness.

6. *What sequence should the session follow?*

The sequencing of programme material was discussed in Chapter 7, and similar guidance applies to the sequencing of the session material:

LEARNING EXPERIENCE	OBJECTIVE	AREAS OF EFFECTIVENESS
Brainstorming – wide-ranging discussion to obtain ideas for solutions	K, A, S	Creativity. New ideas. Problem solving. Decision making.
Buzz groups – groups of 2 to 6 people who discuss a matter for a short time without leaving the training room.	K, A	Encourage reticent people. Ease feedback.
Case study – real or manufactured complex problems analysed in detail for solutions	K, A, S	Encourage application of principles. Group working. Alternative points of view.
Controlled discussion – subjects are discussed under general control of the trainer	K, A, S	Promotes understanding. Allows expression of points of view. How to use discussion. Behaviour identification.
Demonstration – trainer performs an operation or a skill while learners watch	K, S	Practical skill training using real objects to show the elements of the operation.
Instructional talk/Input session – a talk (with visual aids, discussion, activity, handouts etc.) to present information, knowledge and details	K, S	The basic strategy in a training event.

Lecture – an uninterrupted talk by the trainer usually for larger audiences.	K	Provides information.
Question and answer – a series of questions from the trainer to the learning group	K	To check understanding and encourage thought at all levels.
Practical – an activity in which the learners carry out a task or process	K, A, S	Usually following an input to reinforce learning and practise skills and attitudes.
Programmed learning – a text with a series of questions or tasks which must be completed before continuing to next stage	K, S	Individual learning situations. Mixed pace groups.
Project – an exercise in gathering information, performing a task or producing material	K, S, A	To consolidate and extend learning and encourage activity.
Reading – from a book, article or handout, in the training situation or away from it	K	To prepare for learning. To reinforce other forms of learning.
Role play – learners are given roles, real or artificial, in a group or one-to one, to carry out realistically or dramatically	K, S, A	Reinforcing skills. Practising situations. Self-awareness. Attitude change.
Seminars – in one definition, a group or a series of related topics	K	Encourages critical discussion thinking. Group discussion. Presentations.
Simulation – the duplication of a real situation as a complex problem or game with the learners taking on roles or positions	K, S, A	Simulation of an activity which cannot be practised directly. Problem solving. Team building.
Syndicate – or group working. Learners form small groups and are given identical tasks to perform; views or results are presented as a group	K, S, A	Problem solving and decision making in groups. Group behaviour. Leadership.
Video – the viewing by the learners of a pre-prepared video (commercial or internally produced) followed by discussion and review	K	To reinforce learning, change the pace, insert variety.

Figure 9.1   Summary of training approaches and strategies

- *Known to the unknown* – the initial introduction of known material and moving on to new material.
- *Simple to complex* – eases the learners through the new (to them) learning event.
- *Logical stepping in a process* – most session material will benefit from this approach.
- *Interesting material to more serious needs* – can be combined with other sequencing and will need to be taken into account when designing a session of very 'heavy' or complex material.
- *Random sequencing* – some subjects might not require any logical or other sequencing, and planning might depend on the availability of particular trainers or guest speakers, the length of time required for the sessions to ensure that the material is contained effectively, etc.
- *Dependency* – the session material might rely on what is contained in the previous session and this must be taken into account to ensure continuity.
- *Knowledge to doing* – the session starts with an input of knowledge-based material followed by learner practice and is particularly useful when learners have no previous knowledge of the material.
- *Doing to knowledge to doing* – reverses the previous method by using a practical activity to initiate the learning process, followed in the review discussion by reinforcement of the learning points, and is particularly useful where the learners are known to have *some* previous knowledge or experience.

Sessions, like programmes are not (or should not be) fixed and inflexible plans. So many factors can emerge when the session is under way to suggest that the original design must be modified on the spot by the trainer. This modification might be achieved by omitting material or if you identify during the event that there is a significant need for additional material, the design should allow for this, perhaps omitting other material to make way for it.

7. What training aids do you need for the session?

Training aids are usually used in conjunction with an input session and cover a very wide range. In planning you must consider: (a) their use; (b) the nature of the aid; (c) the time that their use will add to the session; and (d) the time and resources necessary for their production.

8. Should you produce a session plan and what form should it take?

There are two stages to this part of the preparation for presenting the sessions: first, deciding what is going to be included and producing a session plan based on these decisions; second, producing a brief for use during the session itself. For the second stage, I prefer to use 'brief' rather than 'script' as both words have specific connotations that describe their use. Whichever stage you are considering, it is recommended that you write down your thoughts and intentions. This is particularly so in the case of the session brief. You may never need to refer to it, but it must always be to hand in case of emergencies.

The session plan follows the more general planning and it is here that more detail starts to be included. In many ways it can be considered as the initial part of the session brief, but many trainers find it useful to look on it as a separate document on which the brief is based. In addition to describing the proposed contents of the session, it can include the stage directions that will need to be incorporated. The amount of detail will depend on your ideas of how your script will look, but the session plan should not be too detailed or reference to it will become too difficult and it may not be used. An example session plan is shown in Figure 9.2.

9. What form of brief are you going to use?

The initial script or brief in which the detail of the session is decided can be in two parts: the first is referred to as the planning script from which the second, the session brief, is produced. The planning script is frequently, though not necessarily, written out in full.

The detailed formats of session scripts will vary according to the experience and preferences of the trainer, but there are five recognized, principal methods of producing planning scripts and session briefs:

- the traditional text form or vertical method
- the headline method
- OHP slides as briefs
- the horizontal plan
- patterned notes.

Some of these scripts can be used directly as the session brief, others need to be modified or converted for practical, session briefs, the amount of modification depending on the preferences and experience of the trainers.

The traditional text form or vertical method

This is a full-script method and although it is a valuable instrument in the preparation and planning stage, it should very rarely be used as the actual session brief. Its foremost principal function is to record all the material that will be used so that a working brief can be constructed.

Writing out the text in full
The text is written out in full, word for word as if it were a report or essay to be read out on some occasion. One difference from the usual form of written report is that the wording should be in the style of the 'spoken' rather than the 'written' word. For example, when speaking we tend to say 'can't' rather than 'cannot', so the former should be used in your script.

SESSION PLAN FOR PRESENTATION SKILLS SESSION

Approx. time

1. Introduce the session and describe the session objectives and methods. Seek information on group's experience of making presentations.   10 minutes

2. Give input session concentrating on skill attributes of session presentation. Include attention span and barriers to communication. 35 minutes

3. During input, when communication barriers are to be introduced. Form buzz groups to identify possible barriers. Take feedback and display OHP slide as summary, adding group ideas.   (12 minutes)

4. Have learning group members present their ten-minute sessions (previously arranged) – two groups of 4 = 4 x 10 minutes plus 4 x 10 minutes review of each presentation plus discontinuity time = 80 + 20 minutes   1 hour 40m

5. Final review session   15 minutes

Total session time   2 hours 40 minutes
(allow 2 hours 45 minutes)

Figure 9.2   An example session plan

Division into paras and subparas
It helps understanding and reference considerably if the script is divided into sections, paragraphs and subparagraphs similar to those of a written report, with headlines for each section. This is not just for the sake of grammatical accuracy, but to make the different parts of the text clearer visually. The script should be laid out with plenty of 'white space', i.e. broad and variable borders, substantial line spaces between sections and paragraphs. Different colours can be used for alternate paragraphs or sections and, if the script is prepared on a computer different fonts can be used to help this clarity.

Underlining for emphasis
It is necessary with a script of this nature to make the separate parts obviously separate and visually impactive. The white space, colours and fonts can help towards this as can underlining words, phrases, sentences or sections, with either single underlining or, to show differences, double underlining linking these with **bold printing** if this is available. *Italics* are frequently used in books instead of

bold printing, so if you are using a computer you may wish to consider this style on occasions.

Colours for emphasis

In addition to using colours to separate parts of the script, they can also produce other forms of emphasis, for example, red lettering in a section written or printed in blue. If the script is hand-written, use coloured pens, or if on a computer, use a colour printer. In the latter case, if a monochrome printer only is available, shades of grey can be used for the printing or as shading blocks, or colours can be added with highlighter pens.

Framing for emphasis or isolation

Adding a frame or boxed border, particularly if combined with some of the previously described emphasizers, can add impact and be attention-grabbing.

The frame or border, in addition to containing words or graphics, can also contain a degree of shading to separate it from another box.

Do not overuse framing, or any other emphasizing effect, otherwise the impact may be lost.

Leaving broad margins

It can be helpful to leave broader than normal borders at both margins of the text so that notes can be added – these might be questions to be raised, amendments necessary, and the stage directions referred to below.

Stage directions

Stage directions, usually entered in the margins of the script, indicate what and when OHPs, handouts, questions are to be used and also timings. Some trainers prefer not to write down actual times – the session may not start at the pre-arranged time, or a spontaneous discussion may arise, and therefore any times will be wrong. An alternative is to enter the time by which that stage of the script should have been reached, or if the session is in very clear sections, a time can be allocated for each section. Remember that any timing entry is only a rough guide and should not be adhered to slavishly if it is going to effect the session adversely.

Timings can be practised in a session rehearsal, but again remember that during the 'real' session anything can happen.

The headline method

The headline method is a simplified and abbreviated form of the full-script approach and produces, by cutting out many of the words and using shorthand-style only, a much clearer and more easily referenced script. The method is summarized as:

1. List the headlines on A4 sheets. First identify the important topics within the subject and list them as the main subject headings, writing them down as you think of them – ordering can follow when you have all the headlines.

2. Enter inter-heading summary notes. Under each heading enter brief, summary notes about that part of the script. The notes should be sufficiently brief for easy reference, but should contain all the significant aspects of that heading in the summary form. Don't worry about writing too much at this stage, as the content can be edited later in the script production.

3. Complete brief with 'impact' techniques. All the techniques described in the traditional text approach for producing impact, clarity and ease of reference can be used in the headline method: upper and lower case; different colours for each heading and sometimes within a heading content; underlining; boxes; marginal stage directions, and so on. Again for the sake of clarity and ease of reference, err on the side of too few directions rather than too many.

In both the traditional script and the headline approach, if more than one sheet is used, number each sheet in case they are dropped or fall out of order.

This approach used as the working session brief, in a modified form, is probably the method used by most trainers. When used as a planning script the titles of the sections of the session are the headlines followed by a summary of the material to be included under that headline. To convert this planning script into a working brief you examine the summaries carefully and reduce them to several isolated words or phrases that remind you of the material to be covered. Consequently, the stages of preparation of a headline brief are:

- construct a full, traditional planning script with all the material included in detail
- contract the full text to headlines followed by summarized notes relating to the headlines
- further contract to headlines followed by key words and phrases relating to the headlines.

Depending on the complexity of the session and the material, it may be possible to restrict the brief to one A4 sheet – this is easier for immediate reference during the session if you want to check the progress of the session and confirm what is to follow. The greater the number of words used, and hence usually the greater the number of sheets, the more difficult this becomes. If the brief becomes longer than desirable, use the impact techniques described for the traditional full script to help in the clarification and identification process.

Leave broad margins on each side of the text so that stage directions can be entered: e.g. 'Show OHP slide 1'; 'Ask question "xxx" at this stage'; 'Put into buzz groups here to discuss x'; 'Issue handout P1.1 here and ask group to read it'. Mark timings in the left margin in a distinctive colour.

Number each sheet clearly and hold them together by means of a tag threaded through a punched hole in the top left corner of the sheet. It is only too easy to drop the sheets during the session and, if they are not held together, the results could be disastrous. (According to a certain law that requires falling toast to land buttered-side down, they will be so!)

The presentation of the brief depends on the complexity and amount of the material, and your personal preferences. Some people use A4 sheets, others prefer index cards. Research suggests that a mixture of upper and lower case text is easier to read, but many trainers prefer entries in upper case – they will help you to find your place without making it too obvious that you are looking at your brief. On this latter point, do not be concerned that looking at your brief will be noticed by the learning group – in my experience it probably will not notice, unless it is very obvious, and even if it does your concern for accuracy and effectiveness will be appreciated. It is unusual to remember everything – text and stage directions – in an extended and complex session. Be accurate and refer to your brief.

The proposed life of the brief and the session to which it refers may affect the way in which it is written. If the session is a one-off, not to be repeated, the brief need only last for the duration of the session, although this short-term nature should not supersede the need for completeness and clarity. The sheets or cards can be handwritten, the colours produced by pens or highlighters, and such aids as boxes may draw attention to certain words. Sheets can be handwritten, typed or, if available, entered on a computer and produced by inkjet or laser printer. The computer, in addition to easing the problems of editing the brief, can produce different fonts, lettering sizes and other effects. Laser printers are particularly clear and colours can be added afterwards by highlighter pens or by means of coloured toners if the printer has this facility.

The aim should be to produce a brief that contains all the keyword reminders in a format that is clear for you to read, whether you are seated or standing near the table.

OHP slides as briefs

Experienced trainers may often use OHP transparencies both as training aids and as their session 'brief'. As each slide is presented, it acts as a reminder of what the trainer needs to discuss. Additional material can be written on the borders of the frame that holds the transparency. As a support you can list the slides and their main messages. If you have a wide selection of OHP slides and you are very familiar with your subject and the session, this is an acceptable approach. But beware. The use depends on an electrical supply, and if this fails during the session (a not uncommon occurrence) or the OHP bulb blows (with no replacement available) you will have to fall back on talking alone. Also, a training session that consists solely of a trainer speaking to a series of OHP slides, can quickly become boring and monotonous. Effective sessions consist of a range of approaches and techniques to introduce variety and retain attention.

Horizontal planning

Horizontal planning is a modification of the headline method. It is probably the most effective planning approach and can be readily converted to a practical session brief. It breaks away from the traditional format and, generally, uses one sheet of paper however complex the session material, although it may be easier to use an A3 size to ensure containment on one sheet if the session material is substantial or complex.

The planning approach is in four stages.

Stage 1
The first stage is similar to the start of the headline approach. Enter first thought headlines, as words or short phrases, across the sheet of paper which should be in the landscape position, i.e. with the longer sides at the top and bottom. Again the headlines need not be in order, nor need they be complete, as both these aspects can be edited later in the process. Other headings may be added as the stage progresses and this might suggest a different order from that originally envisaged.

One example of the practical application of the planning method is the layout of this book. The main headings are the Part headings as shown below:

| IDENTIFYING AND ANALYSING NEEDS | PLANNING AND DESIGNING TRAINING AND DEVELOPMENT PROGRAMMES | PLANNING AND DESIGNING TRAINING SESSIONS | EVALUATING TRAINING AND DEVELOPMENT PROGRAMMES |

Stage 2
At the second stage you consider each subject heading and list below it all the words or short phrases that you can think of that describe the content of that heading. Additional ones can be added later if they come to mind.

IDENTIFYING AND ANALYSING NEEDS	PLANNING AND DESIGNING TRAINING AND DEVELOPMENT PROGRAMMES	PLANNING AND DESIGNING TRAINING SESSIONS	EVALUATING TRAINING AND DEVELOPMENT PROGRAMMES
What it is	Learner qualities	Similar subheadings for these headlines	
Why do it?	Learning models		
Benefits	Learning preferences		
Disadvantages	Sensory learning		
Responsibility for	Learning barriers		
The Training	Attention span		
Quintet	Objectives		
TNIA clients	Design stages		
Stages	Training approaches		
Implementation	On-the-job		
Methods	Off-the-job		
etc	etc		

Many of the subheadings listed above are themselves subject area headings which you will need to break down into greater detail. It may be necessary to have a separate sheet for each main heading, with the subheadings as the headings, and the detail as subheadings.

Stage 3
Now add the stage directions as far the previous method examples. The basic planning sheet may be printed from a computer design: you can add the stage directions with coloured pens, arrow linked items and use all the other impact techniques mentioned. Restrict their use as a mass of added items reduces the clarity significantly.

   Priority annotations can be made, for example, the Must, Should and Could Knows which may be abbreviated to M, S and C.

Stage 4
The final stage is the completion of a fair copy, any reorganization, omissions and additions being recorded, with the stage directions etc. clearly marked.

The use of headlines and subparagraphs alone means that the trainer must be very aware of the material on which the session is to be presented, and the horizontal plan may in some circumstances be preceded by a traditional script or perhaps the headline approach that includes some detail. But the horizontal plan with its headlines and word or short phrase subheadings is clear, can be contained on one sheet of paper and enables any part of the material to be located speedily. Editing does not involve considerable rewriting and the post-addition of clear stage directions means that virtually the complete session can be taken in with one glance.

Patterned notes

The system of patterned notes, mindmaps or spidergrams, pioneered by Tony Buzan, can be and has been successfully applied to the production of session scripts and plans. The method avoids a mass of words that can be unclear and difficult for reference purposes, and places a complete script on one sheet of paper.

The technique is based on research which shows that the brain does not work in a completely logical way, for example the way we follow a traditional script that starts at the beginning or top of the page and works to the end or bottom of the page, reading left to right. The mind is much more chaotic but works to a pattern within this apparent chaos. The patterned note replicates this working of the mind, particularly the right brain, creative faculty. Because the note is directly related to the working of an individual mind, the patterns can take a variety of forms and are frequently unintelligible to another person. Normally the note is for the use of the person producing it, but if a wider distribution is necessary it must be translated into a more traditional form.

The technique has many similarities with the horizontal plan and the modified headlines method. The key elements are identified and summarized in a form that is meaningful to the author. These key words or phrases act as triggers to the memory and enable recall of more details of the topic.

The key words/phrases radiate from the central box that contains the subject theme, and subbranches of these radiating lines give more detail, albeit still in summary form, to the main branch key phrase. Individuals vary in their approaches to these radiating patterns. I use key phrases rather than words on the main branch and, similarly, phrases or even short sentences on the subbranches. I start my pattern at the 11 o'clock position and move round it in a clockwise direction.

Various internal techniques for clarity and impact can be used, as found in the other session planners:

- different colours for each branch or for important aspects
- boxes enclosing the key word or phrase. These boxes need not be rectangular, but with creativity can relate to the theme: for example, if the key phrase is 'Key to the approach', the shape enclosing it can be in the form of a key; if a CCTV use is the key lead into a note, the key word 'CCTV' can be enclosed in a drawing of a TV monitor or camera – the creativity range is endless
- lines with arrows at each end can link related themes in different parts of the pattern
- symbols such as *, !, ?, >, #, can be used with effect as shorthand reminders.

Almost anything can be used in an individual pattern as long as it is meaningful to the constructor and enables recall of the material. The pattern need not be completed in a logical order, as sections can be moved around at a later stage or, for example, numbered according to their position in the note.

The structure of this book might appear as Figure 9.3.

The use of patterned notes as the working brief should be confined to people who are very familiar with the technique and who have produced their own patterns. It has many similarities with the horizontal plan, but following the circle-centred format can be confusing if you are not skilled in its construction and use. Patterns are probably more often used to convert a planning document into another form of brief – headlines or horizontal plan – but they can be a powerful form of brief in their own right.

When converting the patterned planner into a working brief, you can incorporate all the impact techniques and again containment on one sheet will aid clarity and ease of reference. As with the horizontal plan, if you decide during the session to change the logical order of presentation, you can see the material in its new position in the pattern at a glance.

Use of briefs

It was mentioned earlier that some of the approaches can be used simply as planning scripts, others have a dual role of planner and practical brief, and yet others might be suitable only as the session brief. But two factors are common.

A session requires the production of a planning script in which the material is

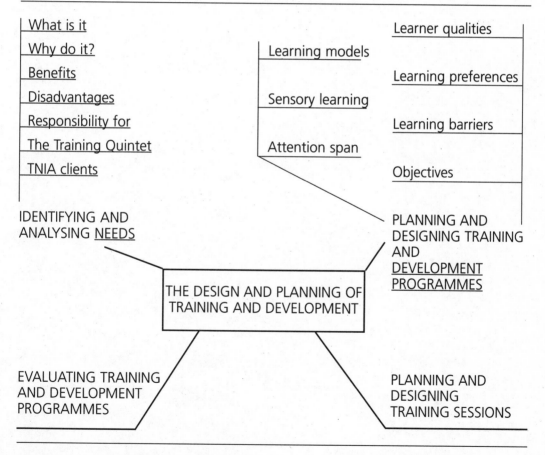

Figure 9.3   **Part of a patterned note planner**

ordered and various aspects identified. A practical session brief is also essential for use in the session. The planning scripts, particularly the traditional method, may not be suitable as working briefs. However, although it is essential to have a brief with you in the session, you do not have to use it. If you know your subject very well and also your approach, the brief will simply be there as an aid if you wish to refer to it. But the risks of not having one available during the session are high. You will have taken a considerable amount of time and effort in producing it in preparation for your session, so why not, at least, take it with you?

Chapter 10

Planning activity sessions

This chapter:

> develops the session planner and brief approach to training programmes other than input sessions or similar.

Planning and brief production are normally regarded as preparation for the various forms of input sessions, but they are equally essential for other forms of training, although there is a tendency not to prepare them as effectively in these cases. Many trainers have fallen into the trap of thinking that there is little planning preparation necessary for activities and role plays, other than the basic materials, but this is far from the truth. This attitude has probably arisen from the fact that the learners are performing the action rather than the trainer, as in the case of an input session, but a little thought will remind you that learners will probably be more concerned with the learning they have to achieve and the strangeness of the situation. These comments are particularly relevant to the use of activities in training and development.

Activities

Activities – games, exercises, small group problem solving, etc. – are now very common inclusions in training programmes either separately or as parts of sessions. The planning for activities is as follows:

- What are my objectives for this session?
- What would be the most effective approach to achieve the session objectives?
- If this effective approach is, or might contain, an activity, will the objectives be achieved through this method?
- Specifically do I want to/need to include a practical activity?
- Have I the programme time to include an activity?
- Why? How many? What form? How? When?

Some of these questions may appear to cover similar ground and may seem to be unnecessary, but it is only too easy to decide on including an activity for its own sake without ensuring that it is the most appropriate approach and the most relevant activity.

Why?

The response to this apparently simple question must be because an activity is the most appropriate and effective instrument to enable the learning to be achieved, not because it is the 'easy way out', because 'the trainer can't think of material for an input', or because the trainer 'likes having activities in the programme'. The activity must be relevant and be able to contribute something to the learning that no other technique could achieve as well or as easily.

There are a number of reasons for including an activity and at what stage in the programme or session it is to be included:

- to consolidate through practice, potential learning from other parts of the programme, e.g. an input session or video
- to introduce learning points, by letting the learners try something out then identify the learning successes or failures and why these occurred
- to lighten the atmosphere, in a realistic way, in a 'heavy' programme, e.g. by a fully relevant or an irrelevant activity, an icebreaker or a session shaker
- to introduce a relevant learning form to an evening session when a more traditional approach would not be well received.

How many?

If you are considering the activity as a complete session, one well-constructed activity should satisfy all the learning aid requirements, but if it is to be part of a full programme, you must ensure a balance with other approaches. It is very easy to create a 'playschool' course with one activity following the other, often with a minimum or even no review and feedback session. Avoid including too many, because of the reasons quoted above, and concentrate on the relevance and singular effectiveness of an activity at any point. Many sessions benefit from inputs, videos or discussions being completed by a practical activity with considerable reinforcement of learning. But if too many activities are included there will be a change of attitude among the learners, with either a spoken or unspoken 'Oh no, not another game!'.

Planning for inclusion of an activity must also take into account, if possible, the nature of the learning preferences of the group. The reflectors and theorists are less likely to accept activities, unless there is substantial opportunity for reflection and discussion, than the activists and the pragmatists, the latter not looking with favour on the apparently non-related game.

Which and what form of activity?

The answer to these questions is defined by the choice between internally-centred and externally-available activities.

Internally-centred activities

One of the accusations levelled at activities in training programmes is that they are too artificial and too unlike the learners' working environments. Although these 'artificial' activities are constructed to include the relevant learning points with consequent significant learning, they are often more acceptable to the learners if they are based on either a real work situation or are introduced by the learners themselves. Where internally-centred activities are produced from work situations, they must be up to date – policies and practices change and the credibility of an activity can be reduced if these are not taken into account.

Externally-available activities

There will be occasions when an internally-centred activity is not available, does not include all the learning points required, or is simply not relevant. Commercial organizations offer activities from a wealth of sources, of almost any type that you would require to include in your programme or session. On the other hand so many collections have been published over the last decade or so, that the main problem becomes finding the most appropriate activity. This assumes that you have access to all the resource collections.

The first step is to seek a suitable activity in use elsewhere in your organization or you may have a collection of your own into which you can tap. Failing this you can invent your own – work-based or artificial – as described above. Otherwise reference should be made to the many collections referred to in Chapter 7 and listed in the 'Index of training resources' (p. 233). You will need to ask yourself:

- In which/whose collections should I look for the appropriate activity?
- I remember seeing an activity that would just fit the bill. Where did I see it?
- Have I recourse to all the possible collections so that I can make the best selection?
- Are there other collections that may contain the activity for which I am searching?

How to plan the introduction of an activity

Once you have decided to use an activity as a session, there are a number of preparatory steps when planning its introduction:

- familiarize yourself with the activity and, if possible, take part yourself, either on someone else's event or by setting up a dummy run
- try out the activity with a group of colleagues or guinea-pig group
- design and/or produce the necessary participant briefs and instruction sheets
- check that all the resources are available that are required by the activity
- decide whether the activity will be for the full group, or whether you will divide the full group into smaller participant groups. How will you do this latter?

- check that you have sufficient and suitable rooms for the participant group(s) and that any necessary material or other resources are available in each room
- check any safety factors necessary
- confirm the activity time requirements
- prepare your introductory verbal description of the activity for the learners
- decide the observation strategy
- decide how the activity is to be reviewed and feedback given.

Observation and review

The last two aspects in the above list are most important. Time must be built into the activity session for review, feedback to the participants, and identification and discussion of the learning points. In many cases, this review session will last as long as the activity, although the available time may mean that this has to be restricted arbitrarily. Observation and feedback are very important factors in activities (and also in videos, case studies and role plays) and considerable attention must be paid to them in the planning process. Which approach will be the most appropriate and effective in the particular situation? The choices include:

- observation by the participants
- observation and feedback by the trainer
- observation by participants withdrawn from the learning group for this purpose
- fishbowl observation
- remote observation and CCTV.

Methods of reviewing include:

- self-feedback by the participants, assisted by self-awareness questionnaires
- group feedback by the trainer and/or member-observers
- subgroup feedback by member-observers followed by full-group plenary
- self-criticism from video recordings.

Methods

By the participants

Observation by the participants themselves is the most difficult approach for learners and therefore the least effective from the trainer's viewpoint. The participants observe their own new skill application and behaviours at the same time as they perform the activity requirements. However, one of the aims in a learning group is for all members to have the opportunity for practice. In a constrained event, this may be difficult if all learners do not take part in all activities.

The basic review approach is to re-assemble the learners in a plenary group after the activity and seek their views on their achievements. The trainer uses a question and answer technique based on the nature of the activity. Responses can be restrained in such circumstances, not only because of the learners' problems in expressing their views, but also because they may have experienced difficulty in both participating and observing. If this is a likelihood, for example with a stranger group that has only recently come together, you can ease the process by using a self-awareness questionnaire. Immediately following the activity, the learners are given a period for reflection before they complete the questionnaire in preparation for the plenary discussion. The questionnaire acts as a memory trigger and also as a comment preparation. If the activity had a leader, a specific leadership questionnaire can be prepared for the leader's completion and questions about the leadership can be included in the members' questionnaires. The trainer will still need to lead the plenary review, but the learners will now be prepared to contribute.

Observation and feedback by the trainer

When all the learners are taking part in an activity the trainer will carry out the observation and feedback. Some trainers try to observe all the groups by moving round from one to another during the activity, but there is a danger that not all behaviours will be observed and a common remark from the learners is 'Oh, we did that, but you weren't in our room at the time!'. It is preferable to have the same number of trainers as groups, but even then there are potential dangers of the different trainers having different observing standards.

Observation by specific participants

In many training courses the most common practice is observation by participants withdrawn from the group for this purpose. Not only are all the learner groups observed, but the observers are in fact receiving training in observation and awareness. The concerns are that the learners are inexperienced and unskilled observers and might miss critical events, or they might misinterpret some observations. This factor may cause disagreement among the learners during the review. Ideally time should be allocated for observer training before an event in which learner-observers are to be used.

Other problems in the post-activity review and feedback session include the length of time that such a session can take because everybody wants to have a say. One method of avoiding this is to require a group's observer(s) to stay with their group after the activity and give immediate feedback to that group alone. The groups eventually come together for a short plenary session to discuss significant events that were common to all groups. By planning for the observers of each group to make a short report to the trainer following their review sessions, the trainer can identify the points to raise in the plenary.

Fishbowl observation

Fishbowl observation is a useful technique for observing both skill application activities and those in which the behaviour of the participants is important. In a group of, say, 12 learners, six are selected to take part in an activity, for example a problem-solving exercise. This group sits in a circle with the remaining members forming a further circle outside them. Each member of the outer group observes one member of the participating group, following clear instructions about what they should be looking for. In behaviourally important events, a form of behaviour analysis might be used, some training in this technique having preceded the event.

At the end of the activity, the observers give feedback to their observed member, thus ensuring that feedback is individual and comprehensive.

The roles are then reversed, the initial observing group becoming the participating group.

All these 'live' observation methods, particularly where the trainer has to give support to inexperienced observers, demand a significant period of the event and require careful planning.

Remote observation and CCTV

Closed circuit television (CCTV) has now taken the place of the once common technique of observing an activity through one-way viewing glass. The TV camera can be operated by the trainer in the room with the activity group or remotely from an observing room. In the latter case the CCTV simply takes the place of live observers, or supplements them. Whether CCTV is used alone or with additional live observers, the session must be planned to allow plenty of time for review and feedback. Use CCTV in the review in some way otherwise the learners might react against not seeing the results of the 'spy in the sky'.

A range of CCTV review methods can be used:

● The trainer (and learner observers) observe at the same time as the CCTV is recording the activity. They give verbal feedback to the participants and illustrate their comments with identified behaviours recorded on the video. This approach involves considerable review time, longer than verbal feedback alone.

● Where another activity follows the observed one, the first group is excused participation to view the video recording of its activity. The group is given a short feedback session in which it is advised to watch for particular incidents. This method, although saving time, means that some learners might miss other parts of the event. It is most useful when the participant 'group' consists of only one or two people, for example the observational results of a presentation or a negotiation between two people.

● Following the activity, a restricted review and feedback session is held, without the use of the video recording, although the participants are advised about critical incidents. The participants are given the video cassette to play outside the course day, for example during the early part of the evening immediately following the day's work. Although this saves time, some feedback possibilities might be lost with the learners observing unsupported.

Whichever CCTV approach is used, there can be no doubt that the review and feedback session is going to be expensive in time if the CCTV is to be used to its best advantage. Session planning includes decisions on whether this time can be afforded within the event or whether some less extensive review methods should be used.

If you have followed the process to this stage, you will have planned most of the aspects of your training and development programme and session content and will be able to see the way ahead clearly. The remaining part in the planning process concerns the very important subject evaluation of the programme: this is the theme of Part Four.

Evaluating training and development programmes

Chapter 11
Evaluating training and development programmes

This chapter:

    identifies the reasons for evaluating training and development
    suggests who should be involved in evaluating
    describes the role of the line managers and gives guidelines for their actions.

Although the subject of evaluation is at the end of this book, this does not imply that it is the last process to be considered at the end of training and development. Too frequently evaluation (or what seems to pass for it) comes to the trainer's mind just before the end of the programme (or even later) and a decision is made to 'evaluate'; it could be only the issue of a 'happiness' sheet two minutes before the end of the course as the learners are leaving to go home, or even some time after the event using the excuse that 'they've had time to settle down now and think about the course'!

Evaluation is too important to be treated in this cavalier fashion and it starts long before the end of a training programme. Its importance is such that I contend that if you do not evaluate your training and development programmes to the maximum extent to which you are allowed or are capable, then it is virtually useless to run the training. If you do not evaluate, apart from highly subjective and personal thoughts, you have no 'evidence' of the success or otherwise of your training. This success is not a measure only of an enjoyable training course that has achieved its objectives. Training is the process of changing people to a more effective state so that the business aspects of the organization are improved. Training without business improvement is usually training for training's sake. Evaluation is the process of 'measuring' this change and achievement from the start of the training process to its final and continued successful application in the workplace. Because of this evaluation over the whole training process, it must be considered early in the design and planning, and must start long before the training event.

Reasons for evaluating

Ask any group of training practitioners if they evaluate their programmes and the

161

answer will be 'yes'. Apart from determining that what they do is actually 'evaluation', the reasons they give can be many and various. Common responses to the question 'Why do you evaluate?' include:

- 'It's a good thing to do – everybody does it, don't they?'
- 'It looks good to show on our records.'
- 'We've been told we have to do it – don't know why!'
- 'The senior management likes reports full of number crunching.'
- 'It's always been done here.'

and rather more practically:

- 'Evaluation is part of the Training and Development National Vocational Qualification.'
- 'Evaluation is part of Investors in People.'
- 'Evaluation is part of Training and Development M.Ed./M.Phil. and similar.'

and what appear to be even more practical and relevant, but on examination are very restricted:

- 'To ensure that the training is achieving its objectives.'
- 'To improve the effectiveness of our training programmes.'

Evaluation appears to be firmly anchored in many people's minds as being restricted to the training and development process only and divorced from business improvement, other than perhaps confirming that the learning achieved is implemented at work.

Reasons for not evaluating

If evaluation is not performed, the responses to the question 'Why not?' are equally revealing of attitudes to evaluation. They include:

- 'You can only *know* whether the course has been successful or not.'
- 'You don't need all those bits of paper to know how successful you've been.'
- 'Evaluation only works for practical training.'
- 'Evaluation is somebody else's responsibility.'
- 'Nobody has ever asked me to evaluate the programmes.'
- 'The client didn't raise the subject of evaluation when the contract was agreed or didn't want to pay for the extra work involved.'
- 'What more do you want? I hand out a questionnaire at the end of the course!'
- 'It would take up so much time I wouldn't have time to train.'

From this negative list, the only answer that has any real substance is the final one, but even that represents restricted thinking without any motivation to evaluate.

Consequences of not evaluating

The absence of much 'real' evaluation in training and development was identified by the Training and Development NVQ Lead Body when TD competences were being investigated. In spite of the low level of practice, the TDLB realized its importance and it immediately became a significant part of the Training and Development NVQ Competence Standards. Whether or not you subscribe to the value of NVQs, competences relate directly to effective job performance and the consequences of not evaluating can be serious and far-reaching. These consequences include:

- valid responses to challenges about your training and development programmes are not possible
- senior sponsors and clients have no concrete evidence or even awareness of your success
- the success of the training design is very difficult to assess
- achievements of the overall training programme are difficult to assess
- learner reactions are not assessable
- learning achievements are not assessable
- trainer self-assessment is not possible in an objective manner
- trainer assessment by their line manager is even more difficult
- learners may be blind to their own changes and improvements
- attribution of change is not assessable.

The last-named consequence is particularly important in the cost- and value-effectiveness evaluation of training programmes, because any business change must be shown to be due to the training and not to other spurious effects, e.g. fear of redundancy, self-motivation to learn without attending formal training, etc.

Who undertakes evaluation?

At one time, the immediate response to the question 'Who undertakes evaluation?' by everyone from learners through line managers to senior management, would be 'the training department' or 'trainers'. But a serious justification for the failure to evaluate was described by one of the reasons listed earlier – 'It would take up so much time I wouldn't have time to train'. Trainers, like most employment practitioners, suffer severe time restraints and if they did not have time to train, there would be no need for evaluation.

Two criteria for action are suggested:

- do something effective, whatever it might be, within the constraints of your resources – it is amazing what can be achieved if the motivation or interest is there
- involve others – there is no reason why the trainer should do it all and, in fact, there are strong arguments why the trainers should not do it all.

Involving the Training Quintet

The Training Quintet was introduced in Chapter 1 in relation to its involvement with the training needs identification and analysis activities at the start of the training process. This Quintet should also be involved in the evaluation process so that much of the resource pressure is taken from the trainers' shoulders and some of it placed where it should really be located.

Figure 11.1 repeats the Training Quintet diagram from Chapter 1 showing the members of the group who must all play their active parts in the evaluation process.

Senior management

The senior group must be involved in evaluation at the earliest stage and should be encouraged to be interested, rather than be considered as nuisances! They should:

● state clearly and authoritatively the responsibilities for evaluation

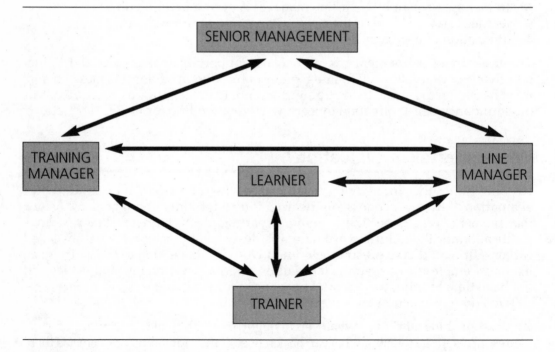

Figure 11.1   The Training Quintet

- require that all training functions are evaluated effectively
- require evaluation analyses and review these regularly.

A bland statement of support for training and evaluation is not sufficient as positive action by this senior group.

The training manager

The training manager performs a range of evaluation activities, principally control measures, including:

- the control of evaluation strategy and practice
- assistance with practical evaluation measures, particularly when a more neutral assessor than the trainer is needed
- close examination of evaluation results and their analyses
- collation of series of evaluation analyses representing the department's range of work
- presentation of analytic results to senior management.

The trainer

Trainers, in spite of their considerable involvement in training itself, must be practically involved in a large proportion of the evaluation. Their responsibilities include:

- designing and implementing validation approaches (validation is defined here as the assessment of the effectiveness of the training events)
- designing implementation evaluation measures and supporting these activities
- supporting line managers in their briefing and debriefing roles, as required
- supporting line managers in their evaluation roles
- providing analyses of evaluation for the training and development programmes for which they are responsible.

The line manager

Traditionally, line management has considered the responsibility for evaluation as the training department's alone. But the line managers *must* have an input, if only because their staff are involved in the training and there is a cost for the training services on their budgets. Only line managers can evaluate those aspects that are linked with the cost- and value-effectiveness of the training and whether, as a result of this expenditure, the business (*their business*) has benefited. Ideally the line managers should participate in:

- evaluation design with the training department – essential as they are a significant party to whatever process is arranged
- pre-programme briefing sessions with their members of staff

- post-programme debriefing sessions with members of their staff
- involvement, if not sole operation, of medium- and/or longer-term evaluation and assessment of business improvement.

The learner

Last, but not least, the learners must be involved as far as possible – they have to be relied on for reliable, accurate and honest reporting and comments.

In the same way that it was suggested the line managers participate in the design and planning of evaluation, so evaluation practitioners should try to involve the learners at all stages. This involvement is a natural extension of the links made with them when training needs were identified and produces a desirable, continuous communication between all participants.

The learners' interest in and support for evaluation must be encouraged at all stages. Too often learners are required to complete evaluation instruments or make effective comments, yet are not told what will be done with them nor given any information about the evaluation. This is because the evaluators either do not think to let them know, or consider that they won't be interested 'because they don't look on evaluation as their concern'. It is their concern and every attempt should be made to acquaint them with the results of the evaluation. The results may suggest a repeat TNIA and these learners will be prime sources of help.

The evaluation process

Twelve stages in an evaluation process can be readily identified and are shown, in a logical process, in Figure 11.2. The first stage, TNIA, was discussed at the start of this book.

TNIA and evaluation and, in fact, all other training and development factors, should be considered as part of one comprehensive effective process. Without TNIA, there is no evidence that training is required; evaluation shows that the objectives of the TNIA and the reasons for those approaches have been achieved.

Design of the evaluation process

The design of the evaluation process should not, as indicated above, be treated as a separate entity, but should be carried out in parallel with the design of the training programmes and sessions. The design will depend on a number of factors including the type of training and development programme.

The evaluation format must be congruent with the type of training and development. Too often one form of evaluation is used for every kind of learning process, whether it is relevant or not. Evaluation in these cases is neither useful nor valid.

The principle behind any evaluation design is that the process must confirm whether or not the training and learning objectives have been achieved, and

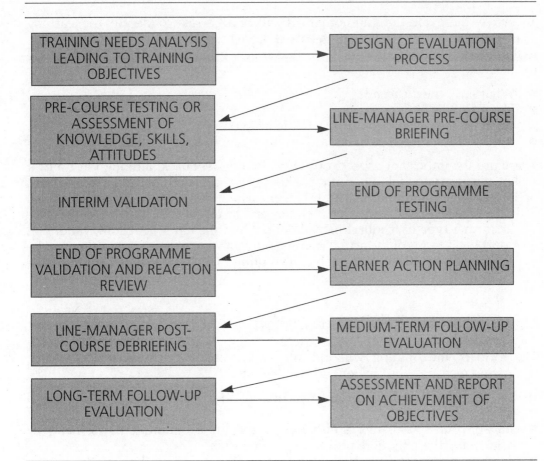

Figure 11.2   The evaluation cycle

subsequently implemented in an effective manner. This requirement includes the validation of the actual training process:

- Was it the most appropriate method?
- Was it presented in the most effective way?
- Did it support the learners and help them to learn?
- Were the training objectives achieved?

and factors relating to the learners:

- Were their starting and finishing levels identified and assessed in any way?
- Were their personal objectives satisfied as far as they correlated with those of the programme?
- Was the learning method the most appropriate for them?
- To what extent did they learn or not learn (and why)?
- What do they intend to do with the learning, and eventually, did they do it?

To answer these questions and others, it will be necessary to identify the learning change of the learners and obtain feedback from them about the quality and value to them of the training process. Obtain as much information about their learning in terms of:

- What have they learned?
- How did this happen?
- What do they intend to do with the learning?
- If they did not learn as much as you/they would have wished, why not?

These are the important aspects of the evaluation feedback, although at times it will be necessary to seek other information, views and opinions on, e.g., the form of the training programme, its length, the most and least useful parts, sessions and activities, the level of the training facilities and so on.

The former type of feedback is 'validation' and the latter 'reaction', validation is important in terms of the actual training and learning, whereas reaction must be a secondary aspect, which although contributing to the learning, has not the same vital nature.

Designing varied forms of evaluation

The form of the training will indicate fairly readily the type and extent of evaluation measures, but in general will include:

- pre-testing or pre-knowledge measures of the learners' existing skills and knowledge
- start-of-course assessments either replacing pre-programme assessments or confirming these in more training-specific forms
- daily or interval interim evaluation approaches, which will normally only be considered if the learning programme lasts more than a day or so, but will certainly be necessary in programmes lasting a week or more
- end-of-programme evaluation and/or reaction and allied activities
- the form of action planning and plans for its use
- arrangements for medium- and long-term evaluation, either by correspondence or visiting, and by whom.

Equally necessary in the planning and design stage will be the confirmation of the Training Quintet involvement and their various responsibilities.

Programme evaluation must be considered at a very early stage in the design and planning process and decisions made on how it is to be achieved, at least in outline format. Most activities can and should be planned and prepared fully in advance, with some of the later actions being outlined for final completion at a later stage. These latter would be the medium and longer-term measures, but even if the detail is not prepared the strategy should be agreed.

Figure 11.3 suggests a checklist of minimum guidelines to assist you in the evaluation planning and design, at the same time as the training itself is being planned.

The line manager's involvement

Of paramount importance in any evaluation programme and process is the active involvement of the learners' line managers. It is they who will (should) have been involved in the training needs analyses and have agreed that their staff should be given the opportunity to learn new skills or procedures, or to undertake remedial training to bring them up to the required competence standards.

Line managers are busy people, usually in a difficult in-between position, and every attempt should be made within the organization to obtain their commitment. This was, in the past, none too easy a task, and in many cases will continue to be so. The more involvement line managers have in the development of their staff, the greater likelihood there will be of a successful learning conclusion, with improved skills, efficiency, attitudes and more effective working as a result.

---

1. Has a training needs analysis been carried out?

2. What are the objectives for the training event?

3. Do the objectives lend themselves to being evaluated? If not, why not and what else could be done?

4. Confirm line management support action.

5. Decide the timing, resourcing and extent of the evaluation process you need to follow.

6. Are you concentrating on full validation or merely reaction?

7. Create instruments that will satisfy your evaluation needs.

8. If possible, test your evaluative instruments against the training programme items.

9. Decide on the form of end-of-programme action planning.

10. Agree post-programme evaluation action – who, what, where, when, how?

Figure 11.3   Checklist for evaluation pre-planning

There are two specific events that the line manager and the learner alone can process, one immediately before the training programme and one immediately afterwards.

1. As the training is a need for learner development, has there been any change since the event was agreed that might alter this need?

2. Is this the most relevant course or other form of programme to satisfy the learner's needs?

3. What are the learner's views about the programme objectives as far as the local organization is concerned – the office, the section, the team, etc?

4. How do the programme objectives affect the learner – at what level of skill and knowledge does the learner self-identify at this programme stage?

5. How will the learner approach the training – specific areas, personal disclosure, etc?

6. Any other aspects not covered by the above.

7. The line manager should guarantee support when the learner returns.

8. A date and time for a post-programme debriefing meeting should be agreed (to be held soon after the training event).

9. Ensure that any pre-programme learning activities are completed and any pre-programme tests of skill and knowledge level take place.

Figure 11.4   Pre-programme briefing checklist

Pre-programme briefing meetings

The pre-programme briefing is a vital stage in the development of people who are to take part in training provided by other than their line managers. There will have been contact regarding the training between the learner and the line manager before this stage and the learner's training needs will have been identified at an appraisal or other career development discussion, or will have come about as the result of the introduction of new tasks or roles.

Shortly, preferably within the fortnight before the start of the training programme, the line manager holds a pre-course briefing with the learner. This will be the last chance to confirm, or agree on cancellation of, the involvement, and will also be an opportunity for them to discuss the training and the hopes and aspirations of both. The line managers should ensure that there is sufficient time for a meaningful discussion to take place, and the learners might have made some preparations by considering the programme objectives and content and identifying their own objectives. This is the occasion for both to discover any differences and agree common objectives.

The event need not be an over-lengthy event. If the relationship between the manager and staff is good, there should be little in the way of surprises, but the line manager must give sufficient time for the discussion, particularly if the learner has concerns or fears that need to be allayed. The event also confirms with the learners that the manager is interested in the learners' development.

Figure 11.4 suggests some guidelines for the line manager. If the learners also see this list it would help in *their* preparation for the discussion.

Post-programme debriefing meetings

In the same way, a post-programme debriefing meeting which is perhaps even more important than the pre-course event, should be held as soon as possible after the learner's completion of the programme, certainly within the first week. Failure to do so will suggest to the learner that their completion of the training is considered of little value, with the result that, unless they are very committed, the action plans will not be implemented.

Figure 11.5 suggests the guidelines for this meeting, perhaps the most important aspects being the agreement by the line manager to give active support to the learner's implementation plans. It should be made clear that this meeting does not wipe the manager's hands of the process, but, with arrangements for at least one further review, it is the start of the implementation process.

The discussion can raise subjects the implementation of which may not be clear to the learner or the manager, or the action may suggest that some further training is required. In such cases, the trainers should be prepared to *assist* with the discussion, offering their knowledge and expertise.

1. How effective was the training programme as far as the learner was concerned? Did this differ from the views of others?

2. How effective were the trainers – approachable, logical, clear in their presentations, good use of visual aids, not too hurried, etc?

3. How appropriate was the training material as far as the learner was concerned?

4. How up to date was the material?

5. Were the programme objectives achieved? If not, why not?

6. Were the learner's personal objectives achieved? If not, why not?

7. What did the learner learn as new material, have usefully confirmed or be timeously reminded of?

8. Discuss with the learner their action plan:
   What is planned to be done?
   How is it to be implemented?
   When and over what period?
   What resources are required?

9. Any other aspects not covered by the above.

10. Arrange a date, between three and six months hence, to discuss with the learner a final implementation review. Offer the availability of interim reviews.

11. Discuss with the relevant trainers, any feedback information about which you feel they should be made aware.

Figure 11.5   **Post-programme debriefing checklist**

Chapter 12
Evaluating before, at the start of and during the programme

This chapter:

    describes knowledge tests and their formats for use at the start of a programme

    details knowledge and skills assessment methods for use at the start of a programme

    suggests some validation activities that can be performed during a programme.

Planning can, and certainly should take place for evaluation approaches before, at the start of and during the training programme itself. 'Before' and 'at the start of' may be interchangeable, depending on the type of training, the extent of knowledge and skills of the learners, and the culture of the organization.

Before or at the start

Training is concerned with improving change in the knowledge and skills of people who attend the programmes. A large part of evaluation is the assessment of this change and in order to perform this assessment you must be aware of the level of knowledge and skills of the learners before they start the programme. Ideally any tests should be completed before the training programme starts, but this is not always (infrequently?) possible. If the environment, the type of training material and other conditions allow, tests (which need not be written tests of the traditional nature) should be sent to the learner as far as possible in advance of the event, to be completed under the supervision of the line manager. Naturally, full information about why this assessment is needed should be sent with the tests, so that the highest degree of accuracy and honesty is achieved, and any suspicions allayed.

The more common approaches used at these stages are:

- knowledge tests
- knowledge/skill assessment
- knowledge/skill *self*-assessment.

Knowledge tests

If the material in the training programme is knowledge-based and is new to the organization, a decision must be made on whether initial testing is worthwhile. If it is known with absolute certainty that the potential learners will have no knowledge of the training material, pre-testing would probably antagonize the learners more than produce any data on knowledge levels. It should therefore be assumed that the knowledge level is nil.

However, if there is any doubt about pre-existing knowledge, tests should be used to confirm the position. The tests (or absence of them) will enable the trainer to:

- assess the general level of the group and individuals and pitch the training level accordingly
- provide the pre-training information for comparison with later assessments to determine the amount of change achieved.

Test formats

Pre-training knowledge tests can be informal or formal, the informal approach being the most subjective and relying on an assessment, perhaps developed from a performance review and appraisal by the line manager. Care must be taken in accepting this information without reinforcement as managers are not necessarily aware of all aspects of knowledge levels of their staff.

Formal tests of knowledge are usually written ones requiring various types of response. The evaluation planning process should include decisions on the type of test that will be the most appropriate and relevant in the circumstances. The range of tests contains:

- open answer
- binary choice
- true/false choice
- multiple choice
- short answer.

Open answer test

The traditional examination is the open answer test in which a question is set to determine the extent of the knowledge possessed and, on occasions, the ability of the person to express themselves in a clear, logical and comprehensive manner. The extent of the knowledge is demonstrated in the written response which has to be assessed by the test-setter or examiner.

The question wording requires considerable skill as it determines the quality and level of the response – specific or general. Sufficient and substantial time must be allowed for the response and for the tester to assess the written answers, the number depending on the potential learning population.

Binary choice test

Other test formats do not require as much time as the open answer approach, the amount of time depending mainly on the number of questions set. Binary choice tests pose questions directly related to the subject under consideration and supply alternative answers from which the person being tested can choose. These alternative answers might be concerned with some information aspect or may even be a simple 'Yes' or 'No'.

Example questions might be:

	Delete inappropriate answer
1. Does your company provide a non-contributory pension plan?	Yes/No
2. To whom would you go to seek information about any plan?	Your boss/The finance manager

This type of test is simple for the learners to complete by deleting the inappropriate answer, and equally simple for the tester to mark. However, this very simplicity can limit the approach and demands excellent knowledge of the subject and the ability to phrase appropriate and unambiguous questions from the tester. Another problem is that the learner may simply guess the response with a fifty-fifty chance of being correct – depending on the laws of probability, it is possible for a person to achieve a 100 per cent correct score without having real knowledge, simply by guessing.

True/False choice test

The true/false choice test is similar to the binary choice test with the response options to a statement being limited to either 'True' or 'False'. For example:

1. The computer is switched on only by depressing the button on the computer main case.	True/False

This simplicity introduces the same problems described for binary choice tests. To ensure the construction of the most effective binary and true/false (and also multiple choice) tests, the following rules must be followed:

1. The test must consist of singular questions and those questions must be clear, unambiguous and not requiring interpretation.
2. One of the answers given in the alternative answer approach must be correct.
3. The statements or questions must be short and in language that is as simple as

appropriate. Unclear and/or long and complex questions tend to test the learners' ability to understand written questions rather than knowledge of the subject.

4.   Use negatives sparingly as the short words 'no' and 'not' can be easily missed when the question is read under conditions of stress. If a negative has to be used, underline it.
5.   Avoid words that may give a clue to the answer – statements that contain absolute words such as 'never', 'always', 'all', 'none' are usually false. True statements are often accompanied by words like 'usually', 'may', 'sometimes'.
6.   Wherever possible , avoid the use of words such as 'frequently', 'most of', 'regularly' and 'at times'; these can mean different things to different people and reduce the validity of the test.
7.   The statement or alternative responses should be sufficiently plausible not to appear obviously false (when this is so) and to reduce the risk of forcing guesswork.

In spite of the above, do not become paranoid about test construction; the most effective test is to do a dummy-run on a group of people who are similar to the potential learners.

Multiple choice test

In order to avoid some of the problems described above you can extend the range of answers from which the choice has to be made. The main difference between the multiple and the various forms of binary tests is that a choice of three or more options is given, usually up to a maximum of five. For example:

1.   Payment to the non-contributor pension plan is:
(a) mandatory for all new employees
(b) voluntary for all new employees
(c) mandatory for all existing employees
(d) voluntary for all existing employees.

In this form of questionnaire, the responder has to choose one answer and either place a tick against it or ring it. The greater the number of options, the less chance there is of random selection producing a high score. The difficulty is in the construction when a number of plausible options, correct and incorrect, have to be found.

The example above is in the form of completing an incomplete statement. One variation poses a question and provides a series of optional answers.

Another variation, used more to establish attitudes and learning rather than obtain singularly correct answers, is the multiple choice in which the tester has a preferred answer in mind – the other options are not wrong, only less preferred by the tester for some reason. For example:

1. Practice interviews are most effective performed with:

   (a) real-life case studies
   (b) case studies based on real-life events
   (c) constructed case studies for the interviewer
   (d) constructed case studies for the interviewee only
   (d) constructed case studies for both.

In a test of this nature it has to be made clear by the tester that a 'correct' answer is not sought, rather the 'best' or 'preferred' option is chosen. Some 'rules' additional to those described under 'binary choice' include:

- try not to repeat the same wording in the various options – put as much information in the question as possible
- if you are using the correct answer approach, ensure that the answer is the only one possible, but make the incorrect options seem plausible
- avoid giving clues to the correct answer – by repetition of words from the question; by giving the correct option in greater detail than the others; or by making the correct answer obviously correct in the way it is expressed
- vary, from question to question, in a random manner the position of the correct answer
- make each answer independent of one another without any co-association that might help in answering the questions
- always identify each question and options within the question, e.g. number the questions 1) 2) etc. and letter the choices a), b) etc.
- if the 'question' is actually a question, make sure that it ends with '?'
- do not end with a full stop if the answer is numerical, to avoid decimal point confusion.

Short answer test

Some tests require the learner to write short answers to the posed questions, rather than selecting one from a prepared list. Consequently the learner has to search for an answer, and there is less likelihood of the 'correct' answer being given by chance. The short answer test is the most effective method, after the full examination approach, and demonstrates the extent of the learners' knowledge without the need for them also to demonstrate skill in grammatical construction – the shorter, yet complete answer, the better.

The constructor of a short answer test must ensure that the questions:

- can produce a short answer
- are clear and unambiguous
- are brief and direct
- require the responses words only – 'a', 'an', 'the', 'some' etc. should not be necessary, although the responder should not be constrained to exclude them

- are consistent in format – the space for the short answer is usually at the end of the question, but can be inserted within the question wording; in the latter case, try to produce all questions in this format, keeping the space in similar positions in each question
- do not have answer spaces that suggest the length of the response
- can be answered correctly with one answer only.

Knowledge/Skills assessment

The assessment or measurement of the learners' skills based on their knowledge prior to the training programme is difficult. It is unlikely, though not impossible, that the trainer will be able to visit the learners' workplaces and assess their skills by direct observation. The learners' line managers are in a better position to do this, particularly if a checklist for the skills is provided for them, containing a means of comparing skill levels such as a scoring rating.

However, on most occasions the assessment of knowledge/skills has to wait until the learners attend the programme, but it is essential that something is attempted at this stage if it has not been achieved previously. The TNIA has described the general needs, but once the training programme is initiated the individual needs become paramount. The tests at the start of the programme should, preferably, not appear to be 'tests', but rather integral parts of the training.

By discussion

A useful method of starting a training programme, and one that satisfies several training course needs, is to hold a discussion with the learning group, perhaps by introducing the subject of the course and inviting comments that will demonstrate the level of the learners' knowledge and their experience. While ensuring that all the learners contribute, remember that some of the contributions may have to be accepted provisionally. The contributors might, for example, have an academic knowledge only that they infer is a practical skill, or some members may simply follow the lead of others. But a discussion of this nature in addition to giving some indication of the learning group level, also acts as an icebreaker by encouraging the learners to speak.

By demonstration

Demonstration by the learners of their practical skills at performing the required operations is of particular value in initial assessment. However, make sure that the participants can perform at least some of the operation, otherwise it may be seen as an attempt to embarrass them. If the operation is completely new, demonstration by the learners would be inappropriate.

Assessment of the learners' skills will be by observation of the demonstrations and by rating their achievements against a pre-formed checklist of operational skills. Anything less than 100 per cent skill (which suggests that the training programme is unnecessary!) will identify the group's learning needs. Observation is at the heart of many areas of evaluation, as it was seen to be in the early stages of the TNIA and this observation extends beyond practical demonstrations.

By activity observation

One method of assessing the skill levels of the learners at the start of a training programme is the observation by the trainer of a relevant activity.

The method of observation will depend on the type of activity and descriptions of these approaches have been made earlier. The activity should be directly related to the subject of the training programme and consequently should not be perceived as a test, although the trainers will be observing and assessing this activity more closely than many of those that will follow during the programme. The basic approach will be to assess the skill performance of the learners against some form of pre-planned checklist or analytical instrument. Specific skill tasks are easier to observe than more general or behavioural activities, but instruments are available for all situations.

Specific skills are assessed against the techniques that are included in the programme, or against an agreed model of, say, behaviour, assertiveness or interviewing, etc. For example, at the start of a programme on negotiation skills, the group can be paired for negotiations designed to demonstrate the extent and nature of the negotiation skills they already possess. Remember that this assessment may not be absolute as the newness of the situation might inhibit the learners from demonstrating all their skills.

Group problem-solving events are particularly difficult to assess, not in the result which is either an accepted or rejected solution, but in the processes and behaviours which the learners use to achieve the ends, particularly if they come to a 'wrong' answer! Two aspects are observable and assessable – the technical processes they follow to achieve the result, and the behaviours they use.

The technical process is observed with the use of a checklist that contains all the steps that should be taken (or will be included in the subsequent training event). As the steps are used they are checked off on the list, the completed list identifying the learning needs. The behaviour processes can be assessed from a similar checklist that details the appropriate and inappropriate behaviours that commonly occur and either contribute to or detract from the success of the event.

Technical and behavioural processes are frequently combined for assessments at this early stage, more detailed observation taking place at later stages. Figure 12.1 is an example of a combined observation checklist for analysing the behaviour of the leader selected for a problem-solving group.

Similar activity analyses can be constructed for observing the group members and of course the post-activity self-assessment and leader-assessment

Did the leader:

TASK	achieve the task requirements? How successfully? analyse and define the problem? work to a plan? test ideas, proposals and solutions? make the best use of resources? use all the information available or obtainable? use any of the techniques to be included as learning points?
GROUP PROCESSES	brief the group effectively about the task? seek and reach agreement about the objectives? agree the aspects of the group process – timing, standards, solution-seeking, decision-making procedures? summarize progress? How often? How well? encourage the group to work together? control the group? keep the group to the task? involve all members?
INDIVIDUAL PROCESSES	give each member a job to do? check the understanding of the individuals about their jobs and the task? investigate special knowledge, experience and skills? monitor the progress of each member with tasks to perform? bring in each member as necessary? ignore any member(s)? visibly develop conflict with any member(s)?

Figure 12.1   Leader observation checklist

questionnaires referred to earlier can be linked to provide an activity review. But the predominating purpose at this stage is to give the trainer(s) a practical assessment of the existing skills and capabilities of the learning group.

Similarly, if the training programme concerns interviewing skills and techniques, a set of paired interviews can be set up and observed to assess initial skills. Figure 12.2 suggests a relatively simple observation checklist to assess the interviewer's first attempts.

Knowledge/Skills self-assessment

The learners can be asked to assess their own skills at the start of the programme, either as the only assessment, or preferably to supplement direct

A useful approach that I have introduced is the three-test, which uses the same questionnaire at three different stages of self-assessment.

The three-test

In the first use of the three-test, the learners complete a questionnaire at the start of the programme – the traditional pre-test – in which they are asked to rate their skills or levels against a number of statements on a scoring range of 1 (low) to 10 (high). The form of the prepared questionnaire will depend on the

---

Please ring the score that you feel represents you at this stage. Enter what you think it really is, not what it should be or what somebody would want it to be.

1. How well do you communicate with your senior managers?
Very well   10 9 8   7   6   5   4   3   2   1   Badly

2. How well do you communicate with your peers?
Very well   10 9 8   7   6   5   4   3   2   1   Badly

3. How well do you communicate with your subordinates?
Very well   10 9 8   7   6   5   4   3   2   1   Badly

4. How well do you communicate in writing?
Very well   10 9 8   7   6   5   4   3   2   1   Badly

5. How well do you communicate orally one-to-one?
Very well   10 9 8   7   6   5   4   3   2   1   Badly

6. How well do you communicate orally to a group?
Very well   10 9 8   7   6   5   4   3   2   1   Badly

7. How well do you question people?
Very well   10 9 8   7   6   5   4   3   2   1   Badly

8. How well do you listen to others?
Very well   10 9 8   7   6   5   4   3   2   1   Badly

9. To what extent do you interrupt others as they are speaking?
Very little   10 9 8   7   6   5   4   3   2   1   Very much

10. How do you rate your communication skills overall?
Very good   10 9 8   7   6   5   4   3   2   1   Poor

Figure 12.3   **Communication skills self-awareness questionnaire**

STRUCTURE	How did the interviewer commence the interview?
	To what extent did the interviewer explain the reason for the interview?
	What form of structure, if any, did the interviewer follow?
	Was the structure explained to the interviewee?
	How did the interviewer end the interview?
	To what extent was the interviewer aware of the interviewee's overt reactions to the interview and the interviewer?
	What summary was used at the end of the interview?
	What form of follow-up, if relevant, was suggested and by whom?
BEHAVIOUR	How quickly was rapport established?
	To what extent was the interviewee encouraged to talk?
	To what extent was the interviewee encouraged to make suggestions?
	How prescriptive was the interviewer?
	How well did the interviewer appear to listen?
	To what extent did the interviewer appear to be interested in the problem and the interviewee?
GENERAL	How would you rate the success of the interview? (A scale range)
	Why do you give this rating?
	How would you rate the behavioural skills of the interviewer (A scale range)
	Why do you give this rating?
	How would you rate the behavioural skills of the interviewer? (A scale range).
	Why do you give this rating?

Figure 12.2   Interviewer observation checklist

observational assessment by the trainer. The normal assessment approach in training programmes is the pre- and post-test as already described, then at the end of the programme the same test is applied. The difference between the results is a measure of the change and the learning. This kind of test is effective only in practical applications that are quantifiable and measurable. Training situations that are concerned with more general skills and behaviours are too susceptible to contamination by this simple method, particularly if self-assessment is invited. This uncertainty is increased by the fact that, at the start of such events, learners may not know in which areas they are deficient. It may not be until they have completed the training process that they realize the limitations they had at the start!

programme content. Figure 12.3 shows a questionnaire for a communication training programme.

In the three-test, a questionnaire of the type shown in Figure 12.3 is completed again at the end of the training programme in a particular way (see Chapter 14).

There are many arguments against testing or assessment at the start of a training programme: 'The type of training cannot be assessed'; 'We haven't the time/resources/opportunity to do these assessments'; 'You can only assess objective training for which measurable results can be obtained'. None of these arguments is valid – it must be accepted that in some cases subjective assessment only can be obtained, usually in the subjective types of training, but if the approach is consistent the results are more acceptable than doing nothing. After all, evaluation is essential if change is to be shown and if no attempts are made to obtain 'evidence', the training cannot be justified. Some form of evaluative assessment is always possible and decisions about this must be part of the design and planning of the training programme.

Evaluation during the event

Planning for the training programme should include an evaluation of its effectiveness as it progresses, usually in an informal manner – observing the activities of the learners, assessing their understanding by questioning, and so on. These observations are subjective, but there are formal and objective approaches that can, and should, be used during a programme, particularly one lasting more than a day. The most frequently used include:

● activity analysis
● behaviour analysis
● practical tests and demonstrations
● diurnal reviews or audits.

The purpose of interim evaluation is to assess how well the training is achieving its objectives and the learners are learning. *Written into the design of the programme must be the direction that if the evaluation shows that all is not progressing as it should, something must be done about it at the time.* You must be certain that programme resources will allow for this use of time. IF IT IS NOT GOING TO BE POSSIBLE TO TAKE THE NECESSARY ACTION, THERE IS LITTLE POINT IN PERFORMING THE EVALUATION AND IDENTIFYING PROBLEMS.

Activity analysis

Activity analysis was described earlier in this chapter as a means of assessing the starting position of the learners. Methods include assessment questionnaires, simple contribution scoring, directional sociograms and the like. All these can be continued during the programme whenever activities take place. They are not performed primarily for evaluation purposes, rather for immediate information feedback to the learners, but if they are written analyses they can be retained and referred to as progressive evaluation measures.

Behaviour analysis

The relatively difficult behaviour analysis is performed more often by the trainers rather than the learners and, particularly in interpersonal programmes, behaviour analysis observation can be planned as a series of observations, a summary and analysis of the data being presented to the learners to demonstrate how they have progressed during the programme. Following this summary, the learners can plan to modify various aspects of their behaviour, the trainer analysis continuing to produce data for this further stage.

Practical tests and demonstrations

Practical tests and demonstrations have been described as initial assessment instruments, which require learners to show the extent of their existing skill, and particular activities or tests are set for this purpose. Interim testing of this nature can be performed in a very natural manner. 'Tests' are planned to be performed after each progressive learning point and are 'disguised' as practices for the learners, but which are also demonstrating the learned skills.

Practical tests are particularly relevant in computer-based training programmes. A new computer program is usually introduced in logical and progressive stages. After each stage the learners practise the new skill, linked to the preceding ones, to demonstrate whether they have in fact learned – evaluation in a natural format.

Diurnal reviews

In programmes lasting more than one day, it is useful to have a daily assessment, which can serve three purposes:

- acts as an interim evaluation of training effectiveness
- gives the learner the opportunity to consolidate their learning through the reflection necessary for the review
- allows the learners to share their learning with others in the group and perhaps remind others of aspects that had slipped their mind.

There are several forms of daily assessment:

- end-of-the-day reviews
- beginning-of-the-day reviews
- written audits
- oral audits

End- and beginning-of-the-day reviews

If the planned review is held at the end of the training day:

- the learning is fresh in the learners' minds
- the learners are accustomed to making comments
- the review 'closes' the day in a neat way.

However:

- immediate comment on learning does not necessarily mean this learning is significant
- immediate recounting of learning may be too facile
- the learners may be tired at the end of a training day and may say anything, simply to finish the review
- the learners may be tired and not sufficiently bothered to make any comments
- immediate feedback does not give the learners an opportunity to reflect and conclude
- there may be insufficient time to discuss the review items.

Alternatively the review can be planned to be held as the first activity of the following day's programme, having asked the learners to consider the day's events during the evening and overnight. If the review is held in this way:

- the learners should have had the opportunity to reflect and conclude on the learning of the day
- if there are no training sessions during the evening on a residential course, the learners should have time to review
- the items mentioned by the learners may not be the ones that would have been commented on the previous day, but they are more likely to be the ones that have had an impact on them
- there is time for a more leisurely and considerative review at the start of the day than at the end
- more methods of review are possible than in an end-of-day review.

However:

- the learners may not take sufficient time during the evening to reflect on and form conclusions about the training/learning
- as a result of minimal reflection, significant learning may not be recalled
- the review may raise items which require immediate resource and programme time – this may not be available unless detailed planning for provision of these resources has been made in case it is needed
- the review may raise requests that the trainers are unable to deal with as required.

Written audits or reviews

In written audits or reviews learners are asked to reflect on the day's learning and write their comments, either as an open response or in answer to specific questions. An example format for such a questionnaire is shown in Figure 12.4. Learners may complete the review at the end of the training day (for which a relevant period of time is allowed) or during the evening, for review the following morning. It is best to keep this type of questionnaire fairly simple if learners have to complete one every day on a longer programme.

As the first activity the following morning the learning group, as one or divided into smaller groups depending on size of the full group, discusses the review questionnaire responses. This discussion can be quite extended, even if the learners have only positive comments, but particularly so if there are problems that need to be discussed and remedied.

Please consider what has happened during today's training and answer the following questions. Your responses, to the extent that you wish, will be discussed at a review session tomorrow morning.

1. What have you learned today?

2. What helped that learning?

3. Was there anything that hindered your learning? If so, please describe it fully.

4. Was there anything on which you would have liked to have spent more time?

5. Was there anything on which you would have liked to have spent less time or had omitted?

6. Was there anything that you did not understand or agree with?

7. Any other comments?

Figure 12.4   Daily review questionnaire

Oral audits or reviews

Oral reviews can replace the written ones if it is felt that the learners, for some reasons, might not take kindly to written requirements, but they are not as satisfactory. When the learners write down their views, a clearer, permanent and more effective consideration is usually possible.

However, if a verbal review is decided on, the questions in Figure 12.4 can be used as prompts to lead the discussion. As before, a large group of learners can be divided into smaller groups to discuss the questions before coming back together as the full group. This approach allows the quieter members the opportunity to speak and a group spokesperson reports back. This neutral approach is particularly useful if the critics do not feel they can verbalize their thoughts.

In addition to these more traditional forms of interim evaluation, there are other approaches that can be usefully considered in the planning process for this stage of evaluation. Chapter 13 describes some of these other approaches.

Chapter 13

Less traditional forms of interim evaluation

This chapter:

> describes a range of validation instruments and approaches
> for use during a programme
> describes in detail the learning log and its use as a validation instrument
> during a programme.

If you want to move away from the more traditional forms of interim evaluation, there are a number of other methods that can be planned, always bearing in mind the interim caveat: 'If there will not be enough time to satisfy any problems that emerge from the evaluation, it may be better not to offer the evaluation at all'.

Some of the other methods include:

- three-word reviews
- spot checks
- session reviews
- logbook reviews.

Three-word reviews

A simple, but very effective form of daily audit, particularly in human relations programmes, can be the three-word review. At the start of the day ask the learners to write down three words or short phrases that describe their feelings at that stage about the training and the learning. Then invite the participants to call out their words or phrases which the trainer enters, verbatim, on a flipchart. Lead a discussion to consider the words and why they were thought to be relevant, and take or promise action wherever necessary. The learners can be invited to question the words used by others and the reasons behind them, and challenge them.

Spot checks

Spot checks are generally shorter forms of evaluation and can be useful when time is limited or in shorter programmes. In a one-day event, a spot check might be held immediately before the end of the morning session or at the start of the afternoon session, with a planned duration of, say, 15 minutes. But again, be careful about offering an evaluation without also ensuring there is time to deal with problems.

These spot check approaches include:

- the thermometer
- the speedometer
- happy faces
- blobs
- progressive blobs.

In these reviews the learners identify their feelings or views at the stage of the spot check, and are then invited to make a mark on a prepared flipchart – the marks may be graphics, ticks, crosses or spots (the spots can be either drawn or self-adhesive).

In all the checks, look for clusters or spots which indicate the majority views of the learners, or groups of learners. If the groups are quite separate in their views, you will need to investigate the reasons for this division: sex or race differences; various departments or organizations; multi-discipline events; wide starting range; and so on. Also look for individual ratings that differ considerably from the remainder, which may suggest an individual need for some form of tutorial while the rest of the group is doing something else, or recommended planned self-study.

When all the marks have been made and any variations noted as above, the reasons for the significant variations have to be sought – this might mean the people who have made particular marks identifying themselves – clarified if possible, or arrangements made for a modified approach.

The thermometer

The thermometer test is a method of taking the 'temperature' of the learning group at a particular point in time. This temperature relates to how the learners are feeling about the event, its process and its progress since its start or since the last review.

A thermometer is drawn on a flipchart sheet (see Figure 13.1) and the learners are asked to come and make a personal mark (full initials, for example) at the 'temperature' they feel best represents their present views or feelings about the programme. Any substantial divergences should be questioned, but no undue pressure should be put on a member to explain their views if they are reluctant to do so.

The completed temperature chart can then be posted on the wall of the training room for later reference or additional review as necessary. In this way the

Figure 13.1   The 'temperature' of the course

variations in the programme reception can be monitored visibly for all to see, and any problems dealt with as they arise or soon after.

The speedometer

In a similar way the speedometer records learners' views on the pace of the course, the speedometer obviously reflecting a car and its speed. Participants enter their personal mark in the sector with which they identify on the prepared flipchart (see Figure 13.2).

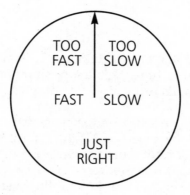

Figure 13.2   The 'speed' of the course

Happy faces

A variation of the thermometer is to display on a chart a number of faces with the mouths and expressions in progressive stages from smiling broadly to scowling or very miserable (see Figure 13.3).

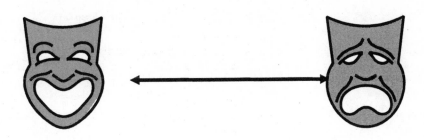

Figure 13.3   **Happy faces**

The learners place a mark beside the face that best represents how they feel, or use self-adhesive faces to place on the chart. Again this process can be repeated several times during the event to show the changes occurring and identify problems that need to be resolved.

Variations to the 'smiling' face can include the size of an open mouth to show how much the members feel they have the opportunity to participate.

The three graphic reviews described above have been suggested as instruments to consider the learners' feelings about the event: the speed, enjoyment or satisfaction with the programme. All the reviews can be used otherwise to test interest, participation possibilities, usefulness, understanding, form of the event – too much x, too little y – and so on.

Blob review

The blob review is another instant form of checking progress. The review can be very short or can extend over an hour or more, but will be worth the time if you are unsure about how an event is progressing. In the more extended form, you must plan for its inclusion.

The short form is very similar to the previous approaches. A prepared flipchart is exhibited showing aspects of the event up to that stage, or questions about views on the training or learning. These might be objective – for example, the learning points covered – or more reactive – seeking views on the learners' reactions to the programme. Figure 13.4 demonstrates an example of the reaction type of blob review.

Please consider the programme so far and place a blob – ● – in the box that you feel represents most closely your views on the programme. The boxes in between the extremes are for levels between these extremes.

Interesting	☐ ☐ ☐	Boring
Clear	☐ ☐ ☐	Confusing
Simple	☐ ☐ ☐	Complicated
Time too short	☐ ☐ ☐	Too long
Visual aids good	☐ ☐ ☐	Aids poor
Session should be retained	☐ ☐ ☐	Session should be omitted
Learned a lot	☐ ☐ ☐	Learned little
Confirmed usefully a lot	☐ ☐ ☐	Confirmed little
Pace too fast	☐ ☐ ☐	Pace too slow
Good interaction within group	☐ ☐ ☐	Poor interaction within group
Good interaction with trainer	☐ ☐ ☐	Poor interaction with trainer
Have no problems	☐ ☐ ☐	Have a lot of problems

Figure 13.4   Blob review

The learners are asked to go to the flipchart and put a pen-marker or self-adhesive blob in the space representing their current views or feelings. The placement of these blobs will indicate the overall and individual views that may need to be discussed and taken into account by the trainer.

Extended blob review

One variation of the blob review is to ask each learner to consider three significant statements they would like to make about the programme and write them clearly and briefly on a flipchart or whiteboard mounted at the front of the group. When all statements have been entered, the learners are asked to make or place their blobs against the statements with which they agree. Commonly agreed views will soon become evident from the clustering, as will individual ones – the 'owners' of the latter might be invited to comment on their entries (without any challenge or value judgement being expressed or implied).

Progressive blob review

Another variation of the straightforward blob activity is to:

1. Ask each individual to write down three significant statements that they would like to make about the programme so far.
2. Divide the learning group into pairs. Decide from their six statements which three they wish to carry forward.
3. When the three statements have been decided upon, form them into groups of four with the similar brief of deciding on three statements from the six brought to the group.
4. If time and numbers permit, groups of eight can then be formed to decide on *six* statements to be the final agreed comments.
5. The six final statements are entered on a chart (see Figure 13.5) and clarified if necessary by the originators.
6. All the learners then come to the chart and place a blob in the column relating

SET OF STATEMENTS	SD	D	A	SA

Figure 13.5   **Blob validation chart**

to the rating with which they agree. The columns are headed SD strongly disagree; D disagree; A agree; SA strongly agree.

Once all the blobs have been entered, a pattern will emerge about the views of the learning group that will indicate if there are any problems requiring immediate action.

Session reviews

It is sometimes necessary to make more detailed plans for assessing the progress of the programme than in the case of a day's training. Particularly in the longer and more complex programmes, it may be too much to ask the learners to add extensive reflection to their other difficulties. In such cases reviews of individual sessions or groups of associated sessions and activities can be conducted. Different parts of a programme, although appearing separate, may relate to each other, and if the earlier sessions are reviewed, this may be done in isolation. Consequently the learners' responses may be negative because they have not then had the benefit of the further material. This presents no problems if the session or group of sessions are self-contained, and the review directed to these. Often a day's training has a single theme – a useful link with the previously described end-of-day review – and the review can concentrate on this. The session review becomes more difficult for the learners if a day's training with a number of separate session groups is being considered. In this latter case, it may be more effective to conduct the reviews following each discrete group.

Before planning this type of review decide what type of feedback is required, why, and what you are going to do with the responses.

The form of session reviews

Session or group session reviews can take a number of forms, some similar to the end-of-day review. They include:

- oral reviews
- simple written reviews
- questionnaires, particularly justifiable questionnaires.

Oral and simple written reviews were discussed in Chapter 12.

Justifiable questionnaires

Tick-list questionnaires may sometimes ask the completers to justify their ratings. Because they require more consideration by the learners these justifiable questionnaires require accurate planning and must be comprehensive.

The simple tick-list questionnaire can be modified easily to the justified example by adding a space that asks for specific comments about the rating. Many trainers complain that they rarely receive any comments, but this is because a space annotated 'comments' is added with no further instructions The learners must comment in addition to placing their marks and the trainer may return a questionnaire if any significant comments have been omitted. An example of this type of questionnaire, again principally based on reaction, is shown in Figure 13.6.

SESSION: THE BARRIERS TO LEARNING

Please consider the session that has just ended and circle the scoring number that most closely represents your answer to the question.

In addition, under every rating please comment on the reasons why you have given that rating – these comments will be as important as the ratings.

Interesting	6	5	4	3	2	1	Boring
Why have you given this rating?							
Clear	6	5	4	3	2	1	Confusing
Why have you given this rating?							
Simple	6	5	4	3	2	1	Complicated
Why have you given this rating?							
Time too short	6	5	4	3	2	1	Too long
Why have you given this rating?							
Visual aids good	6	5	4	3	2	1	Aids poor
Why have you given this rating?							
Session should be retained	6	5	4	3	2	1	Session should be omitted
Why have you given this rating?							
Learned a lot	6	5	4	3	2	1	Learned little
What have you learned? (rating 6–4)							
Why have you only learned a little? (rating 3–1)							
Confirmed usefully	6	5	4	3	2	1	Confirmed little
Why have you given this rating?							

Figure 13.6   **A justified session reactionnaire**

Logbook reviews

Many activities in training and development programmes have a number of uses – aids to learning, aids to recall, evaluation, encouragement of confidence, learner inter-sharing, and so on. The logbook is valuable in all these aspects of the programme.

A learning log is an instrument in which learners record, during and after a training event, the learning points that have been significant and which they want to recall. For a training event, the logbook consists of an introductory section (see Figure 13.7) followed by a number of sets of three sheets, one set for each day of the training event. A log would normally be contained in a ring-binder with the introductory page and title sheets followed by sets of three sheets for use on the course, the number of sets depending on the number of days of the event – a five-day event would have five sets of three pages.

A LEARNING LOGBOOK

Keeping a learning log

The objective of attending a learning event is to learn something you can use. A complex event can contain a number of ideas, concepts, activities etc. that you might wish to implement at work. It can be difficult, particularly over an extended period, to remember all these ideas, even some of the important ones.

A Learning Log:

- gives you a permanent document in which to record these ideas as they occur
- helps you at a later stage to recall what you have experienced and learned, particularly the key ideas
- helps you to consider at leisure which aspects you want to implement and how
- is a reminder for you about your intentions when you get back to work
- is a permanent record of your progress and development and of what you have learned.

The other notes you have taken and the handouts issued during the training programme are then combined with this log to give you a full record of your training to which you can refer at any time.

Your Learning Log should be completed at stages during the event, preferably during periods allocated for this purpose, or during the evening following the training day. Do not leave its completion any longer than this otherwise some useful and/or important ideas or learning may be lost.

From your ongoing notes section, select the ideas, techniques, suggestions, activities that you feel could be important or significant for you.

In the second section of the log, describe these selections in as much detail as necessary so that you will be able to recall them later.

In the third section, first prioritize your list in the second section and then decide on the following:

- WHAT are you going to do?
- HOW are you going to implement or action it?

- WHEN AND/OR BY WHEN are you going to implement it?
- WHAT resources will you need?
- WHO can or should be involved?
- WHAT implications are there for effects on others?

Continued use of the learning log

On the training programme

At the start of the day following the one for which you have completed your log you will, in a small group, be asked to describe the entries you have made. This presentation will:

- help you to clarify your thoughts on the area presented
- help you in the recall process
- widen the views of the remainder of the group who may not have seen the implications of the areas you have highlighted
- raise the opportunity for clarification of doubtful points.

As a continuous process

A Learning Log is not intended for use only on training programmes. We are learning all the time, in every type of situation and a log can help us to capitalize on these opportunities. If you read a book and there are ideas that you want to remember and implement, enter these in the log. If in discussion with others, ideas are suggested that you feel may be of use to you, remember them and enter them in your log at the first opportunity. Keep referring to your log constantly to remind you of activities that you have not yet implemented.

Your line manager in his/her process of your continuing assessment will not only find your log entries valuable, assessing your development but could be impressed by your intent and persistence.

Remember that if eventually you decide to seek the award of the Training and Development National Vocational Qualification, this record can form a useful part of the portfolio you will need to produce.

Figure 13.7   **The introductory section of a learning logbook**

Set sheet 1 can be used instead of or in addition to any notes that the learner might make during the training day of interesting, useful or significant learning points (see Figure 13.8).

Set sheet 2 is used by the learners to sort and summarize the points from sheet 1 that they particularly want to recall, perhaps adding references to handouts and other information (see Figure 13.9).

Set sheet 3 is a mini-action plan, detailing from sheet 2 entries about learning

DAY ONE

* *

SECTION ONE   SET SHEET 1

RUNNING RECORD OF ITEMS OF WHICH YOU
WISH TO REMIND YOURSELF

xxxxxxxxxxxxxxxxxxxxxxxxxxxxxxxxxxxxxxxxxxxxxxxxxxxxxxxxxxxxxxxxxxxxxxxxxxxxxxxx

Figure 13.8   Set sheet 1 of a Learning Logbook

SECTION TWO   SET SHEET 2

DETAILED DESCRIPTIONS OF YOUR
SELECTED ITEMS

xxxxxxxxxxxxxxxxxxxxxxxxxxxxxxxxxxxxxxxxxxxxxxxxxxxxxxxxxxxxxxxxxxxxxxxxxxxxxxxx

Figure 13.9   Set sheet 2 of a Learning Logbook

that the learner intends to implement and how this action will be taken (see Figure 13.10). The various sheet 3s can be used to formulate a final action plan.

The log is issued at the start of the learning event and set sheets 2 and 3 are completed during the evenings, giving the learners an opportunity to reflect on the events of the day and their significance.

At the start of the following day, allocating about 45 minutes, divide the full learning group into smaller groups of four to six and ask each group to give a short presentation based on their previous evening's log entries. The learners find

---

SET SHEET 3

SECTION THREE

IMPLEMENTATION DECISIONS

xxxxxxxxxxxxxxxxxxxxxxxxxxxxxxxxxxxxxxxxxxxxxxxxxxxxxxxxxxxxxxxxxxxxxxxxxxxxxxxx

---

Figure 13.10   Set sheet 3 of a Learning Logbook

that in addition to consolidating further their learning they are reminded of other learning points by hearing the presentations of their colleagues. At the same time the trainer receives feedback on what has been learned to that stage and can compare this with the anticipated learning from the programme objectives, hence obtaining a continuous review of the training programme.

Chapter 14

Evaluating at the end of the training programme

This chapter:

> describes the most effective methods of validating training and development at the end of the programme
> discusses the use and value of reactionnaires and questionnaires
> describes subjective and self-awareness reviews
> recommends an effective end-of-programme instrument
> discusses effective action planning.

Evaluation at the end of a course, workshop or programme fulfils a number of purposes. It:

- validates the effectiveness of the training and development programme in terms of the satisfaction of the programme objectives and the learners' objectives
- identifies the learning achieved by the learners
- provides a means for the learners to reinforce what they intend to do with the learning they have achieved
- acts as a continuous link between the programme and the learners' implementation of their learning, leading to the improvement in business activity.

Guidelines to end-of-programme validation

Before we progress to the specific forms of validation that can be used with effect, some general guidelines include:

- *Allow sufficient time for the validation to be completed.* Do not, as is all too common, hand out any end-of-programme instruments two or three minutes before the end of the event and ask the learners to fill them in before they leave. Or even worse, hand the learners the instruments as they are actually leaving.

    Part of your design of any end-of-programme instruments will be to assess how long people will take to complete them effectively. This is the minimum time that should be allocated at the end of the training event, and should be part of the programme.

- *KISS.* Keep it short and simple, as far as you can. The longer and more complicated the questionnaires, the less likely you are to receive them realistically completed.

- *Make evaluation important to the learners.* Evaluation is important (especially the learners' part in it) and you can make this clear in your introduction to the period allocated it. Tell the learners what you want them to do, and why; tell them what you will do with the responses and who will see them, or whether there will be an anonymous summary. If it is feasible, and there are few reasons why it should not be, promise the learners a copy of the validation results, for example a summary of the comments made by their learning group and what you are going to do about any problems.

- *Don't try to have an effect on the responses.* Your tests and questionnaires should be so designed that they give no indications of your personal preferences. They should relate to the learning and the training provided for this purpose.

End-of-event validation formats

Satisfaction of the validation requirements of the effectiveness of the training and development programme can be achieved in a number of ways. Many of the evaluation approaches used at the start of and during training programmes can be used at the end of the event. Knowledge tests will normally be repeated in exactly the same form as the beginning or before the event – the hope will always be that the scoring of the second test will be higher than the first, showing that:

- the learning approach was necessary
- the learning approach achieved its objectives.

Tests or assessments of skills at the end of the event will usually continue the initial and progressive assessments made from the observation and review of activities and demonstrations that have taken place during the event, again in the expectation that the learners are performing the skills more effectively and are using the techniques and models suggested to them.

These end-of-event assessments will demonstrate the effectiveness of the learning programme and justify its inclusion in the organization's training budget by acknowledging the skill changes of the learners so that they can progress when they return to work.

Group reviews

Oral and written group reviews were described in Chapter 13 when interim, diurnal and session reviews were considered. These approaches can be replicated as end-of-programme reviews, the group's brief being to review and comment on the event/programme as a whole. The groups can be given an open brief to comment on whatever they feel is significant, or can be posed specific questions.

The group review can be one of the least effective methods as so many aspects can contaminate the responses: end-of-course fatigue or euphoria; thoughts of going home; over-contribution by some members and under- or non-contribution by others; comments selected on the basis of pleasing/displeasing the trainer; and so on. However, occasionally this will be the most relevant method of obtaining validation views and at least there will be a sharing of views with some possible consequent learning.

Reactionnaires

Many programmes include reactionnaires as the end-of-event attempt at validation. The reactionnaire obtains (whether this was intended or not) the reactions, views, feelings and personal opinions of the learners to a range of features of the programme, rather than information about the learning achievements and justification of these responses. The 'happy' or 'happiness' sheet so often referred to in training circles is a poor example of a reactionnaire which is usually biased so that the responses are always in the good to excellent area, or otherwise tend to reflect the euphoria felt at the end of a course.

The typical 'happy' sheet

A typical 'happy' sheet (see Figure 14.1) shows the general nature of the questions in these reviews. Note that the questions are very general, are not separated into types and are selected from those to which good responses are usually obtained. The scales of response are not consistent and the words describing them are designed, even in the worst case, not to be damning. Finally, it is simply a tick-list that can be completed in a minute with little or no consideration of the responses.

More-valid reactionnaires

The valid type of reactionnaire seeks to obtain responses about important aspects of the programme, in particular those that are concerned with the learning. Of course it may be said that questions and responses about the comfort of the hotel, the facilities of the conference centre and how much the participants 'enjoyed' the event, may have an influence on the learning, but they are not concerned with validation of the learning itself. If that information is required, by all means ask relevant questions, but remember that they do not directly concern the validation of the learning and it will be more appropriate to use a separate reactionnaire.

COURSE REACTIONNAIRE

Please consider the following questions and ring the scale number that most closely represents your views.

1. How interesting did you find the course?
   Very   5   4   3   2   1   Not too interesting

2. How much new information did you acquire?
   Quite a lot   5   4   3   2   1   Not too much

3. How would you rate the following:

	Good	Fair	Poor
content of the sessions?	3	2	1
the hotel?	3	2	1
sequence of the sessions?	3	2	1
the trainers?	3	2	1
the seating arrangements?	3	2	1
the videos?	3	2	1
the visual aids?	3	2	1
the course overall?		3	2 1

Figure 14.1   A typical 'happy' sheet reactionnaire

The limitations of reactionnaires

Reactionnaires:
- give only a very limited indication of learning and usually fail either to justify or quantify the amount of learning
- give little indication of the transfer of the learning to the work environment and the likelihood of its implementation
- give no real measure of the extent of the learning, in spite of their tick-boxes and scoring approaches which seem to indicate a mathematically-based approach
- can be completed with little thought, especially if tick-boxes alone are provided
- provide at most an impression of what the learners *think* they have learned.

The value of reactionnaires

Reactionnaires are generally subjective, rough and ready means of obtaining feedback from a programme's participants, but:

- if responses are favourable, they can provide useful material for programme publicity by the use of the quasi-arithmetical analyses

- they provide information about the subjective views of the learners, perhaps the highest level of views that can be obtained for a particular programme

- they can provide a warning signal where something has gone badly wrong in a programme

- if broad objectives have been stated at the beginning of the programme, the broad brush of the reactionnaire can be used to test the satisfaction of these objectives

- they give responses to questions seeking useful reactive data – how effectively the training need was identified; whether there was a pre-course briefing and views on its effectiveness; environmental factors that worked against full learning during the event; programme design that the learners could identify as unhelpful; the acceptability or otherwise (as opposed to value) of the learning methods used; and so on.

The value of a reactionnaire increases if it is improved beyond the simple tick-list, so that the learners can justify their scorings, comment fully on their scorings, compare and contrast levels of information, and so on. Unfortunately, on too many occasions, a tick-list happiness sheet is accepted as realistic validation of a programme if it supports the programme, but decried as subjective if it doesn't!

Subjective reactionnaires

Fully objective approaches are not always possible and reliance sometimes has to be placed on subjective measures of learning. Such an event would be, for example, an interpersonal skills training programme in which the learning changes are attitudinal, subjective and difficult to identify objectively. It may be that obtaining reactions or even feelings is the only method possible – if this is so, do not decry the subjectivity of the approach; it's all you have and you will obtain some information. Figure 14.2 demonstrates an example of this 'feelings review' questionnaire used at the end of an interpersonal skills programme during which 'feelings' have been the main approach and in which the emphasis has been on behavioural change. The latter can be observed and recorded by behavioural analysis methods described earlier, but even these are based on what must be a subjective and controversial model.

Self-awareness reviews

Continuing the theme of the more subjective form of end-of-event reviews, although taking one step nearer to objectivity, is a return to the three-test approach. This was introduced in Chapter 12 as one of the start-of-programme approaches and as an alternative to the traditional pre/post-test. If inclusion of this 'test' has been planned for the start of the programme, using the questionnaire

INTERPERSONAL SKILLS REVIEW

1.   The main feeling I have about this learning event is ...

2.   If this course had been a film, a play or a book, the title would have been ...

3.   The part(s) of the event I enjoyed most ...

4.   The part(s) of the experience I can make most use of ...

5.   Something I learned, or had strongly confirmed about myself is ...

6.   Something I learned or had usefully confirmed about other people is ...

7.   The part(s) of the event that I enjoyed the least was (were) ...

8.   The part(s) of the event from which I learned the least was (were) ...

9.   The part(s) of the event I can make least use of is (are) ...

10.   If I were starting this event again I would ...

11.   One thing I regret having done is ...

12.   One thing I regret not having done is ...

13.   I would/would not attend another event of this nature

14.   Right now I am feeling ...

Figure 14.2   Feelings review reactionnaire

in Figure 12.3, it is relevant to repeat it at the end of the event, using the same questionnaire. As a result we appear to have a 'what I felt I knew then' and a 'what I feel I know now' comparison. The words 'appear to have' are used, because the comparison is not necessarily, and usually not, valid.

Self-assessment in practice

If a self-assessment reactionnaire such as Figure 12.3 is used for the pre-test instrument, it might include a question about the learner's awareness of their communication skills in writing:

	High								Low
4. How well do you communicate in writing?	10 9	(8)	7	6	5	4	3	2	1

At the start of the course the self-assessment might be at the scale point 8, the learner describing him/herself as very, although not completely, aware of their failings and their modification needs.

The same test instrument is used at the end of the course in an attempt to 'measure' the changes that the learner was able to self-assess. On this occasion, the learner might give a rating of 9, indicating that his/her awareness had increased during the course and that now, although not complete, is very significant. Taking into account that comparison is subjective and not strictly arithmetical, it suggests that there has been an increase in awareness of about 10 per cent. This is not exceptional bearing in mind the training and learning opportunities offered, but if you look back at the pre-test the initial scoring was 8, a not insubstantial level of awareness. But the subjectivity and self-assessment raise suspicions about the initial assessment in particular. To what extent was there any self-delusion in this initial statement? The suspicion might be supported by the facilitator's observations during the event and the more objective evidence of behaviour analysis.

The three-test extended

Completion of the self-awareness questionnaire a third time, immediately following the second completion, will make it possible to assess more accurately the amount of change. It is helpful to the learners if a comment is made on the possible contaminatory aspects introduced by self-awareness and that this is an attempt to determine the real level of change. On this third occasion the learners are asked to complete the reactionnaire *'as if they were doing so at the start of the programme, but with their current perception of their skills'* - in other words, knowing what they know now.

The results of this third completion can fall within a wide range, depending on the awareness of the learners at both the start and finish of the programme, their level of self-deception or self-delusion, and so on. For example, the learner who has previously rated 8 then 9, now rates the awareness score on the third completion for this question as 3. This considerably lower revised starting score may be a truer estimate of their skill at that pre-training stage. As a result, the percentage learning change (from 3 to 9) is an increase of 60 per cent, a much more worthwhile value for expensive training and a realistic validation of the content. Some learners may even revise their initial awareness to 1 or 2, the increase to 9 representing a substantial change over the training programme and an indication of its true value and validity.

Anomalies can become evident in the three tests and these apparent (or real) anomalies need to be examined by the learner and the trainer before the real reasons can be considered, rather than the ones assumed by, say, a *drop* in skill rating. Other changes may need to be queried, and compared with, say, behaviour analyses to ensure that the full picture emerges. This type of analysis and comparison can require a substantial amount of time which must be included in the planning.

The three-test produces more realistic (not necessarily 'better') results than the pre/post-test and compares well with other assessments, such as behaviour analyses made during the programme. However, the method is still sensitive to subjective treatment, which of course is found in any form of self-assessment other than direct, practical testing.

Effective evaluation

Where objective evaluation measures can be achieved, they must be introduced at the end of the programme, bearing in mind the guidelines suggested at the start of this chapter. The two types of evaluation used for this purpose are:

- justified evaluation learning questionnaires
- action planning.

Justified evaluation learning questionnaires

My concept of an 'evaluation questionnaire' is an instrument that concentrates on validating the training programme methods and objectives and the learners' objectives by investigating the learning achieved and the learners' intentions of implementing this learning back at work.

Further, it is an instrument that defines the amount and range of *learning* achieved by a learner within a training programme, and also identifies the reasons why (some) learning did not occur. Notice that the emphasis all the time is on the *learning* – this is what training, in whatever form, is all about. A properly-constructed and administered questionnaire should be able to stand up to scrutiny and answer the basic question that will be posed by an interested senior and line management: 'Am I getting my money's worth from your training? Prove it!'.

Recommended questionnaires

Some people may disagree with this concentration on learning and feel that other, perhaps wider questions, should be posed. If this is what is required, a well-constructed reactionnaire could supplement the questionnaire. This approach will provide information, but the basic requirement of *validation* and *evaluation* must remain the assessment of *learning*.

Planning the questionnaire format

When planning an end-of-event evaluation questionnaire there are a number of construction criteria that must be considered.

The semantic differential questionnaire
Most validation questionnaires are of the semantic differential type. The basic part of the questionnaire is a scoring bar or row of boxes between a set of opposite, polarized descriptions which are different semantically and are usually in the form of antonyms. An example of the simplest SDQ is:

How hard did you work today?

Very hard_____**Not at all hard**

Of course this simple use of two polarized statements is not sufficiently sensitive to shades of meaning and usually the score bar is divided into sections, for example:

Very hard |__|__|__|__|__|__|__|__|__| **Not at all hard**

Very hard   ☐ ☐ ☐ ☐ ☐ ☐ ☐ ☐ ☐   **Not at all hard**

Very hard   9   8   7   6   5   4   3   2   1   **Not at all hard**

In the first two examples, the learners are asked to place a tick or cross in the space or box the position of which away from the poles represents closest their views. In the numbered example, a circle is placed around the relevant number or a stroke marked through it.

Score identification
In some scoring bars with spaces or boxes, the bars are left as shown above; in others, numbers are placed above them to identify the discrete position of the scoring tick. In this way the tick position on each scoring bar used can be used arithmetically to analyse the results of the questionnaire. Some questionnaire designers argue that the use of numbers gives the incorrect impression that the analysis is a mathematically valid calculation, whereas this is not the case in such a subjective and arbitrary area.

Scale anchors
Each end of the scoring scale is anchored by a word or short phrase, antonyms being used to provide the semantic differential. The necessity to use suitable words has already been mentioned. Other anchor factors can determine the value of the scale. A consistent approach to placing the anchors should be followed – to avoid confusion and/or unconsidered completion of the scales, the 'good/very' and 'bad/not at all' anchors should be placed in the same position for all the scales. Use the positioning consistently to avoid errors or confusion.

Scale scoring positions
The scale scoring position is probably the most discussed, unresolved aspect of questionnaire construction. Two questions are raised:

● Should there be an even or odd number of score positions?
● How many score positions should be offered?

The principal argument against an odd number of rating positions is that there will always be a mid-number which will be viewed by many completers as the 'average' scoring, and they will use it to avoid having to give a definite response. The supporters of the odd-numbered scale suggest that instruction in its completion should be given to the learners, to encourage them to think more deeply about their score and use the mid-position only if it is appropriate.

Number of scale points

Questionnaire constructors can be torn between a minimum number of scorings entries on the basis that this increases the chance of the learners completing it effectively rather than having to produce what the learners might see as an over-imposing document. On the other hand, a simpler scoring scale will not allow people to define their views as accurately as they might wish.

At the simplest, the rating scale contains two scoring possibilities – 1 or 2 – corresponding to the Yes/No or the Agree/Disagree of the knowledge tests. The number of stages you feel can be identified without too much trouble will determine the number of rating points above two. Too long a scale can confuse the completer who might be tempted, because of too many doubts about the fine details, to place the scoring marks in a haphazard way, concentrating about the central areas. The three-test described previously has a ten-point scale, but this version is used in a particular situation and normally ten points might be too much to ask the completers to use in defining their views.

In most cases a six-point scale gives sufficient latitude but does not confuse. However, eight points also seems to be quite acceptable.

Questions to ask

Any questions posed in an evaluation questionnaire must relate to the purpose of the evaluation, namely the assessment of achievement of the training programme's objective and methods, and the satisfaction of the learners' objectives – that is to say, the extent of the *learning*. For example:

- How much have you learned?
- What have you learned?
- If you haven't learned in all aspects, why not?

Answers to these questions should be sufficient to validate the learning. Some of this information – the extent of learning – will be obtained from a scoring scale:

During the programme, how much have you learned?
A lot   6   5   4   3   2   1   **A little**

In programmes where earlier assessments have shown a wide variety of knowledge and skill within the learning group, it may also be necessary to ask:

During the programme, how much have you usefully confirmed?
A lot   6   5   4   3   2   1   **A little**

Justification

The scales do not tell you everything you need to know. Full validation will require information on:

- what has been learned
- what is going to be done with that learning
- why learning hasn't occurred.

Completers of questionnaires should be asked to justify their ratings, both good and bad. This is achieved by adding, after the rating scale, questions that seek responses to the information requested above. Ask the learners, if they have given a 'good' rating to learning, to state what they have learned, and also what they are going to do with that learning. If they have given a 'bad' rating, ask them for the full reasons why they have given this rating.

The inclusion of a specifically-designed reactionnaire has been mentioned earlier and this can be added to the justified questionnaire on particular occasions. You may want to use this additional sheet:

- when a new programme is starting
- at the mid-point in an extended programme
- if there have been substantial changes in a programme
- when there are indications that all is not going correctly.

The 'reaction' questions can reflect these reasons.

Figure 14.3 is an example of this recommended form of end-of-programme validation questionnaire, with a supporting, additional reactionnaire.

Action planning

Although action planning is not a direct form of validation or assessment, it is

---

END-OF-PROGRAMME VALIDATION QUESTIONNAIRE

Please consider the learning programme that you have attended and complete the following, being completely honest in your assessments and answering the questions as fully as possible.

PART ONE: LEARNING

To what extent do you feel you have learned from the programme? (Please ring the score number that you feel most closely represents your views.)

Learned a lot   6   5   4   3   2   1   Learned nothing

If you have rated 6, 5 or 4, please describe (a) what you have learned, and (b) what you intend to do with this learning on your return to work.

If you have rated 3, 2 or 1, please state as fully as possible the reasons why you gave this rating.

PART TWO: CONFIRMATION OF LEARNING

To what extent do you feel you have had previous learning (perhaps some you have forgotten) confirmed in a useful manner?

Confirmed a lot   6   5   4   3   2   1   Confirmed little

If you have rated 6, 5 or 4, please describe (a) what has been confirmed, and (b) what you intend to do with this learning on your return to work.

If you have rated 3, 2 or 1, please state as fully as possible the reasons why you gave this rating.

PART THREE: ADDITIONAL INFORMATION (Alternative 1)

For every item, place an 'X' in the scoring box that most closely represents how you feel about the programme. Please comment briefly on each item about your reasons for giving this score, particularly if your scorings are 3, 2 or 1.

	6	5	4	3	2	1	
Stimulating Please comment briefly why you have given this score	☐	☐	☐	☐	☐	☐	Boring
Useful for my work Please comment briefly why you have given this score	☐	☐	☐	☐	☐	☐	Useless
Relevant to my work Please comment briefly why you have given this score	☐	☐	☐	☐	☐	☐	Irrelevant
Good discussions Please comment briefly why you have given this score	☐	☐	☐	☐	☐	☐	Limited discussions
Flexible Please comment briefly why you have given this score	☐	☐	☐	☐	☐	☐	Rigid structure
Well conducted Please comment briefly why you have given this score	☐	☐	☐	☐	☐	☐	Poorly conducted
Demanding Please comment briefly why you have given this score	☐	☐	☐	☐	☐	☐	Undemanding
Challenging Please comment briefly why you have given this score	☐	☐	☐	☐	☐	☐	Patronizing
Well spaced out Please comment briefly why you have given this score	☐	☐	☐	☐	☐	☐	Too condensed
Coherent Please comment briefly why you have given this score	☐	☐	☐	☐	☐	☐	Fragmented
My objectives achieved Please comment briefly why you have given this score	☐	☐	☐	☐	☐	☐	Objectives not achieved

Good level of activity	☐ ☐ ☐ ☐ ☐ ☐	Poor level
Please comment briefly why you have given this score		of activity

Good use of time	☐ ☐ ☐ ☐ ☐ ☐	Poor use of time
Please comment briefly why you have given this score		

I would recommend the programme to my colleagues   YES ☐   NO ☐
Any other comments

PART THREE: ADDITIONAL INFORMATION (Alternative 2)

1. Which parts of the event did you find most useful?
2. Which parts of the event did you find least useful?
3. Are there any parts you would have omitted? If so, which and why?
4. Is there anything you would have liked to have seen added to the event? What should have been removed to make room for it?
5. Which of your personal objectives were satisfied?
6. Which of your personal objectives were not satisfied?
7. Have you any other comments you wish to make?

Name...
Date....................................

Figure 14.3   End-of-programme validation questionnaire
(In reproducing this questionnaire for use, leave sufficient space between items to permit all the comments the learners would wish to make.)

such a powerful tool with a range of uses, that it must be considered as a key part of evaluation. *In fact, if no other evaluation tool can be used or is available, the action plan must be used, hopefully with the opportunity for follow-up at a later date.*

Consequently, I would recommend that planning for *every* training and learning programme includes closure with an action plan.

The action plan is a commitment by the learners to implement, when they return to work, the learning they have achieved and identified in the end-of-programme validation. Items included in the plan will be learning points taken from the programme, and the results will show whether the intended objectives of the programme have been understood and accepted. Variation between the action plans of the learners is natural and some, by their inclusions or exclusions, may indicate particularly good or bad aspects of the programme.

The action plan is one of the most effective instruments for strengthening the links between training and work. The simple act of planning action based on the learning immediately relates the learners to their working environment. If the action plan is used by the learner in the implementation of the learning, and by their managers in performing longer-term evaluation and control of implementation, no forced or artificial links are necessary. It becomes part of the work ⇨ training/learning ⇨ work-integrated cycle.

An action plan format

A good action plan:

- is simple and straightforward
- is clear and unambiguous
- contains items that can be implemented by the learner, with or without other resources
- is owned by the learner
- contains specific information that is time-bounded for implementation.

Figure 14.4 suggests a simple format for the action plan, leading the learners in only three headings and leaving them to decide on the detail and amount of planning to include. The number of action items should not be too many, three or four is reasonable. In the 'How to' column, the learner should consider materials, resources etc. that might be needed. The plans should always be time-bounded with a starting/finishing commitment or a start-by time.

Producing the action plan

1. The action plan should follow the justified end-of-programme validation questionnaire in which the learners identify and reflect on what they have learned and what they wish to do with this learning. (If a Learning Log has been used, this will also prove useful in reminding them of lessons learned.)

PERSONAL ACTION PLAN

ACTION PLAN ITEMS	HOW TO IMPLEMENT	WHEN, BY WHEN
1.		
2.		
3.		
4.		

Figure 14.4   **Action plan format**

2. Give ample time for the learners to consider:
    - their personal action objectives
    - priorities among these objectives.

3. The learners complete their action plans, taking special note of:
    - the implementability of their plans
    - what materials and other resources (including people) they might need
    - the time factors involved
    - strategies and tactics for implementing the plans
    - the effect of their plans on others
    - any possible obstacles to implementation
    - any special factors that will help their implementation.

4. Once the learners have identified their planned items, it is useful for them to prioritize the items, rather than taking them as they thought of them, or implementing first the least important (often the simplest) items.

5. Planning for the programme could allow time for the learners to pair off so that they can enter into one-to-one discussions with a partner of their choice.

6. Ask the learners to commit themselves to implementing their plan by discussing it with their line manager immediately on return (hopefully a post-programme debriefing session has been arranged).

7. Agree, if possible without the presence of the line manager, how the implementation will be monitored and by whom.

8. The trainer might find it useful to keep a copy of the action plan, with the learner's agreement, to help in the medium- and longer-term evaluation processes.

Chapter 15

Evaluating after the training programme

This chapter:

>   describes the evaluation action to be taken after the programme to ensure 'value for money'
>   details the types of medium- and long-term evaluation methods
>   discusses approaches to analysing the cost and value effectiveness of training.

Learning and the application of training does not stop at the end of the programme with the production of an action plan. Training and learning are concerned with change – the improvement of the business at the bottom line – and change is the practical demonstration of training and learning in the workplace. The best planned and designed training will never be more than an expensive interesting exercise if what has been learned is not put into action in the work environment. The planning of the training programme must include at least the outline introduction of medium- and longer-term evaluation.

The cardinal responsibility for post-programme implementation lies with the line manager, who selected the training, paid for it and will expect a return on the investment. Naturally, trainers will retain an interest in the results of their labours long after the event, even if they play no practical part in a follow-up. However, as members of the training quintet, they can strengthen the links by continuing their involvement.

Medium/Longer-term evaluation methods

The final stages in the evaluation process are assessment of the extent to which the training has been implemented effectively and has had a positive effect on the work of the organization. The first post-programme action is putting into practice the items of the action plan as a minimum objective, preferably with the active and continuing support of the line manager. Subsequent to this, the assessments can be made after an interval of, say, three months – the medium-term evaluation – and then/or at a longer interval of twelve months – the longer-term evaluation.

Provided that the outline agreement to post-programme evaluation has been made, working out of the details of how this should be done is not urgent at the initial planning stage, but obviously must be completed as soon as possible.

Post-programme evaluation can be made by:

- line manager observation and assessment of the performed activities
- trainer observation and assessment of the performed activities
- follow-up questionnaire sent to both the learners and their line manager
- structured interview conducted by the line manager or trainer
- telephone follow-up interview by the trainer
- critical incident analysis
- Learning Logs
- repertory grid.

Line manager or trainer observation and assessment of the performed activities

Observation at work must be the most effective method of evaluating the learning and confirming its performance. The observation technique will depend on whether it is an operational task, a behavioural role, or a mixture of both. Activity and behaviour analysis instruments such as those described earlier can be used according to the training applications.

The line manager can make such observations within the routine of the daily work, perhaps with some special efforts to observe particular, possibly infrequent, elements of the task. A record can be maintained of observations made and to be made, so introducing a discipline that ensures that the practice is carried out. Otherwise it is too easy to allow the follow-up to fall by default.

The manager cannot always afford the time to carry out the observation. Or, as often happens, the line manager is not in a practical position to observe the learner. An agreement might be reached with the training organization for observation support or to carry out the observations in lieu of the manager. However, using the trainer for post-programme observation is not desirable because the trainer may be seen as an observer whereas the manager becomes part of the scenery.

One approach that is effective in both practice and the saving of expensive time in some cases is *activity sampling* in which the observer spreads the observing periods over time – hours, days, even weeks – ensuring that all aspects are seen and assessed. In some circumstances this may be the only possible approach.

The follow-up questionnaire

The follow-up questionnaire is probably the most frequently used of all longer-term evaluation approaches, is the simplest and also the least expensive, but it is not necessarily the most effective. The questionnaire must be planned to obtain comprehensive and objective responses and there must be an effective method of ensuring that responses are made and questionnaires returned.

The follow-up questionnaire is based on the learners' action plans and the key objective is to determine to what extent the action plans have been implemented and with what effectiveness. A secondary objective might be post-programme consideration of the training course where care must be taken to include only the minimum number of questions. Too many may complicate the questionnaire to the extent that the real reason for its use is not fulfilled.

Construction of follow-up questionnaires

The objectives in the construction of the questionnaire include:

- confirmation of the learning achieved during the training programme
- action taken to implement the action plan
- assessment of the effectiveness of the learning implementation.

To achieve these objectives questions include:

- Which items of the action plan have been implemented?
- What degree of success has been achieved from this?
- Which items have not (yet) been implemented?
- What are the reasons for their non-implementation?
- Did any planned actions fail in implementation?
- What reasons emerged for their failure?
- What are the plans for further action:
  - on unsuccessful or non-implemented plans?
  - beyond this stage?

If you have newly instituted a scheme whereby the line managers are more involved in training and evaluation further questions might be added to this innovation. These will be about:

- the nature of the debriefing meeting and its outcomes
- the support promised and received from the manager
- the support arranged and received from colleagues
- the extent of the value of post-programme support.

Figure 15.1 suggests a questionnaire in this format.

One of the arguments against the use of the validation questionnaires immediately at the end of the course, is that the learners may not be in a position or mood to give a full and reflected response. The medium-term evaluation approach can be an opportunity to seek more reflected views about the training if it is felt that the immediate ones were contaminated in some way and an additional questionnaire can also be sent.

If you decide to extend the range of the approach, a questionnaire such as that shown in Figure 15.2 can be used.

MEDIUM-TERM EVALUATION ACTION QUESTIONNAIRE

COURSE ATTENDED..DATES..............................

PART ONE: When you completed the training programme, you contracted to implement an action plan which detailed the following items:

1.
2.
3. etc.

Would you please answer the following questions as completely as you can.

1. Which items of your action plan have you implemented so far?
2. What degree of success have you achieved in respect of these items?
3. To what factors or reasons do you attribute your success in implementing these items?
4. Which items of your action plan have you not yet implemented?
5. Which of these items have you tried but failed to implement?
6. Why did this occur?
7. Which items have you not yet attempted to implement?
8. Why have you not yet attempted these?
9. What plans do you have to:
       attempt to rectify your unsuccessful items?
       implement the as yet unattempted items?
10. Have you any additional plans? Please comment.

PART TWO: It will help our organization of training and the involvement of different people if you could answer the following questions, the responses to which will be confidential.

Did you have a debriefing meeting with your manager on your return to work?
If so, how quickly after the course did this take place?
What was the nature of the debriefing meeting and its outcomes?
What was the extent of the support promised by your manager?
What was the extent of the support received from your manager?
What was the extent of any support arranged with colleagues?
What was the extent of any support received from colleagues?
How valuable do you feel was the post-programme support?
Any other comments you wish to make?

Figure 15.1   Medium- and longer-term evaluation questionnaire
(In reproducing this questionnaire for use, leave sufficient space between items to permit all the comments the learners would wish to make.)

COURSE ATTENDED...DATES...................................

Now that some time has passed, please consider the learning programme that you attended and complete the following, being completely honest in your assessments and answering the questions as fully as possible.

PART ONE: LEARNING

To what extent do you feel you learned from the programme? (Please ring the score number that you feel most closely represents your views.)

Learned a lot   6   5   4   3   2   1   Learned nothing

If you have rated 6, 5 or 4, please describe what you learned.

If you have rated 3, 2 or 1, please state as fully as possible the reasons why you gave this rating.

PART TWO: CONFIRMATION OF LEARNING

To what extent do you feel you have had previous learning (perhaps some you have forgotten) confirmed in a useful manner?

Confirmed a lot   6   5   4   3   2   1   Confirmed little

If you have rated 6, 5 or 4, please describe (a) what has been confirmed, and (b) what you intend to do with this learning on your return to work.

If you have rated 3, 2 or 1, please state as fully as possible the reasons why you gave this rating.

Figure 15.2   Post-programme learning questionnaire
(In reproducing this questionnaire for use, leave sufficient space between items to permit all the comments the learners would wish to make.)

Follow-up with the line manager

You may wish to involve the manager in the evaluation when using the questionnaire method and it can be useful to inform them of the progress of the evaluation by sending the questionnaire through them. In such cases it can be politic to ask for the questionnaire to be returned direct to the originator to avoid inhibition in the responses of the learners.

The other method of involving the line manager in this first stage of post-programme evaluation is to send them a progress questionnaire (see Figure 15.3) at the same time as the one sent to the learners. With the learners' agreement, it would include a copy of the action plan.

When you are planning and designing your medium- and longer-term questionnaires, ask yourself the following:

COURSE REVIEWED...
DATES............................

PART ONE: When ....completed the training programme, they contracted to implement an action plan which detailed the following items:

1.
2.
3. etc.

Would you please answer the following questions as completely as you can from your own knowledge or observation.

1. Which items of the action plan do you know that they have implemented so far?
2. What degree of success have they achieved in respect of these items?
3. To what factors or reasons do you attribute their success in implementing these items?
4. Which items of the action plan have they not yet implemented?
5. Which of these items have they tried but failed to implement?
6. Why did this occur?
7. Which items have they not yet attempted to implement?
8. Why have they not been attempted?
9. What plans have you discussed with the learner to:
    attempt to rectify the unsuccessful items?
    implement the as yet unattempted items?
10. Have you any other comments?

PART TWO: It will help our organization of training and the involvement of different people if you could answer the following questions.

Did you have a debriefing meeting with the learner on their return to work?
If so, how quickly after the course did this take place?
What was the nature of the debriefing meeting and its outcomes?
What was the extent of the support you promised?
What was the extent of the support you gave?
What was the extent of any support arranged with colleagues?
What was the extent of any support received from colleagues?
How valuable do you feel were the post-programme interactions?
Any other comments you wish to make?

Figure 15.3   Medium-term evaluation questionnaire (line manager version)
(In reproducing this questionnaire for use, leave sufficient space between items to permit all the comments the learners would wish to make.)

- What do I want to know that will form part of a realistic evaluation? (normally this will relate directly to the action plan completed by the learner)
- What form of questionnaire will be the most effective?
- How can I ensure that the line managers' responses will be based on observation or specific knowledge?
- How can I ensure a satisfactory (complete) rate of return?

Structured follow-up interviews

The other main method of performing a medium- and longer-term evaluation is by follow-up interview. Interviews are usually more expensive than questionnaires, particularly if the learners are located throughout the country, or internationally. Many of the cost problems can be avoided if the line manager conducts the interview rather than a remote trainer, but you must be assured that the line manager is not too 'close' to the learner, and has the necessary skills to conduct effective interviews.

The interview approach

The interview is based closely on the follow-up questionnaire, with the important points being:

- What do I want to know that will form part of a realistic evaluation? (normally this will relate directly to the action plan completed by the learner)
- What form of interview will be the most effective?
- Who is the most appropriate person to conduct the interview?
- Is the interview approach the most (cost-) effective one?

The interview consists of a discussion between the interviewer and the learner, and separately with the line manager, and the format must be the same. In this way, in addition to obtaining information, valid comparisons can be made between the reactions of learners.

Interview structures

The structure of the interview will depend on the circumstances prevailing, but a general, consistent structure should be used. Use the same questions for any follow-up of a similar group and, wherever possible, the same words. But the interviewer should avoid making the interview so inflexible that other subjects are not allowed to enter the discussion or the interviewer misses valuable clues by concentrating on the narrow path.

Although groups of interviews will differ because of the different circumstances, Figure 15.4 summarizes the format you might follow.

FORMAT OF STRUCTURED FOLLOW-UP EVALUATION INTERVIEW

1. Describe the reasons for, purpose and objectives of the interview concerned with the '*x*' training programme that the learner had followed some three months earlier.

2. Referring to the action plan ask:

    (a) Which items of the action plan have been implemented so far?
    (b) What degree of success has been achieved in respect of these items?
    (c) To what factors or reasons is the success in implementing these items attributed?
    (d) Which items of the action plan have not yet been implemented?
    (e) Which of these items have been tried but couldn't be implemented?
    (f) Why did this occur?
    (g) Which items have not yet been attempted?
    (h) Why have they not been attempted?
    (i) What plans does the learner have to:
         attempt to rectify unsuccessful items?
         implement the as yet unattempted items?
    (j) Are there any additional plans? If so, obtain similar comments or full details.

3. Seek other comments relating to the action plan, particularly about any other learning achieved.

4. Seek general comments about the training programme now that the learner has had time to reflect:

    (a) Which parts of the event were found to be the most useful?
    (b) Which parts of the event were found to be the least useful?
    (c) Are there any parts that should have been omitted? If so, which parts and why?
    (d) Is there anything that should have been added to the event? What should have been removed to make room for it?
    (e) Which personal objectives were satisfied?
    (f) Which personal objectives were not satisfied?
    (g) Any other comments?

5. Seek comments about the follow-up procedure and its outcomes. Confidentiality of responses and comments must be stressed and adhered to:

    (a) Was a debriefing meeting with the manager held on return to work?
    (b) If so, how quickly after the course did this take place?
    (c) What was the nature of the debriefing meeting and its outcomes?
    (d) What was the extent of the support promised by the manager?
    (e) What was the extent of the support received from the manager?
    (f) What was the extent of any support arranged with colleagues?
    (g) What was the extent of any support received from colleagues?
    h) How valuable was the post-programme support felt to be?
    (i) Any other comments?

Figure 15.4   **Format of structured follow-up evaluation interview**

Telephone follow-up interview

Follow-up by telephone is an extension of the face-to-face interview approach and is a way of reducing costs yet still maintain the advantages of the interview. The time and cost are still obviously greater than using the questionnaire follow-up, but less than the face-to-face interview. The interview can suffer to some degree, depending on the skills of the interviewer, by the absence of face-to-face interaction and possible reduction of rapport, and the interviewee may not give it the same depth of attention.

The telephone interview follows the same pattern as the structured, face-to-face interview with a planned pattern of appropriate questions the responses to which can be clarified or followed up to a greater depth.

Arrangements for the telephone interview may need to be more strictly controlled than for the face-to-face event:

- A telephone appointment must be made beforehand to ensure availability of the interviewee and to give them time for preparation.
- The interviewee must guarantee (as far as possible) that there will be no interruptions while the interview is taking place – the same as for the face-to-face event.
- The interviewee must be in a private environment so that there are no inhibitions about what might be said.
- The interviewer must ensure that the questions are posed clearly and that the listener has heard and understood them.
- Cost must be understood so that this does not become a factor in the pace of the interview.
- The interviewer must be aware that some people are unable to be as natural when using the phone as when in a face-to-face situation.

Long-distance telephone/television conferences facilities can also be considered although this approach is not used frequently. Or, by using modern IT methods, the interview might be conducted over local networked computer facilities or over the Internet.

Critical incident analysis

Critical incident analysis used in the medium/longer-term review is usually a self-reporting exercise, although interviews or even group discussion can be held. The normal approach is with the use of diaries, followed by an analysis of the critical incidents that these documents show.

The learners keep a diary in which they write down critical incidents soon after they occur, particularly those relating to the learning area being evaluated, and the learners then reflect on these incidents and make simple judgements about them – when they happened, how they happened, why they happened, and what learning can be extracted from them.

The critical incidents recorded are then analysed by:

- an extraction and consideration by the learner of relevant incidents

- a meeting with the line manager or a trainer who assists in the extraction, discussion and interpretation of relevant incidents
- a group discussion during which the critical incidents are compared, discussed and analysed.

How long a diary should be maintained will depend on the complexity of the learning, the occurrence and frequency of the incidents, coverage of a range of

---

A CRITICAL INCIDENT DIARY

DATE......................................
DIARY SHEET NUMBER.............................

Include in this diary what you consider as critical incidents concerned with your work and your relationships with your colleagues, particularly those relating to the learning you have achieved from the training programme .... , although you need not restrict yourself to this area. Include incidents of both a satisfactory and unsatisfactory nature.

1. What happened; how did it happen; when did it happen; who was involved; and why did it happen?
2. What was the outcome of the incident? Was it satisfactory or unsatisfactory?
3. Who or what was responsible for this outcome?
4. If the outcome was satisfactory, what have you learned from the processes that made it so?
5. If it was unsatisfactory, what made it so and what can you learn from this?
6. Was the incident relevant to the training you followed? If so, did the training help you to cope with the incident? To what extent?
7. Did the incident expose any further training needs you might have?

Figure 15.5   A critical incident diary

similar but not exactly the same incidents, and so on. The format of the diary is not critical, as long as the learner records and can identify the relevant material and incidents. Guidance can be given to the learner about effective approaches and Figure 15.5 shows a suggested format.

Learning logs

Learning logbooks were described in Chapter 13 as instruments designed to help the learners remember, recall, share and reinforce their learning during the training programme. They can become part of the learner's continuing professional development after the formal programme and, as such, valuable post-programme evaluation tools.

At the end of a training programme during which learning logs have been completed, used for review and accepted as useful instruments, learners should be encouraged to carry on using the logs as a record of their continuous learning and development. Incidents from which they have learned something are entered in the continuing log with comments and form an effective action plan. These entries and plans can be considered at an evaluation review, perhaps accompanying other approaches, as helpful indicators of the implementation and continuation of their learning in much the same way as the critical incident diary was used.

Repertory grid

The repertory grid is an instrument with many uses, including evaluation. It is, however, a complex, complicated and time-consuming technique and its application in evaluation, apart from perhaps in research, is rare. In order to obtain the maximum benefit from its use, the practitioner must preferably be trained and certainly experienced in the technique. Mention of it is included here for the sake of completeness.

The basis of a repertory grid is the comparison of effective and ineffective behaviours and behaviour analysis, based on an acceptable model, can be more effective. The technique is derived from the personal construct work (each person's unique framework for understanding the world) of George Kelly.

Long-term evaluation

The proof of effective training and development and its consolidation into the work, with beneficial effects on the business, is its ability to stand the test of time. Learning and its implementation do not necessarily remain over a long period, even if they are relevant. Learners can forget the techniques and methods learned, or slip back to the pre-training state of 'unconscious incompetence'.

Long-term evaluation is carried out (when it is part of the evaluation process) between nine months and a year following the end of the training programme. The approaches used for the earlier, medium-term stage apply equally at this time, namely a concentration on the long-term implementation of the learning, in particular the items included on the action plan and the continuing positive effect on business achievement.

The evaluation may be carried out by either the line manager or, perhaps if the medium-term evaluation was performed by the trainer, by face-to-face visit or telephone interview, again by the trainer. If everything seems to be well and the learning is still being implemented (if appropriate), the evaluation process for this training series can be ended. Otherwise the cycle will need to start again, perhaps even as far back as the initial TNIA.

Is it worth it?

The longer-term evaluation completes the practical evaluation process and the planned training process, but there is still the question of the value-effectiveness of the training to the organization – is it worth it? Some assessment of value-effectiveness can be included in the early part of the planning – How much will the training cost? Have we a budget to cover this cost? Does the budget place cost limits on the training? And so on. The wider aspects of value-effectiveness will only be known when the training has taken place and the medium- and long-term evaluations have been performed. However, both intentions to cover the full range of value-effectiveness should be considered at the relevant stages of planning.

Cost-effectiveness

This is the relatively simple part of value effectiveness calculations. The costing of training programmes consists of cost inputs and outputs. The key headings in cost inputs are:

- fixed capital costs
- maintenance or working capital costs
- administrative costs
- trainer costs
- direct training costs
- external agent costs
- trainee costs.

They give the planner information about:

- How many trainers must be employed to perform the training required?
- How much does a trainer cost?
- What is the total cost of the training to the organization?
- What is the cost of a training day? How many training days can the organization afford?
- What is the comparable cost of an open learning package and can the organization afford the requisite number of packages?
- What is the cost of training in relation to production or provision of services costs?
- Is the training worth the expenditure?

Fixed capital costs

Fixed capital costs include the running of the parts of the organization's building(s) that can be fully or partly attributable to training purposes.

Maintenance or working capital costs

Maintenance or working capital costs include:

- consumables, e.g. stationery
- routine maintenance and repair contracts
- other materials used during the training by trainers and trainees.

Administrative costs

Administrative costs include:

- cleaning costs
- support service staff accommodation, materials and salaries attributable to training-related duties
- telephone, electricity, gas etc. charges attributable to the training function
- computer time charges where appropriate.

Trainer costs

Trainer costs, which are usually expensive, include;

- costs of employing a training manager, where relevant, or apportioned costs, and the part attributable costs of more senior managers with some role responsibility for the training function
- trainer/programme designers' and writers' salaries and expenses, whether or not they are engaged on training activities
- continued training and development of training staff costs when attending internal or external programmes or completing other types of developmental programmes
- professional fees for training staff
- subscriptions to professional journals and purchase of training resources
- licence fees.

Direct training costs

Some costs will be incurred directly in relation to the training itself, such as fees and expenses for guest speakers.

External agent costs

External agent costs may include (as relevant):

- consultant fees and expenses
- external course fees and expenses
- purchase of open-learning programmes if not accounted for elsewhere.

Learner costs

Finally, account must be taken of the costs attributable to the learners themselves:

- apportionment of salary for period of travelling to and from and attending the training programme
- cost of pre-programme action with line manager (also apportioned to line manager costs)
- travel and accommodation costs
- cost of replacement staff where relevant
- opportunity costs.

Cost analysis

The figures obtained under the headings described above are used to produce a monetary summary statement from which a number of conclusions are made, including:

- direct cost of the training programme
- direct cost of the total training function
- cost of the training function per individual within the organization
- cost of the training programme per learner.

From these calculations the training and development planner will be able to assess whether the programmes can go ahead within existing budgetary constraints.

Value-effectiveness

The costs of training show but one side of the equation. No account has been taken of the value obtained from the training – the increase in knowledge, skills and attitudes; the increase in work capacities; the decrease in undesirable practices and events; and, above all, the effect on the business achievement. This second stage is not simple: it is not always easy to obtain the financial information or produce real attribution or apportionment to assess costs, but obtaining the value of the training is much more difficult – some people suggest that it is impossible. Certainly it is often impossible in quantitative terms and in many cases it will be necessary to accept subjective and qualitative assessments, perhaps relying on a consistency of approach to produce acceptable, comparative results.

Some aspects are *easier* to assess for value. Changes might be observed following training and development programmes which include aspects of the back-at-work implementation of the learning, although care must be taken in attributing all changes to the training. Some of these changed aspects might include:

- efficient time usage – meetings are kept to time and are time-effective; appointments are kept efficiently; reports submitted at the due time, and so on

- effective work practices – stricter adherence to health and safety practices; effective operating procedures adhered to

- output of products or services – an increase in the amount of work produced, sales or other visits made etc.

- costs – many of the endless list of organizational costs are seen to be reduced

- people – team development, interpersonal skills and people relationship programmes result in improvements in effectiveness and efficiency in the way people undertake tasks

- individual development – increased creative ability of people, they present themselves in more favourable lights, they demonstrate their promotability and, in general, are more effective

- quality of products and services – a reduction in the number of rejects of projects and customer complaints, reduced operating costs, increased business etc.

- improvements in the organizational climate and culture (the most difficult to assess) – reduction in number of resignations and discharges, fewer sick absences, increased production, reduction in number of customer complaints – these and other indicators may give the opportunity to assess a change, but all are highly subjective, particularly when confirmation of a direct link with a training/learning programme is attempted.

Guidelines for value-effectiveness analysis

When the training and development programmes and evaluation measures have been completed and the early costing measures weighed against the assessments of the value achieved, the value-effectiveness of the programmes can be assessed. It will be assessment, rather than measurement because of the myriad of difficulties in measuring value, but in most cases some approach to objectiveness can be made. Even if this is not possible, in the same way that we considered subjective evaluation, subjective value-assessment if applied in a consistent manner can provide a great deal of information. Guidelines that should help in the analysis in this difficult area include:

1   Don't be put off by the apparent, or real, difficulties and subjective nature of the areas to be assessed – try something.

2.   In subjective assessment use comparisons with similar events under similar conditions.

3.   Seek the views, albeit subjective, of others – for example, from customers, internal and external.

4. Compare results against models or even concepts when the areas are completely subjective in nature.

5. Only gather information or data that you will be able to use, however interesting or easy to obtain other 'data' might be.

6. Ask the line manager of the learners before the events for their estimate of how much it will be worth to them and their operation to have an effective person. After the training evaluate the success and again ask the line manager whether their initial estimates have been achieved. The line managers are usually in the most favourable position to assess the value-effectiveness, particularly if they are responsible for most or all of their budgeting.

7. Seek, but do not necessarily take as positive proof, organizational effects linked to the training areas – increased productivity, decreased absences, discipline incidents, grievances, etc. Link these to other evaluation processes to ensure that contamination has not occurred.

ENVIRONMENT

Training room booked
Access method
Suitability of room for event
Parking facilities
Seating arrangements
Toilets locations and availability
Fax availability (if relevant)
Clerical/secretarial contact
Wall space for posters etc.
Ventilation regulations
Refreshments ordered
Posters, screen shots visible

Syndicate rooms booked
Electrical sockets needed
Other required rooms available
Porterage access
Sufficient chairs, tables etc.
Telephone access
Computer availability (if relevant)
Lighting control
Cleanliness
Refreshment availability
Photocopier availability
Messages arrangements

EQUIPMENT

Audio recorder and tapes
Video camera, camcorder, mixer, tapes
Extension cords
Overhead projector
Film projector and screen
Whiteboard and wiper
Power points – available and compatible

Video recorder, monitor and tapes
Computers, projectors and networks
Microphones
Flipchart and stand
Slide projector and screen
Lectern

MATERIALS

Visual aids
Small felt tip pens or similar
Drymaker pens
Highlighter pens
Pencils
Blutack
Scissors
Hole punch
A4 lined/plain paper
Clipboards
Water carafes and glasses
Bowls of sweets etc
Direction signs

Blotter pads
Large felt tip pens or similar
Lumocolour pens – Water and spirit based
Acetate sheets and rolls
Masking tape
Paperclips
Stapler
Flipchart paper
File folders
Reference books
Bottled water, juices etc
Nameplates

IMMEDIATELY BEFORE TRAINING EVENT

Get into training room about an hour before the event is due to start
Check all seating, tables, extra seating available
Check all other rooms available
Check refreshments – water and other supply available
Air conditioning working/too audible
Confirm refreshment arrangements
Own brief and other resources available and in order
Confirm guests coming
Clock available, working and correct

Check power points
Check clear vision for self and group
Silence any telephone in room
Check equipment available and working
Windows openable/open
Hotel speaker system off
Confirm availability of hotel/centre contact
Copies and spare copies of handouts etc available
Secretarial assistance available

Figure 15.6   Example of a pre-training checklist
Of one thing you can be almost certain: 'If something can go wrong, it will' ('Murphy's Law'); and from 'Paddy's Law' – 'Murphy was an optimist!'

Pre-training checklist

As a final aid the designer can provide the programme practitioners with a pre-course checklist to ensure that nothing has been forgotten (see Figure 15.6). This is a guide only and any items that are not relevant to your environment can be omitted and others added as necessary.

Conclusion

By this stage in the design and planning of training and development you should be ready to hand over your detailed programme to the trainer(s) responsible for implementing it (this may, of course, be yourself). Further action is personal to the trainers who should be responsible for ensuring that all environmental resources are suitable and available; all relevant and related material for the sessions and programme are complete and available; all training aids have been produced; and that they possess all the skills necessary to implement the programme in the most effective manner.

Index of training resources

Activities

The following list includes a selection of the collections of training activities of various kinds that are currently available. It makes no pretence at being complete, although the number of collections listed should give any trainer or programe designer sufficient activities from which to choose for almost any type of programme (4,271 activities are included).

Title	Author	Publisher	No. of activities
20 Training Workshops for Customer Care, Vol. 1	Gillen	Gower	20
20 Training Workshops for Customer Care, Vol. 2	Cook	Gower	20
20 Training Workshops for Developing Managerial Effectiveness, Vols 1 and 2	Lewis, Kelly and Armstrong	Gower	40
25 Interventions for Team Development	Woodcock and Francis	Gower	25
25 Role Plays for Assertiveness Training	Bishop	Gower	25
25 Role Plays for Developing Counselling Skills	Couper and Stewart	Gower	25
25 Role Plays for Developing Management Skills	Kamp	Gower	25
25 Role Plays for Interview Training	Cox and Dufault	Gower	25
30 Activities for Internal Customer Care	Hill, Tullock, Garai	Gower	30
30 Training Sessions for Effective Meetings	Bray	Gower	30
30 Training Sessions for Effective Presentation	Denham and Naylor	Gower	30
35 Ways to Start a Training Event	Rae	Fenman	35
38 Activities for Handling Difficult Situations	Stewart and Couper	Gower	38
40 Activities for Improving Customer Service	Linton	Gower	40

Title	Author	Publisher	No. of activities
40 Activities for Training in Self-empowerment	Seifert	Gower	40
40 Activities for Training with NLP	Johnson	Gower	40
50 Activities for Achieving Change	Fletcher	Gower	50
50 Activities on Creativity and Problem Solving	Cox, Dufault and Hopkins	Gower	50
50 Activities for Developing Counselling Skills	Bailey	Gower	50
50 Activities for Developing Management Skills Vols 1 to 8	Various authors	Gower	400
50 Activities for Managing Stress	Bailey	Gower	50
50 Activities for Self-development	Francis and Woodcock	Gower	50
50 Activities for Self-directed Teams	Parker and Kropp	Gower	50
50 Activities for Teambuilding	Woodcock	Gower	50
50 Activities for Unblocking Organisational Communication, Vols 1 and 2	Francis	Gower	100
50 Activities for Unblocking your Organisation 1 & 2	Francis and Woodcock	Gower	100
50 Problem Solving Activities	Badger and Chaston	Gower	50
75 Ways to Liven up your Training	Orridge	Gower	75
A Compendium of Icebreakers, Energizers and Introductions	Edited by Kirby	Gower	75
A Manual of Management Training Exercises	Payne	Gower	20
Activities for Achieving Managerial Effectiveness	Wilson	Gower	35
Activities for Developing People Skills	Stewart and Couper	Gower	50
Activities for Developing Project Management Skills	Stokes	Gower	34
Activities for Developing Project Management Techniques	Stokes	Gower	33
Activities for Developing Supervisory Skills	Nicholls	Gower	50
Activities for Public Sector Training	Editor: Griffiths	Gower	40
Assertiveness Skills Training	Bishop	Kogan Page	50
Beginnings and Endings	Barca and Cobb	Gower	70
Connections: 125 Activities for Faultless Training	Hart	Gower	125
Customer Service Triggers	Kelly, Roger and Watson	Gower	40
Delegation Skills	Bray	Fenman	26
Developing Cross-Cultural Communication	Oomkes and Thomas	Gower	70

Title	Author	Publisher	No. of activities
Effective Meetings	Richards	Fenman	20
Exercises for Developing First-line Managers	Payne and Payne	Gower	20
Flexible Flipcharts	Richards	Fenman	50
Games for Trainers, Vols 1, 2 and 3	Kirby	Gower	225
Handbook of Management Games	Elgood	Gower	300
Icebreakers	Jones	Kogan Page	48
Icebreakers	Kirby	Gower	75
Imaginative Events, Vols 1 and 2	Jones	McGraw-Hill	48
Influencing Skills	Cleeton and Sharman	Fenman	22
Insights: A Collection of Incidents for Developing Managers	Armstrong and Kelly	Gower	31
Internal Customers: 21 Tried and Tested Training Activities for Improving Internal Customer Care	Bailey	Fenman	21
Interpersonal Skills Training	Burnard	Kogan Page	110
Interviewing Skills	Davies	Fenman	19
Interviewing TOPPICS	Leigh	Gower	25
Leadership Training	Christopher and Smith	Kogan Page	74
Managing Change	Mann	Fenman	19
Meetings Management	Rae	McGraw-Hill	17
Mentoring	Clarke	Fenman	20
Negotiation Skills: 19 Tried and Tested Training Activities for Developing Effective Negotiators	Clarke, Steers and Simmonds	Fenman	19
Outdoor Games for Trainers	Consalvo	Gower	63
Outdoor Training	Krouwel and Goodwill	Kogan Page	50
People Problems At Work: 40 Roles for Managers	Smith	Fenman	40
Presentation Skills	Fenwick	Fenman	20
Reaching Agreement: 26 Exercises, role plays and simulations	Smith	Fenman	26
Role Plays	Turner	Kogan Page	60
Role Plays for Interpersonal Skills	Williams	Gower	25
Session Shakers	Cook	Fenman	50
Team Building	Parker and Kropp	Kogan Page	50
Teams in Action	Bray	Fenman	22

Title	Author	Publisher	No. of activities
The Assertiveness Skills Pack	Gutman	Fenman	24
The Customer Care Pack	Bray	Fenman	20
The Supervisor Development Pack	Fenwick	Fenman	15
The Trainer's Pocketbook of Ready to Use Exercises	Townsend	Mgt. Pocketbooks	40
The Trainer's Quality Pack	Bray	Fenman	23
The Trainer's Toolkit	Melrose Mitchell	Melrose	17
Time Management Triggers	Kamp	Gower	35
Time Management TOPPICS	Leigh	Gower	25
Toolkit for Trainers	Pickles	Gower	60
Training for Assertiveness	Seifert	Gower	40
Training for Change	Bishop and Taylor	Kogan Page	50
Training for Time Management	Moon	Gower	22
Training Workshops for Supervisors	Atkinson and Feathers	Gower	5
Unlocking your People's Potential	Davies	Fenman	20
Workshops that Work	Bourner, Martin and Race	McGraw-Hill	100

Other learning packages and resources

A very extensive range of learning packages, videos, CD-Is, and computer programs is available. The following lists includes a representative selection of some of these other resources, concentrating on those that link directly or peripherally with design and planning, although some examples of complete, specific training resources are also given. Information about specific subject resources suitable for including in extended programmes or in the ways described earlier in this book – for example negotiations, written communication etc. – can be obtained from the relevant publishers who all produce extensive catalogues. More and more videos are being offered in video CD or CD-I form – if you are interested in these media, you should contact the relevant supplier (Video Arts and Melrose are among the leading producers).

Training and workshop resources are suggested, complete programme plans, usually consisting of session briefs, OHP masters and handouts. Total training kits can include a number of different media resources to enable a training programme to be held with minimal additional preparation.

Title	Medium	Publisher
20 Workshops for Developing Leadership (Villiers)	Workshop resource	Gower
25 Team Management Training Sessions (John Allan)	Workshop resource	Gower

Title	Medium	Publisher
Body Talk	Video + Trigger video	Fenman
Brief Encounters: Training for team briefing	Total training kit	Melrose
Can We Please Have That The Right Way Round:	Video	Video Arts
How to use visual aids		
Coaching Skills	Video + Trigger video	Fenman
Complete Communication	Total training kit	Melrose
Complete Resource Kits for Training and Development	Resource packages	Kogan Page
(Kits on Evaluation and The Use of Training Aids		
are now available, to be followed by kits on		
Training Needs Analysis, Design and other		
training skills)		
Customer Care on the Telephone	Video	Gower
Developing Training Skills (Pickles, Britton and	Training resource	Longman
Armstrong)		
Customer Service Triggers (Descriptions of situations	Resource ringbinder	Gower
designed to act as triggers to stimulate discussion)		
Effective Listening Skills	Video + Trigger video	Fenman
Handling Customer Complaints on the Telephone	Video	Gower
Letter Writing Made Easy (Bray)	Workshop resource	Fenman
Making your Case: Planning and making a presentation		Video
Video Arts		
Management Matters: Coaching and Training	Video	Video Arts
Memories are Made of This (John Townsend)	Video	Melrose
One-day Workshop Packages (two-volume	Resource packages	Kogan Page
ringbinders including a trainer's guide and a		
participant's guide on subjects that include coaching		
and counselling skills; presentation skills; delegation		
skills; negotiation skills; trainer's companion volume;		
time management; etc.)		
Problem Solving and Decision Making Toolkit		
(Woodcock/Francis)	Training resource	Gower
Problem Solving in Groups	Video	Gower
Quality Triggers (descriptions of situations	Resource ringbinder	Gower
designed to act as triggers to stimulate discussion)		
Ready, Steady, Go: A guide to presentations	Video	Video Arts
Report Writing Made Easy (Bray)	Workshop resource	Fenman
Team Development Toolkit (Woodcock/Francis)	Training resource	Gower
Teambuilding Blocks: Practising group collaboration	Teambuilding game	Gower
Teams	Management game	Gower
Ten Training Tips (Presenter John Townsend)	Video and Video CD	Melrose
The Audience is Yours, Now	Video	Gower
The Complete Presenter	Total training kit	Melrose
The Floor is Yours, Now	Video	Gower
The Great Communicator: Communication Skills		
for all	Video	Melrose

Further reading

The following are some of the many publications relating to training and development which are relevant to the planning and design of training. The list is not exhaustive, but if you do not find what you are seeking, most of the publications have further reading lists that should lead you to the information. A number of the books relate to specific areas, whereas others cover wider fields perhaps in less detail and the list is divided into these interest areas.

General

Argyle, Michael (1988) *Bodily Communication*, Routledge.
Baguley, Phil (1994) *Effective Communication for Modern Business*, McGraw-Hill.
Rae, Leslie (1992) *Guide to In-Company Training Methods*, Gower.
Rae, Leslie (1995) *The Techniques of Training*, 3rd edition, Gower.
St Maur, Suzan (1991) *Writing your own Scripts and Speeches*, McGraw-Hill.
Stimson, Nancy (1991) *How to Write and Prepare Training Materials*, Kogan Page.
Townsend, John (1996) *The Trainer's Pocketbook*, Management Pocketbooks.

Training needs identification and analysis

Bartram, Sheila and Gibson, Brenda (1994) *Training Needs Analysis*, Gower.
Craig, Malcolm (1994) *Analysing Learning Needs*, Gower.
Fletcher, Shirley (1991) *NVQs, Standards and Competence*, Kogan Page.
Holyfield, James and Moloney, Karen (1996) *Using National Standards to Improve Performance*, Kogan Page.
Honey, Peter (1979) 'The Repertory Grid in Action', *Industrial and Commercial Training*, vol. II, nos 9, 10 and 11.
Kelly, G.A. (1953) *The Psychology of Personal Constructs*, Norton.
Odiorne, G.S. (1970) *Training by Objectives*, Macmillan.
Ollin, Ros and Tucker, Jenny (1994) *The NVQ and GNVQ Assessor Handbook*, Kogan Page.
Peterson, Robyn (1992) *Training Needs Analysis in the Workplace*, Kogan Page.

Reay, David G. (1994) *Identifying Training Needs*, Kogan Page.

Planning and designing training programmes

Bentley, Trevor (1994) *Facilitation: Providing opportunities for learning*, McGraw-Hill.
Bourner, T., Martin, V. and Race, P. (1993) *Workshops that Work; 100 ideas to make your training events more effective*, McGraw-Hill.
Buckley, Roger and Caple, Jim (1995) *The Theory and Practice of Training*, Kogan Page.
Corder, Colin (1990) *Teaching Hard Teaching Soft*, Gower.
Davis, John (1992) *How to Write a Training Manual*, Gower.
Harrison, Nigel (1995) *Practical Instructional Design for Open Learning Materials*, McGraw-Hill.
Hart, Lois B. (1991) *Training Methods that Work*, Kogan Page.
Honey, Peter and Mumford, Alan (1992) *The Manual of Learning Styles*, Honey.
Kolb, D.A., Rubin, I.M. and McIntyre, J.M. (1974) *Organizational Psychology – An experiential approach*, Prentice-Hall.
Leatherman, Dick (1990) *Designing Training Programmes*, Gower.
Morris, Desmond (1978) *Manwatching: A Field Guide to Human Behaviour*, Grafton.
Munson, Lawrence S. (1992) *How to Conduct Training Seminars*, McGraw-Hill.
Pinnington, Ashley (1992) *Using Video in Training and Education*, McGraw-Hill.
Rae, Leslie (1994) *How to Design and Introduce Trainer Development Programmes*, Kogan Page.
Rae, Leslie (1994) *The Trainer Development Programme*, Kogan Page.
Reay, David G. (1994) *Selecting Training Methods*, Kogan Page.
Sheal, Peter R. (1994) *How to Develop and Present Staff Training Courses*, Kogan Page.

Planning and designing training sessions

Cartey, Ron (1996) *Inspirational Training*, Gower.
Elgood, Chris (1996) *Using Management Games*, 2nd edition, Gower.
Fenwick, Mike (1994) *Presentation Skills*, Fenman Training.
Forsyth, Patrick (1992) *Running an Effective Training Session*, Gower.
Jones, Ken (1993) *Imaginative Events*, vols 1 and 2, McGraw-Hill.
Kirby, Andy (1993) *A Compendium of Icebreakers, Energizers and Introductions*, Gower.
Piocotto, M., Robertson, I. and Colley, R. (1989) *Interactivity: Designing and Using Interactive Video*, Kogan Page.
Rackham, Neil and Morgan, Terry (1977) *Behaviour Analysis in Training*, McGraw-Hill.
Rae, Leslie (1996) *Using Activities in Training and Development*, Kogan Page.
Rawlinson, J.G. (1981) *Creative Thinking and Brainstorming*, Gower.
Russell, Tim (1994) *Effective Feedback Skills*, Kogan Page.
Spinks, Terry and Clements, Phil (1993) *A Practical Guide to Facilitation Skills*, Kogan Page.

Evaluation

Bramley, Peter (1996) *Evaluating Training Effectiveness*, 2nd edition, McGraw-Hill.
Fletcher, Shirley (1991) *Designing Competence-Based Training*, Kogan Page.
Hamblin, A.C. (1974) *The Evaluation and Control of Training*, McGraw-Hill.
Newby, Tony (1992) *Cost-Effective Training*, Kogan Page.
Newby, Tony (1992) *Validating your Training*, Kogan Page.
Rae, Leslie (1983) 'Towards a More Valid End-of-course Validation', *Training Officer*, October 1983.
Rae, Leslie (1991) *Assessing Trainer Effectiveness*, Gower.
Rae, Leslie (1997) *How to Measure Training Effectiveness*, 3rd edition, Gower (includes Chapter 4 for Repertory Grid practice in evaluation).
Reay, David G. (1994) Evaluating Training, Kogan Page.
Warr, P.B., Bird, M. and Rackham, N. (1970) The Evaluation of Management Training, Gower.

Index